# PRAY *In* GOD'S WORD *for* Encouragement and Change

CRAIG WILLIAMS

ISBN 979-8-89345-092-7 (paperback)
ISBN 979-8-89345-093-4 (digital)

Copyright © 2024 by Craig Williams

All rights reserved. No part of this publication may be reproduced, distributed, or transmitted in any form or by any means, including photocopying, recording, or other electronic or mechanical methods without the prior written permission of the publisher. For permission requests, solicit the publisher via the address below.

Christian Faith Publishing
832 Park Avenue
Meadville, PA 16335
www.christianfaithpublishing.com

Printed in the United States of America

# Contents

| | | |
|---|---|---|
| Part 1: | God's Assurance | 1 |
| | Invitation for All to Come to Christ Jesus | 3 |
| | The Warfare: Flesh versus the Spirit | 7 |
| | The Purpose of the Book | 13 |
| | Praising God through the Difficulties | 17 |
| | Please, Lord, Let Today Be My Breakthrough | 20 |
| | Lord, Please Comfort My Soul | 26 |
| | The God of Israel Is Awesome in All His Ways | 30 |
| | My God Is Faithful | 34 |
| | Just Praise Him | 38 |
| | Lord, Remember Me in Mine Affliction | 43 |
| | The God Who Answers Prayers | 49 |
| | Lord, My Soul Is Discouraged and Turmoiled | 53 |
| | Thanking Abba for My Covenant Blessings | 58 |
| | Lord, I Am Trapped, When Will You Come? | 64 |
| | A Declaration of Praise | 68 |
| | God Cares for the Backslider | 74 |
| | Be Encouraged | 79 |
| | Love | 82 |
| | God's Love | 83 |
| | Adoration to God | 85 |
| | God Saves the Righteous | 89 |
| | Joy | 94 |
| | God's Joy | 95 |
| | To Be Blessed by God | 97 |
| | Security in the Lord | 100 |

| | |
|---|---|
| Praising God for Our Children | 105 |
| By God's Grace and Mercy | 108 |
| God's Favor | 113 |
| Peace | 116 |
| God's Peace | 117 |
| Reflecting on God's Miracles | 120 |
| Forgiving | 123 |
| Trust in the Lord Your God | 126 |
| The Honor of God's Name Upheld | 129 |
| Patience | 132 |
| God's Patience | 133 |
| Reflections | 136 |
| I Have Been Chosen | 137 |
| Kindness | 142 |
| God's Kindness | 143 |
| God's Blessings and Promises | 145 |
| Receiving God's Spiritual Gifts | 148 |
| Goodness | 153 |
| God's Goodness | 154 |
| A Promise | 157 |
| Blessings | 160 |
| Faithfulness | 163 |
| God's Faithfulness | 164 |
| Boasting in the Lord | 166 |
| My God Is Faithful | 169 |
| God's Promise of Protection | 173 |
| God Is Able | 178 |
| I Believe | 188 |
| Speak a Word | 192 |
| Reflections | 195 |
| Gentleness | 196 |
| God's Gentleness | 197 |
| Giving Thanks to God Almighty | 199 |
| Communing with God | 205 |
| Self-Control | 208 |
| God's Temperance | 209 |

|  |  |  |
|---|---|---|
|  | Confession and Repentance | 211 |
|  | Reflections | 215 |
|  | The Two Shall Be One | 216 |
|  | Walking in God's Plan | 220 |
|  | It Is Written | 222 |
|  | Lord, Give Me Your Desires | 226 |
|  | Ungodly Desires You Want God to Change | 229 |
|  | Reflections | 230 |
|  | Honoring the Sabbath | 231 |
|  | Be Ye Holy | 235 |
| Part 2: | Winning the Battle through the Word of God | 241 |
|  | Petition for God's Help | 243 |
|  | Prayer of Victory | 247 |
|  | The Lord's Vengeance on My Enemies | 252 |
|  | The Righteous Vindicated | 256 |
|  | God's Provision and Protection | 260 |
|  | A Solitude Cry for Help | 263 |
|  | The Lord Is Our Intercessor | 267 |
|  | God's Protection for His Servants | 271 |
|  | Reflections | 275 |
|  | Desperation | 276 |
|  | Supplication for God's Help against Attackers | 281 |
|  | Assurance from God | 284 |
|  | Lord, Rescue Me | 287 |
|  | God's Sheltered Protection and Promises | 291 |
|  | Help for the Righteous and Wrath to the Wicked | 295 |
|  | Betrayal | 298 |
|  | Longing for God's Help | 301 |
|  | The Lord Is Our Covering in Battle | 304 |
|  | Introduction to the Author | 307 |
|  | Reflections | 311 |
|  | Source Notes | 313 |
|  | The Reason for Our Faith | 315 |
|  | Bless My Day, Lord | 317 |
|  | Covered Prayer | 321 |
|  | Closing Prayer | 323 |

# Part 1

## God's Assurance

*"ALL that the Father giveth me shall come to me; and him that cometh to me I will in no wise cast out."* (John 6:37 KJV)

*"And I give unto them eternal life; and they shall never perish, neither shall any man pluck them out of my hand."* (John 10:28 KJV)

# Invitation for All to Come to Christ Jesus

> For with the heart one believes and is justified, and with the mouth one confesses and is saved. For the scripture says, "Everyone who believes in him will not be put to shame." For there is no distinction between Jew and Greek; for the same Lord is Lord of all, bestowing His riches on all who call on Him. For "everyone who calls on the name of the Lord will be saved." (Rom. 10:10–13 ESV)

The world system has deceived society in believing that if you have great wealth, influence, earthly accomplishments, material possessions, and social status, then you will have personal peace. Finally being free from life's daily toils, worries, and pain. Influencing a false sense of euphoria, of being complete and whole. The Bible teaches us that we should not be surprised when offenses come/happen for this is the natural order of things essential for believers to grow in faith. "Beloved, do not be surprised at the fiery trial when it comes upon you to test you. But rejoice insofar as you share Christ's sufferings, that you may also rejoice and be glad when his glory is revealed" (1 Pet. 4:12–13 ESV). The Bible wants us to train ourselves to be godly. Since we don't live by ourselves in the world, this can be challenging at times. "This is why we work hard and continue to struggle, for our hope is in the living God, who is the savior of all people and particularly of all believers" (1 Tim. 4:10 NLT). The only way to be made whole is by accepting Jesus Christ as your Lord and savior over your life. Furthermore, God promised us: "If you are insulted for the name of Christ, you are blessed, because the Spirit of glory and of God rests upon you" (1 Pet. 4:13 ESV).

"Jesus said to him, I AM the way, and the truth, and the life. No one comes to the father except through me" (John 14:6 ESV).

If you're not yet a believer in Christ Jesus, I invite you to say the following prayer, before reading "Pray in God's Word," to fully experience the fullness of God through reading His words. God loves us dearly. For the Word of God says: "Come to me, all who labor and are heavy laden, and I will give you rest" (Matt. 11:28 ESV).

"Take my yoke upon you and learn from me (following me as my disciple), for I AM gentle and humble in heart, and you will find rest (renewal, blessed, quiet) for your souls" (Matt. 11:29 AMP).

## Prayer

Now, Father God, I ask you to forgive me of my transgressions, my iniquities, and my trespasses that you, O Lord, went to the cross to give me. I ask you, Lord, to come into my heart, my life and be my Lord and savior.

Hope, deliverance, peace, and a new life.

"Peace I leave with you; my peace I give you. I do not give to you as the world gives. Do not let your hearts be troubled and do not be afraid" (John 14:27 NIV). "Create in me a clean heart, O God; and renew a right Spirit within me" (Ps. 51:10 KJV).

Lord, I believe *you* went to the cross and died for my sins. I believe you rose three days later and ascended into heaven and is now sitting at the right hand of God, interceding on my behalf. In Jesus name, amen.

If you have prayed this prayer, welcome to the family of believers in Christ Jesus!

Now as a new creation by Christ Jesus, you are to:

"Love the Lord your God with all your heart and with all your soul and with all your mind and with all your strength" (Mark 12:30 NIV).

"The second is equally important: 'Love your neighbor as yourself.' No commandment is greater than these" (Mark 12:31 NIV).

Secondly, model your life after Jesus's character:

"Since you have been raised to new life with Christ, set your sights on the realities of heaven, where Christ sits in the place of honor at God's right hand" (Col. 3:1 NLT).

"Set your affection on things above, not on things on the earth" (Col. 3:2 KJV).

Let the peace of God be released in your life. It's your birth right as a believer to have the gift of peace and operate in peace.

Next, establish roots. Find a good Bible-based church, which teaches there is no inerrancy in the Bible. Get water baptized, which is an act of obedience that should be an immediate part of our acceptance of the precious, unmerited gift of grace offered by Jesus Christ our Lord.

"He who believes and is baptized will be saved; but he who does not believe will be condemned" (Mark 16:16 NKJV).

Finally, share the gospel of Jesus Christ with others, as Jesus commanded.

"And He said to them, go into all the world and preach the gospel to all creation" (Mark 16:15 AMP).

Keep the faith, God will fulfill the destiny He has for your life.

*In Jesus name, amen.*

# The Warfare: Flesh versus the Spirit

In thinking on the subject of the flesh versus the spirit is not merely choosing right from wrong when it suits us, it also shows who we identify with. Who is our lord and how deep is the bond? This notion of picking when to obey God is a false concept of Christianity. This false sense of Christianity makes us think—if we choose more good things than bad ones—we are good Christians. It doesn't. Like my social media mentor and pastor, Dr. Tony Evans says, "Partial obedience is complete disobedience to God." In fact, all our best attempts of righteous deeds are as filthy rags. "We are all infected and impure with sin. When we display our righteous deeds, they are nothing but filthy rags. Like autumn leaves, we wither and fall, and our sins sweep us away like the wind" (Isa. 64:6 NLT).

Yes, choosing between the flesh versus the Spirit is making a decision to choose God or the world principles, but it's much more damaging than that with adverse repercussions. As Christians, because of our own lust, we indoctrinate this worldly ideal that it's okay to choose or adopt a lifestyle of the world that doesn't entirely disrupt our Christian beliefs is acceptable to God. It's not! It's absurd and insulting to the creator of the universe and everything we come to know of Him. God looks at this kind of mindset as being on the fence, the culture, the grey area, that lukewarm state, which God dislikes. In Revelation 3:16 KJV, God says it like this: "So then because thou art lukewarm, and neither cold nor hot, I will spue thee out of my mouth." I can't imagine anything worse than being separated from God.

When we choose the world, we are saying we want to be independent of God. We are married to God when we choose Jesus

Christ as our Lord and Savior. To follow the world standard makes us adulterers and adulteresses, as well as God being in enmity with us. "Ye adulterers and adulteresses, know ye not that the friendship of the world is enmity with God? Whosoever therefore will be friend of the world is the enemy of God" (James 4:4 KJV). When we choose the world morals, God considers us hostile. "The mind governed by the flesh is hostile to God; it does not submit to God's law, nor can it do so" (Rom. 8:7 NIV). Rightly so! Go is our creator! As a Christian, God is our burden bearer, He is the Author and Finisher of our faith. "Looking unto Jesus the author and finisher of our faith; who for the joy that was set before him endured the cross, despising the shame, and is sat down at the right hand of the throne of God" (Heb. 12:2 KJV). God had Jesus to die on the cross for us, which is the deepest expression of love. "Greater love hath no man than this, that a man lay down his life for his friends" (John 15:13 KJV). God loves us deeply and want us to live an abundant life with Him, both here and in the next (in glory, heaven).

Furthermore, choosing the world's ideology is arguing with God.

> What sorrow awaits those who argue with their creator. Does a clay pot argue with its maker? Does the clay dispute with the one who shapes it, saying, "Stop, you're doing it wrong!" Does the pot exclaim, "How clumsy can you be?" How terrible it would be if a newborn baby said to its father, "Why was I born?" Or if it said to its mother, "Why did you make me this way?" (Isa. 45:9–10 NLT)

Choosing the world's belief over God's, we are in reality, questioning the validity of the one true God—the God of Abraham, Isaac, and Jacob. This is completely unacceptable in the eyes of our creator.

> This is what the Lord says—the Holy One of Israel and your creator: "Do you ques-

tion what I do for my children? Do you give me orders about the work of my hands? I am the one who made the earth and created people to live on it. With my hands I stretched out the heavens. All the stars are at my command." (Isa. 45:11–12 NLT)

You might be wondering at this point—in light of everything you have known and now know to be factual characteristics of Elohim, our Creator—it should be an easy decision to choose God over the world. It is, but there are numerous reasons and circumstances why someone would choose the world over God despite knowing His character and even having a relationship with Him. I will touch on five root causes that is at the center of every decision, tempting us to choose the world over Yahweh.

First, sinful emotion that causes us not to choose God but the world is covetousness. Covetousness means "to be marked by inordinate desire for wealth or possessions or for another's possessions or having a craving for possession covetous of power." The Bible breaks it down further for us at the root. To be covetous is to operate in greed.

Greed means "to have an intense desire to accumulate large amounts of something; such as food or money, especially if you try to acquire more than you need or more than your fair share."

We've seen this before in the book of Exodus 16:19–20 (ERV):

> Moses told them, "Don't save that food to eat the next day." But some people did not obey Moses. They saved their food for the next day. But worms got into the food and it began to stink. Moses was very angry with the people who did this.

Those people who chose not to listen, to be obedient to God's instructions. They failed to recognize the surety that He, God, is a provider, and if He allows you to see tomorrow, He will provide for you. "And my God will liberally supply (fill until full) your every need according to His riches in glory in Christ Jesus" (Phil. 4:19 AMP). Greed always demands independence from God. The reason the people of God in Exodus hoarded the manna was one of greed, but also because they did not want to rely on God for their daily bread, which is a direct contradiction to God. In the Lord's Prayer, we are taught to honor God as our only source. Matthew 6:9–11 (AMP) says, "Pray, then, in this way: 'Our Father, who is in heaven, Hallowed be Your name. Your Kingdom come, Your will be done On earth as it is in heaven. Give us this day our daily bread." We are to be dependent on Abba, Father physically, mentally, and definitely spiritually. Why?

> For ye have not received the spirit of bondage again to fear, but ye have received the Spirit of adoption, whereby we cry, Abba, Father. The Spirit itself beareth witness with our spirit, that we are the children of God. (Rom. 8:15–16)

We belong to God. We've been redeemed. God doesn't want us making a decision before first seeking Him or us going outside of Him for help.

> Woe to them that go down to Egypt for help; and stay on horses, and trust in chariots, because they are many; and in horseman, because they are very strong; but they look not unto the Holy One of Israel, neither seek the LORD! (Isa. 31:1 KJV)

Greed is a desire from the devil.
Biblical commentator, John Ritenbaugh, describes greed as a ruthless self-seeking and an arrogant assumption that others and things exist for one's own benefit.
If you're struggling under the weight of greed or simply want to ensure that you don't succumb to the sin of greed, God can equip

us with the spirit of contentment, through receiving the Holy Spirit, by accepting Jesus's gift on the cross. Contentment is a godly desire to combat the sin of greed. "And he said unto him, Take heed, and beware of covetousness: for a man's life consisteth not in the abundance of the things which he possesseth" (Luke 12:15 KJV).

Contentment means "a state of happiness and satisfaction."

The world motto teaches us to not to be satisfied with what we have or where we are, even if we are comfortable. The Word of God teaches us that contentment is great gain. "But godliness with contentment is great gain" (1 Tim. 6:6 KJV). Moreover, we didn't come into this world with anything, so we certainly will not leave with anything. "For we brought nothing into this world, and it is certain we can carry nothing out" (1 Tim. 6:7 KJV).

If you've been keeping track, greed is a desire from the devil. It's a learned behavior, so it can be changed. To be content, we have to come to the knowledge and understanding which is true wisdom, that we are to reject all forms of covetousness and know that God will never leave us nor forsake us, "Let your conversation be without covetousness; and be content with such things as ye have: for he hath said, I will never leave thee, nor forsake thee" (Heb. 13:5 KJV), no matter the circumstance we find ourselves in.

In knowing that God will never leave us nor forsake us, we can rely and trust on His provisions, His protection and presence, no matter the situation we find ourselves in. This state of contentment is achieved through learning to operate in a season of being abound and abased. "I know both how to be abased, and I know to abound: everywhere and in all things I am instructed both to be full and to be hungry, both to abound and to suffer need" (Phil. 4:12 KJV).

Abound means "to be full to be overflowing." Abase means (archaic) "to lower physically or depress; to throw or cast down."

There is a constant battle that rages continually between the flesh and the Spirit, well after a person chooses to operate in the character of Christ till the day this physical life ceases.

> But I say, walk habitually in the [Holy] Spirit [seek Him and be responsive to His guid-

ance], and then you will certainly not carry out the desire of the sinful nature [which response impulsively without regard for God and His precepts]. For the sinful nature has its desire which is opposed to the Spirit, and the [desire of the] Spirit opposes the sinful nature; for these [two, the sinful nature and the Spirit] are in direct opposition to each other [continually in conflict], so that you [as believers] do not [always] do whatever [good things] you want to do. (Gal. 5:16–17 AMP).

To help us navigate this walk in the Spirit, God gives us this encouraging word: "I can do all things through Christ which strengtheneth me" (Phil. 4:13 KJV). God says with Him and through Him operating within us, we can do all things. That bad habit. That bad temper. Even choosing godly things over the sinful nature of the flesh can be accomplish with Christ living on the inside of us. The strength of the Christian believer is in direct connection to our relationship with God.

In conclusion, deciding whether to choose the things of the flesh versus the Spirit, I implore you to choose the Spirit of God, He will reward you. "Cast not away therefore your confidence, which hath great recompense of reward" (Heb. 10:35 KJV). Operating in the Spirit God requires walking in faith, trusting and believing, that what God says is true. Not choosing the Spirit of God will undoubtedly ruin your life. You will be engulfed by the entrapment of the world's greedy desires to satisfy the flesh.

## Notes

# The Purpose of the Book

In this present life, it is impossible not to have troubles. At times, for me, it seems like, trouble searches for me. As soon as one ordeal is finish, another even more diabolical one appears. This constant bombardment of troubles is to be expected. The Bible says, "Woe unto the world because of offences! For it must needs be that offences come; but woe to that man by whom the offence cometh!" (Matt. 18:7 KJV). Unless we start one, we don't have any control over the troubling circumstances that confronts us, but we do have a choice has to how we react to it and a stern warning not instigate one.

For a long time, I was lost in the world, trying to find purpose in my existence, then I was introduced to Christ. I was led to believe that once I come to Christ, life would be easy street. That was detrimental and false. God does not say we will not have storms. In fact, Jesus sent his disciples directly in the path of a storm. "And the same day, when the even was come, he saith unto them, Let us pass over unto the other side...And arose a great storm of wind, and the waves beat into the ship, so that it was now full" (Mark 4:35, 37). Not because he wants to punish them, but to build their faith. "And he said unto them, why are ye so fearful? How is it that ye have no faith?" (Mark 4:40 KJV). Once I read this, my life was changed. I no longer look at bad circumstances as a potential setback, but rather a door way to a breakthrough to grow deeper in my faith in Christ Jesus. There are no bad days. God doesn't make bad days. There are only bad circumstances.

Not long after, I went through several difficult, challenging, heartbreaking trauma in my life, which caused me, at that time, to question God—questioned my faith in Him. These series of troubles challenged everything I know and believed about God. I wanted it to be over instantly. I asked God to rebuke the trouble like Jesus did for his disciples in the storm. "And he arose, and rebuked the wind, and said unto the sea, Peace, be still. And the wind ceased, and there was a great calm" (Mark 4:39). But He didn't. I knew enough that if God did not stop the storm, He would be with me through it. The only problem is that I took my focus off God and fixed them on my troubles and pain. I started sinking in self-pity and despair. Peter, a disciple of Jesus, took his focus of Jesus as well. "But when he saw the wind boisterous, he was afraid; and beginning to sink, he cried, saying, Lord, save me" (Matt. 14:30).

Before I knew it, I was overwhelmed by my circumstances and bound by depression. I thought maybe I am not praying enough? So I prayed at sundown. I prayed in the morning and at noonday. Physically, my bad circumstances didn't change. I remained persistent, I didn't give up praying, because I knew God is a covenant keeper and is my only hope of a recompense. "I will not violate my covenant or alter what my lips have uttered" (Ps. 89:34 NIV). "So do not throw away this confident trust in the Lord! Remember the great reward it brings you!" (Heb. 10:35 NLT).

One day, while I was praying, I hear the Holy Spirit saying to me, "Pray in God's Words." I thought, *Uh?* Then one day, while watching television, I heard "Pray in God's Word." Then another day, as I was traveling in my vehicle, I heard over the radio "Pray in God's Word." So I seek God on what He meant. In my prayer time with Him, He gave me the rest of the title—"for encouragement and change." The Word of God is indeed encouraging, it's powerful, it's the truth, and it will bring about a change in you. Then He said to me, "It's not how much you say, but rather, what you say." But when ye pray, use not vain repetitions, as the heathen do: for they think that they shall be heard for their much speaking" (Matt. 6:7). As I read His word in my Bible, I started having scriptures coming to me to confront a problem I was dealing with. So as I give God a particular problem I was facing (giving it a title) and seek Him in His word, scriptures would come to me. After I wrote a prayer, I would read it aloud, to my LORD and savior. In doing so, that took my focus off my situation and back on God, with the confidence that He heard me and He will take care of it. In fact, it is already done!

During my ordeal, I learn to be patient in God and know, "The Lord is not slow to fulfill His promise as some count slowness, but is patient toward you, not wishing that any should perish, but that all should reach repentance" (2 Pet. 3:9 ESV). The Word of God is life and is alive. The Word of God is practical. So it should be of no surprise that His Word will not be constrained nor be confined to a chapter or verse in a particular section of a book in the Bible. The Bible is chronological, but the Words of God all flow together. There is no contradiction or error in God's words. God's words fit and flow together. No matter the period, BC or AD. The Word of God transcends all time periods, generations, culture, or financial and social status. God is spreading His Word around the world.

The first publication of the Bible in its present form, English, started in 1604 and was completed in 1611. Exactly seven years. The number of perfection and completion. Nothing with God is coincidental, it's purposeful. I did not know it would take seven years for God to give me the victory in my situation. I just knew if I continue to trust Him, He will bring me out in His timing, which is always perfection. God didn't just change my attitude to trust in Him and be confident in His Word, not being a mocker (disbeliever), but He also has brought about a change to my adverse situation, my battle, my struggle and gave me the victory! He defeated all my foes, the oppressor, the deceiver, that false friend in sheep clothing, those brood of vipers (those with malice in their hearts), the real enemy (Satan), and restored everything that I had loss/stolen and added a double portion blessing for my troubles. Through the healthy fear (reverence) of the LORD, I know He will add years to my life by the wisdom I've received from praying in His Word.

> The fear of the LORD is the beginning of wisdom, and knowledge of the Holy One is understanding. For through wisdom your days will be many, and years will be added to your life.

If you are wise, your wisdom will reward you; if you are a mocker, you alone will suffer" (Prov. 9:10–12 NIV)

May the Word of God richly bless and inspire you, as you read this book, *Pray in God's Word for Encouragement and Change*, lead you and usher you to repentance and to cultivate a continuous prayer life. I pray the Spirit of God motivate and elevate you to pray for others and to pray in the Holy Ghost!

"Praying always with all prayer and supplication in the Spirit, and watching there unto with all perseverance and supplication for all saints" (Eph. 6:18 KJV).

"This is good, and it is pleasing in the sight of God our Savior" (1 Tim. 2:3 ESV).

"Who desires all people to be saved and to come to the Knowledge of the truth" (1 Tim. 2:4 ESV).

My hope for those of you reading *Pray in God's Word for Encouragement and Change*, who are not yet a believer in Christ Jesus, is to have your hearts and minds be transformed to model Jesus Christ and enjoy all the blessings God has for you. For believers, for your mind to be renewed. Whether you have been a believer for a while or a new one, always remember to: "Seek the Kingdom of God above all else, and live righteously, and he will give you everything you need" (Matt. 6:33 NLT).

Be wise and be blessed.

*In Jesus name, amen.*

# Praising God through the Difficulties

## (Prayer)

"Let God arise, let his enemies be scattered: let them also that hate him flee before him" (Ps. 68:1 KJV).

"Sing unto God, sing praises to his name: extole him that rideth upon the heavens by his name JAH, and rejoice before him" (Ps. 68:4 KJV).

"I will praise the LORD at all times. I will constantly speak his praises" (Ps. 34:1 NLT).

"I will boast only in the LORD; let all who are helpless take heart" (Ps. 34:2 NLT).

"O God, thou art my God; early will I seek thee: my soul thirsteth for thee, my flesh longeth for thee in a dry and thirsty land, where no water is" (Ps. 63:1 KJV).

"To see thy power and thy glory, so as I have seen thee in the sanctuary" (Ps. 63:2 KJV).

"Because thy lovingkindness is better than life, my lips shall praise thee" (Ps. 63:3 KJV).

"O LORD, God of my salvation, I cry out day and night before you" (Ps. 88:1 ESV).

"Let my prayer come before you; incline your ear to my cry!" (Ps. 88:2 ESV).

"Attend unto my cry; for I am brought very low: deliver me from my persecutors; for they are stronger than I" (Ps. 142:6 KJV).

"I am ready to give up. I am losing my courage" (Ps. 143:4 ERV).

"Hurry and answer me, Lord! I have lost courage. Don't turn away from me. Don't let me die and become like the people lying in the grave" (Ps. 143:7 ERV).

"Be merciful unto me, O God, be merciful unto me: for my soul trusteth in thee: yea, in the shadow of thy wings will I make my refuge, until these calamities be overpast" (Ps. 57:1 KJV).

"My life is in danger. My enemies are all around me. They are like man-eating lions, with teeth like spears or arrows and tongues like sharp swords" (Ps. 57:4 ERV).

"Like a deer drinking from a stream, I reach out to you, my God" (Ps. 42:1 ERV).

"I will cry unto God most high; unto God that performeth all things for me" (Ps. 57:2 KJV).

"God, don't keep quiet! Don't close your ears! Please say something, God" (Ps. 83:1 ERV).

"The Lord made it known to me and I knew; then you showed me their deeds" (Jer. 11:18 ESV).

"And the word of the Lord came to me a second time" (Jer. 13:3 ESV).

"Great blessings belong to those who trust in the Lord, for those who do not run to demons and false gods for help" (Ps. 40:4 ERV).

"So through Jesus we should never stop offering our sacrifice to God. That sacrifice is our Praise, coming from lips that speak his name" (Heb. 13:15 ERV).

"And don't forget to do good and to share with those in need. These are the sacrifices that please God" (Heb. 13:16 NLT).

"For who is God save the Lord? Or who is a rock save our God?" (Ps. 18:31 KJV).

"It is God that girdeth me with strength, And maketh my way perfect" (Ps. 18:32 KJV).

"My heart is fixed, O God, my heart is fixed: I will sing and give praise" (Ps. 57:7 KJV).

"I will sacrifice a voluntary offering to you; I will praise your name, O Lord, for it is good" (Ps. 54:6 NLT).

"Praise ye the LORD. O give thanks unto the LORD; for he is good: for his mercy endure for ever" (Ps. 106:1 KJV).

"Who can utter the mighty acts of the LORD? Who can shew forth all his praise?" (Ps. 106:2 KJV).

"LORD, remember me when you show kindness to your people. Remember to save me too!" (Ps. 106:4 ERV).

"Let me share in the good things that you do for your chosen people. Let me rejoice with your nation. Let me join with your people in praise" (Ps. 106:5 ERV).

"I will sing forever about the LORD's love. I will sing about his faithfulness forever and ever!" (Ps. 89:1 ERV).

"I will say, "Your faithful love will last forever. Your loyalty is like the sky-there is no End to it!" (Ps. 89:2 ERV).

"The LORD taketh my part with them that help me: therefore shall I see my desire upon them that hate me" (Ps. 118:7 KJV).

"The LORD is my strength and song, and is become my salvation" (Ps. 118:14 KJV).

"The voice of rejoicing and salvation is in the tabernacles of the righteous: the right hand of the LORD doeth valiantly" (Ps. 118:15 KJV).

"The right hand of the LORD is exalted: the right hand of the LORD doeth valiantly" (Ps. 118:16 KJV).

"Thou art my God, and I will praise thee: thou art my God, I will exalt thee" (Ps. 118:28 KJV).

"Let the people praise thee, O God; let all the people praise thee" (Ps. 67:5 KJV).

"Then shall the earth yield her increase; and God, even our own God, shall bless us" (Ps. 67:6 KJV).

*In Jesus name, amen.*

## Notes

_____

_____

_____

# Please, Lord, Let Today Be My Breakthrough

## (Prayer)

"O Lord of hosts, God of Israel, enthroned above the cherubim, you are the God, you alone, of all the Kingdoms of the earth; you have made heaven and earth" (Isa. 37:16 ESV).

"Look to the right and see: there is none who takes notice of me; no refuge remains to me; no one cares for my soul" (Ps. 142:4 ESV).

"My eyes are awake before the watches of the night, that I may meditate on your promise" (Ps. 119:148 ESV).

"Remember your word to your servant, in which you have made me hope" (Ps. 119:49 ESV).

"Thus says the Lord who made the earth, the Lord who formed it to establish it—the Lord is his name" (Jer. 33:2 ESV).

"Call to me and I will answer you, and will tell you great and hidden things that you have not known" (Jer. 33:3 ESV).

"Be glad, O children of Zion, and rejoice in the Lord your God, for he has poured down for you abundant rain, the early and the latter rain, as before" (Joel 2:24 ESV).

"The threshing floors shall be full of grain; the vats shall overflow with wine and oil" (Joel 2:24 ESV).

"I will restore you the years that the swarming locust has eaten, the hopper, the destroyer, and the cutter; my great army, which I sent among you" (Joel 2:25 ESV).

"You shall eat in plenty and be satisfied, and praise the name of the LORD your God, who has dealt wondrously with you. And my people shall never again be put to shame" (Joel 2:26 ESV).

"And my tongue shall declare Your righteousness (justice), And Your praise all the day long" (Ps. 35:28 AMP).

"I bless the LORD who gives me counsel; in the night also my heart instructs me" (Ps. 16:7 ESV).

"O God, you are my God; earnestly I seek you; my soul thirst for you; my flesh faints for you, as in a dry and weary land where there is no water" (Ps. 63:1 ESV).

"God has taken his place in the divine council; in the midst of the gods he holds judgment" (Ps. 82:1 ESV).

"To hear the groans of the prisoners, to set free those who were doomed to die" (Ps. 102:20 ESV).

"So I have looked upon you in the sanctuary, beholding your power and glory" (Ps. 63:2 ESV).

"Give attention to the sound of my cry, my King and my God, for to you do I pray" (Ps. 5:2 ESV).

"Who can utter the mighty deeds of the LORD, or declare all his praise?" (Ps. 106:2 ESV).

"But may all who seek you rejoice and be glad in you; may those who love your salvation say continually, 'Great is the LORD!'" (Ps. 40:16 ESV).

"The LORD has established his throne in the heavens, and his Kingdom rules over all" (Ps. 103:19 ESV).

"To you I lift up my eyes, O you who are enthroned in the heavens!" (Ps. 123:1 ESV).

"You are the God who works wonders; you have made known your might among the peoples" (Ps. 77:14 ESV).

"You with your arm redeemed your people, the children of Jacob and Joseph" (Ps. 77:15 ESV). *Selah.*

"You led your people like a flock by the hand of Moses and Aaron" (Ps. 77:20 ESV).

"You split open springs and brooks; you dried up ever-flowing streams" (Ps. 74:15 ESV).

"He it was who struck down the first born of Egypt, both man and of beast" (Ps. 135:8 ESV).

"He rebuked the Red Sea, and it became dry, and he led them through the deep as through a desert" (Ps. 106:9 ESV).

"Who struck down many nations and killed mighty kings" (Ps. 135:10 ESV).

"Sihon, king of the Amorites, and Og, king of Bashan, and all the kingdoms of Canaan" (Ps. 135:11 ESV).

"You crush Rahab like a carcass; You scattered your enemies with your mighty arm" (Ps. 89:10 ESV).

"Oh, continue your steadfast love to those who know you, and your righteousness to the upright of heart!" (Ps. 36:10 ESV).

"Let not the foot of arrogance come upon me, nor the hand of the wicked drive me away" (Ps. 36:11 ESV).

"Let not the flood sweep over me, or the deep swallow me up, or the pit close its mouth over me" (Ps. 69:15 ESV).

"Hide not your face from your servant, for I am in distress; make haste to answer me" (Ps. 69:17 ESV).

"My spirit is broken; my days are extinct; the graveyard is ready for me" (Job 17:1 ESV).

"Summon your power, O God, the power, O God, by which you have worked for us" (Ps. 68:28 ESV).

"For you, O Lord, good and forgiving, abounding in steadfast love to all who call upon you" (Ps. 86:5 ESV).

"Even now, behold, my witness is in heaven, and he who testifies for me is on high" (Job 16:19 ESV).

"Whom have I in heaven but you? And there is nothing on earth that I desire besides you" (Ps. 73:25 ESV).

"If you, O Lord, should mark iniquities, O Lord, who could stand?" (Ps. 130:3 ESV).

"You have caused my companions to shun me; you have made me a horror to them. I am shut in so that I cannot escape" (Ps. 88:8 ESV).

"My eyes long for your promise; I ask, 'When will you comfort me?'" (Ps. 119:82 ESV).

"Will the Lord spurn forever, and never again be favorable?" (Ps. 77:7 ESV).

"Has his steadfast love forever ceased? Are his promises at an end for all time?" (Ps. 77:8 ESV).

"Has God forgotten to be gracious? Has he in anger shut up his compassion?" (Ps. 77:9 ESV). *Selah.*

"My God, my God, why have you forsaken me? Why are you so far from saving me, from words of my groaning?" (Ps. 22:2 ESV).

"O my God, I cry by day, but you do not answer, and by night, but I find no rest" (Ps. 22:2 ESV).

"Why, O Lord, do you stand far away? Why do you hide yourself in times of trouble?" (Ps. 10:1 ESV).

"How long, O Lord? Will you forget me forever? How long will you hide your face from me?" (Ps. 13:1 ESV).

"How long must I take counsel in my soul and have sorrow in my heart all the day? How long shall my enemy be exalted over me?" (Ps. 13:2 ESV).

"O Lord, rebuke me not in your anger, nor discipline me in your wrath!" (Ps. 38:1 ESV).

"I am utterly bowed down and prostrate; all the day I go about mourning" (Ps. 38:6 ESV).

"I am feeble and crushed; I groan because of the tumult of my heart" (Ps. 38:8 ESV).

"O Lord, all my longing is before you; my sighing is not hidden from you" (Ps. 38:9 ESV).

"My heart throbs; my strength fails me, and the light of my eyes – it also has gone from me" (Ps. 38:10 ESV).

"I have become like a man who does not hear; and in whose mouth are no rebukes" (Ps. 38:14 ESV).

"For I am ready to fall, and my pain is ever before me" (Ps. 38:17 ESV).

"Hear, O Lord, and be merciful to me! O Lord, be my helper!" (Ps. 30:10 ESV).

"Hear a just cause, O Lord; attend to my cry! Give ear to my prayer from lips free of deceit!" (Ps. 17:1 ESV).

"Restore to me the joy of your salvation, and uphold me with a willing spirit" (Ps. 51:12 ESV).

"O Lord, open my lips, and my mouth will declare your praise" (Ps. 51:15 ESV).

"Because your steadfast love is better than life, my lips will praise you" (Ps. 63:3 ESV).

"I will rejoice and be glad in your steadfast love, because you have seen my affliction; you have known the distress of my soul" (Ps. 31:7 ESV).

"So I will bless you as long as I live; in your name I will lift up my hands" (Ps. 63:4 ESV).

"Oh, guard my soul, and deliver me! Let me not be put to shame, for I take refuge in you" (Ps. 25:20 ESV).

"Do not sweep my soul away with sinners, nor my life with bloodthirsty men" (Ps. 26:9 ESV).

"Deliver me from all my transgressions. Do not make me the scorn of the fool!" (Ps. 39:8 ESV).

"Keep steady my steps according to your promise, and let no iniquity get dominion over me" (Ps. 114:133 ESV).

"Let your steadfast love come to me, O Lord, your salvation according to your promise" (Ps. 119:41 ESV).

"Confirm to your servant your promise, that you may be feared" (Ps. 119:38 ESV).

"Let your hand be ready to help me, for I have chosen your precepts" (Ps. 119:173 ESV).

"For you O Lord, are my hope, my trust, O Lord, from my youth" (Ps. 71:5 ESV).

"Let me dwell in your tent forever! Let me take refuge under the shelter of your wings!" (Ps. 61:4 ESV). *Selah*.

"Take away from me scorn and contempt, for I have kept your testimonies" (Ps. 119:22 ESV).

"Turn away the reproach that I dread, for your rules are good" (Ps. 119:39 ESV).

## PRAY IN GOD'S WORD FOR ENCOURAGEMENT AND CHANGE

"Let my soul live and praise You, And let Your ordinances help me" (Ps. 119:174 AMP).

"I Know, O Lord, that your rules are righteous, and that in faithfulness you have afflicted me" (Ps. 119:75 ESV).

"Bring me out of prison, that I may give thanks to your name! The righteous will surround me, for you will deal bountifully with me" (Ps. 142:7 ESV).

*In Jesus name, amen.*

## Notes

_____
_____
_____

# Lord, Please Comfort My Soul

## (Prayer)

"To you, O Lord, I lift up my soul" (Ps. 25:1 ESV).

"My soul longs for your salvation; I hope in your word" (Ps. 119:81 ESV).

"I know that you can do all things, and that no purpose of yours can be thwarted" (Job 42:2 ESV).

"Be gracious to me, O Lord, for I am languishing; heal me, O Lord, for my bones are troubled" (Ps. 6:2 ESV).

"My soul also is greatly troubled. But you, O Lord -how long?" (Ps. 6:3 ESV).

"From your presence let my vindication come! Let your eyes behold the right" (Ps. 17:2 ESV).

"My steps have held fast to your paths; my feet have not slipped" (Ps. 17:5 ESV).

"I have not hidden your deliverance within my heart; I have spoken of your faithfulness and your salvation; I have not concealed your steadfast love and your faithfulness from the great congregation" (Ps. 40:10 ESV).

"My frame was not hidden from you, when I was being made in secret, intricately woven in the depths of the earth" (Ps. 139:15 ESV).

"Your eyes saw my unformed substance; in your book where written, everyone of them, the days that were formed for me, when as yet there was none of them" (Ps. 139:16 ESV).

"Be merciful to me, O God be merciful to me, for in you my soul takes refuge; in the shadow of your wings I will take refuge, till the storms of destruction pass by" (Ps. 57:1 ESV).

"O Lord, I call upon you; hasten to me! Give ear to my voice when I call to you" (Ps. 141:1 ESV).

"Let my prayer be counted as incense before you, and the lifting up of my hands as the evening sacrifice!" (Ps. 141:2 ESV).

"O Lord, what is man that you regard him? Or the son of man that you think of him?" (Ps. 144:3 ESV).

"Man is like a breath; his days are like a passing shadow" (Ps. 141:2 ESV).

"The Lord is gracious and merciful, slow to anger and abounding in steadfast love" (Ps. 145:8 ESV).

"The Lord is good to all, and his mercy is over all that he has made" (Ps. 145:9 ESV).

"All your works shall give thanks to you, O Lord, and all your saints shall bless you!" (Ps. 145:10 ESV).

"The Lord upholds all who are falling and raises up all who are bowed down" (Ps. 145:14 ESV).

"The eyes of all look to you, and you give them their food in due season" (Ps. 145:15 ESV).

"You open your hand; you satisfy the desire of every living thing" (Ps. 145:16 ESV).

"The Lord is righteous in all his way and kind in all his works" (Ps. 145:17 ESV).

"The works of his hands are faithful and just; all his precepts are trustworthy" (Ps. 111:7 ESV).

"The Lord is near to all who call on him, to all who call on him in truth" (Ps. 145:18 ESV).

"He fulfills the desire of those who fear him; He also hears their cry and saves them" (Ps. 145:19 ESV).

"Gladden the soul of your servant, for to you, O Lord, do I lift up my soul" (Ps. 86:4 ESV).

"The Lord will perfect that which concerneth me: Thy mercy, O Lord, endureth for ever: Forsake not the works of thine own hands" (Ps. 138:8 KJV).

"Be surety for thy servant for good: Let not the proud oppress me" (Ps. 119:122 KJV).

"Deliver me from mine enemies, O my God: Defend me from them that rise up against me" (Ps. 59:1 KJV).

"Deliver me from my enemies, O Lord! I have fled to you for refuge" (Ps. 143:9 ESV).

"The Lord is my chosen portion and my cup; You hold my lot" (Ps. 16:5 ESV).

"Blessed are you, O Lord; teach me your statutes!" (Ps. 119:12 ESV).

"Teach me to do your will, for you are my God! Let your Spirit lead me on level ground!" (Ps. 143:10 ESV).

"How precious to me are your thoughts, O God! How vast is the sum of them!" (Ps. 139:17 ESV).

"O Lord, you have searched me and know me!" (Ps. 139:1 ESV).

"I have stored up your word in my heart, that I might not sin against you" (Ps. 119:11 ESV).

"You know when I sit down and when I rise up; you discern my thoughts from afar" (Ps. 139:2 ESV).

"For you formed my inward parts; you knitted me together in my mother's womb" (Ps. 139:13 ESV).

"I praise you, for I am fearfully and wonderfully made. Wonderful are your works; my soul knows it very well" (Ps. 139:14 ESV).

"Be the guarantee for Your servant for good [as Judah was the guarantee for Benjamin]; Do not let the arrogant oppress me" (Ps. 119:122 AMP).

"Listen carefully, I have created the smith who blows on the fire of coals And who produces a weapon for its purpose; And I have created the destroyer to inflict ruin" (Isa. 54:16 AMP).

> "No weapon that is formed against you will succeed; And every tongue that rises against you in judgment you will condemn. This [peace, righteousness, security, and triumph over opposi-

tion] is the heritage of the servants of the LORD,
And this is their vindication from Me," says the
LORD. (Isa. 54:17 AMP)

"You will be firmly established in righteousness: You will be far from [even the thought of] oppression, for you will not fear, And from terror, for it will not come near you" (Isa. 54:14 AMP).

"Indeed, all those who are angry with you will be put to shame and humiliated; Those who strive against you will be as nothing and will perish" (Isa. 41:11 AMP).

"The LORD has heard my plea; the LORD accepts my prayer" (Ps. 6:9 ESV).

"Your promise is well tried, and your servant loves it" (Ps. 119:140 AMP).

"All my enemies shall be ashamed and greatly troubled; they shall turn back and be put to shame in a moment" (Ps. 6:10 ESV).

*In Jesus name, amen.*

## Notes

_____
_____
_____

# The God of Israel Is Awesome in All His Ways

## (Prayer)

"Be gracious to me, O Lord, for to you, do I cry all the day" (Ps. 86:3 ESV).

"I cry aloud to God, aloud to God, and he will hear me" (Ps. 77:1 ESV).

"In the day of my trouble I seek the Lord; in the night my hand is stretched out without wearing; my soul refuses to be comforted" (Ps. 77:2 ESV).

"Because of the noise of the enemy, because of the oppression of the wicked. For they drop trouble upon me, and in anger they bear a grudge against me" (Ps. 55:3 ESV).

"Preserve my life, for I am godly; save your servant, who trusts in you- you are my God" (Ps. 86:2 ESV).

"Rescue the weak and the needy; deliver them from the hand of the wicked." (Ps. 82:4 ESV).

"Do not deliver the soul of your dove to the wild beasts; do not forget the life of your poor forever" (Ps. 74:19 ESV).

"My soul longs, yes, faints for the courts of the LORD; my heart and flesh sing for joy to the living God" (Ps. 84:2 ESV).

"Remember this, O LORD, how the enemy scoffs, and a foolish people reviles your name" (Ps. 74:18 ESV).

## PRAY IN GOD'S WORD FOR ENCOURAGEMENT AND CHANGE

"Destroy, O Lord, and divide their tongues: For I have seen violence and strife in the city" (Ps. 55:9 ESV).

"For, lo, thine enemies make a tumult: And they that hate thee have lifted up the head" (Ps. 83:2 KJV).

"O my God, make them like whirling dust, like chaff before the wind" (Ps. 83:13 ESV).

"As fire consumes the forest, as the flames sets the mountains ablaze" (Ps. 83:14 ESV).

"So may you pursue them with your tempest and terrify them with your hurricane" (Ps. 83:15 ESV).

"Fill their faces with shame, that they may seek your name, O Lord" (Ps. 83:16 ESV).

"Let them be put shame and dismayed forever; let them perish in disgrace" (Ps. 83:17 ESV).

"Let him rain coals on the wicked; fire and sulfur and scorching wind shall be the portion of their cup" (Ps. 11:6 ESV).

"Blessed are those whose strength is in you, in whose heart are the highway to Zion" (Ps. 84:5 ESV).

"For a day in your courts is better than a thousand elsewhere. I would rather be a doorkeeper in the house of my God than dwell in the tents of wickedness" (Ps. 84:10 ESV).

"You are the God who works wonders; you have made known your might among the peoples" (Ps. 77:14 ESV).

"For the Lord God is a sun and shield; the Lord bestows favor and honor. No good thing does he withhold from those who walk uprightly" (Ps. 84:11 ESV).

"For your way, O God, is holy. What god is great like our God?" (Ps. 77:13 ESV).

"When the waters saw you, O God, when the waters saw you, they were afraid; indeed, the deep trembled" (Ps. 77:16 ESV).

"The clouds poured out water; the skies gave forth thunder, your arrows flashed on every side" (Ps. 77:17 ESV).

"The crash of your thunder was in the whirlwind; your lightnings lighted up the world; the earth trembled and shook" (Ps. 77:18 ESV).

"Ascribe power to God, whose majesty is over Israel, and whose power is in the skies" (Ps. 68:34 ESV).

"I consider the days of old, the years long ago" (Ps. 77:5 ESV).

"You with your own hand drove out the nations, but them you planted; you afflicted the peoples, but them you set free" (Ps. 44:2 ESV).

"And he brought them to his holy land, to the mountain which his right hand had won" (Ps. 78:54 ESV).

"Truly God is good to Israel, to those who are pure in heart" (Ps. 73:1ESV).

"I will remember the deeds of the LORD, yes, I will remember your wonders of old" (Ps. 77:11 ESV).

"I will ponder all your work, and meditate on your mighty deeds" (Ps. 77:12 ESV).

"You with your arm redeemed your people, the children of Jacob and Joseph" (Ps. 77:15 ESV). *Selah.*

"In the sight of their fathers he performed wonders in the land of Egypt, in the fields of Zoan" (Ps. 78:12 ESV).

"Your way was through the sea, your path through the great waters; yet your footprints were unseen" (Ps. 77:19 ESV).

"In the daytime he led them with a cloud, and all the night with a fiery light" (Ps. 78:14 ESV).

"He split rocks in the wilderness and gave them drink abundantly as from the deep" (Ps. 78:15 ESV).

"He made streams come out of the rock and caused waters to flow down like rivers" (Ps. 78:16 ESV).

"There is none like you among the gods, O Lord, nor are there any works like yours" (Ps. 86:8 ESV).

"For you are great and do wondrous things; you alone are God" (Ps. 86:10 ESV).

"Send out your light and your truth; let them lead me; let them bring me to your holy hill and to your dwelling!" (Ps. 43:3 ESV).

"I entreat your favor with all my heart; be gracious to me according to your promise" (Ps. 119:58 ESV).

"Surely his salvation is near to those who fear him, that glory may dwell in our land" (Ps. 85:9 ESV).

"Your decrees are very trustworthy; holiness befits your house, O LORD, forevermore" (Ps. 93:5 ESV).

"Uphold me according to your promise, that I may live, and let me not be put to shame in my hope!" (Ps. 119:116 ESV).

"One thing have I asked of the LORD, that will I seek after: that I may dwell in the house of the LORD all the days of my life, to gaze upon the beauty of the LORD and to enquire in his temple" (Ps. 27:4 ESV).

"My lips will shout for joy, when I sing praises to you; my soul also, which you have redeemed" (Ps. 71:23 ESV).

"For who is God, but the LORD? And who is a rock, except our God?" (Ps. 18:31 ESV).

"The God who equipped me with strength and made my way blameless" (Ps. 18:32 ESV).

"You have given me the shield of your salvation, and your right hand supported me, and your gentleness made me great" (Ps. 18:35 ESV).

"You gave a wide place for my steps under me, and my feet did not slip" (Ps. 18:36 ESV).

"He brought me out into a broad place; he rescued me, because he delighted in me" (Ps. 18:19 ESV).

"Blessed is the one you choose and bring near, to dwell in your courts! We shall be satisfied with the goodness of your house, the holiness of your temple!" (Ps. 65:4 ESV).

"Awesome is God from his sanctuary; the God of Israel-he is the one who gives power and strength to his people. Blessed be God!" (Ps. 68:35 ESV).

*In Jesus name, amen.*

## Notes

_____
_____
_____

# My God Is Faithful

## (Prayer)

"I rise before dawn and cry for help; I hope in your words" (Ps. 119:147 ESV).

"I cry out to God Most High, to God who fulfills his purpose for me" (Ps. 57:2 ESV).

"O Lord, in the morning you hear my voice; in the morning I prepare a sacrifice for you and watch" (Ps. 5:3 ESV).

"Then shall I have an answer for him who taunts me, for I trust in your word" (Ps. 119:42 ESV).

"For thus says the One who is high and lifted up, who inhabits eternity, whose name is Holy: "I dwell in the high and holy place, and also with him who is of a contrite and lowly spirit, to revive the heart of the contrite" (Ps. 57:15 ESV).

"O God, hear my prayer; give ear to the words of my mouth" (Ps. 54:2 ESV).

"The wicked are estranged from the womb; they go astray from birth, speaking lies" (Ps. 58:3 ESV).

"But I, O Lord, cry to you; in the morning my prayer comes before you" (Ps. 88:13 ESV).

"Make haste, O God, to deliver me! O Lord, make haste to help me!" (Ps. 70:1 ESV).

"My soul is in the midst lions, I lie down amid fiery beasts- the children of man, whose teeth are spears and arrows, whose tongues are sharp swords" (Ps. 57:4 ESV).

"Whose mouths speak lies and whose right hand is a right hand of falsehood" (Ps. 144:8 ESV).

"For all day long I have been stricken and rebuked every morning" (Ps. 73:14 ESV).

"They make their tongue sharp as a serpent's and under their lips is the venom of asps" (Ps. 140:3 ESV).

"But I will sing of your strength; I will sing aloud of your steadfast love in the morning. For you have been to me a fortress and a refuge in the day of my distress" (Ps. 59:16 ESV).

"Behold, God is my helper; the Lord is the upholder of my life" (Ps. 54:4 ESV).

"He will send from heaven and save me; he will put to shame him who tramples on me. *Selah*. God will send out his steadfast love and his faithfulness!" (Ps. 57:3 ESV).

"He alone is my rock and my salvation, my fortress; I shall not be greatly shaken" (Ps. 62:2 ESV).

"On God rests my salvation and my glory; my mighty rock, my refuge is God" (Ps. 62:7 ESV).

"By awesome deeds you answer us with righteousness, O God of our salvation, the hope of all the ends of the earth and of the farthest seas" (Ps. 65:5 ESV).

"Trust in him at all times, O people; pour out your heart before him; God is a refuge for us" (Ps. 62:8 ESV). *Selah*.

"Therefore, since we have been justified by faith, we have peace with God through our Lord Jesus Christ" (Rom. 5:1 ESV).

"The Lord looks down from heaven on the children of man, to see if there are any who understand, who seek after God" (Ps. 14:2 ESV).

"I will look with favor on the faithful in the land, that they may dwell with me; he who walks in the way that is blameless shall minister to me" (Ps. 101:6 ESV).

"Those of low estate are but a breath; those of high estate are a delusion; in the balances they go up; they are together lighter than a breath" (Ps. 62:9 ESV).

"Put no trust in extortion; set no vain hopes on robbery; if riches increase, set not your heart on them" (Ps. 62:10 ESV).

"Better is the little that the righteous has than the abundance of many wicked" (Ps. 37:16 ESV).

"Once God has spoken; twice have I heard this: that power belongs to God" (Ps. 62:11 ESV).

"Who made heaven and earth, the sea, and all that is in them, who keeps faith forever" (Ps. 146:6 ESV).

"Who executes justice for the oppressed, who gives food to the hungry. The Lord sets the prisoners free" (Ps. 146:7 ESV).

"He provides food for those who fear him; he remembers his covenant forever" (Ps. 111:5 ESV).

"He raises up the poor out of the dust, And lifted the needy out of the dunghill" (Ps. 113:7 KJV).

"To make them sit with princes, with the princes of his people" (Ps. 113:8 ESV).

"My soul makes its boast in the Lord; let the humble hear and be glad" (Ps. 34:2 ESV).

"Say to those who have an anxious heart, "Be strong; fear not! Behold, your God will come with vengeance, with the recompense of God. He will come and save you." (Isa. 35:4 ESV).

"Then the eyes of the blind shall be opened, and the ears of the deaf unstopped" (Isa. 35:5 ESV).

"Then shall the lame man leap like a deer, and the tongue of the mute sing for joy. For waters break forth in the wilderness, and streams in the desert" (Isa. 35:6 ESV).

"The burning sand shall become a pool, and the thirsty ground springs of water; in the haunt of jackals, where they lie down, the grass shall become reeds and rushes" (Isa. 35:7 ESV).

"And a highway shall be there, and it shall be called the Way of Holiness; the unclean shall not pass over it. It shall belong to those who walk on the way; even if they are fools, they shall not go astray" (Isa. 35:8 ESV).

"No lion shall be there, nor shall any ravenous beast come up on it; they shall not be found there, but the redeemed shall walk there" (Isa. 35:9 ESV).

"And the ransomed of the Lord shall return and come to Zion with singing; everlasting joy shall be upon their heads; they shall obtain gladness and joy, and sorrow and sighing shall flee away" (Isa. 35:10 ESV).

"The LORD is the strength of his people; he is the saving refuge of his anointed" (Ps. 28:8 ESV).

"My times are in your hand; rescue me from the hand of my enemies and from my prosecutors!" (Ps. 31:15 ESV).

"In you, O LORD, do I take refuge; let me never be put to shame!" (Ps. 71:1 ESV).

"For you have been a stronghold to the poor, a stronghold to the needy in his distress, a shelter from the storm and a shade from the heat; for the breath of the ruthless is like a storm against a wall" (Isa. 25:4 ESV).

"Like heat in a dry land, You will subdue the noise of foreigners [rejoicing over their enemies]; Like heat in the shadow of the cloud, the song of the tyrants is silenced" (Isa. 25:5 AMP).

"Let me hear in the morning of your steadfast love, for in you I trust. Make me to know the way I should go, for to you I lift up my soul" (Ps. 71:8 ESV).

"Into your hand I commit my spirit; you have redeemed me, O LORD, faithful God" (Ps. 31:5 ESV).

"You guide me with your counsel, and afterward you will receive me to glory" (Ps. 73:24 ESV).

"Blessed is he whose help is the God of Jacob, whose hope is in the LORD his God" (Ps. 146:5 ESV).

*In Jesus name, amen.*

## Notes

_____
_____
_____

# Just Praise Him

## (Prayer)

"I have been as a potent to many, but you are my strong refuge" (Ps. 71:7 ESV).

"My mouth is filled with your praise, and with your glory all the day" (Ps. 71:8 ESV).

"I was glad when they said to me, "Let us go to the house of the Lord!" (Ps. 122:1 ESV).

"Great is the Lord, and greatly to be praised, and his greatness is unsearchable" (Ps. 145:3 ESV).

"For you are great and do wondrous things; you alone are God" (Ps. 86:10 ESV).

"To you I lift up my eyes, O you who are enthroned in the heavens!" (Ps. 123:1 ESV).

"Those who trust in the Lord are like Mount Zion, which cannot be moved, but abides forever" (Ps. 125:1 ESV).

"As the mountains surround Jerusalem, so the Lord surrounds his people, from this time forth and forevermore" (Ps. 125:2 ESV).

"Great is the Lord, and greatly to be praised, and his greatness is unsearchable" (Ps. 145:3 ESV).

"He changes times and seasons; he removes kings and sets up kings; he gives wisdom to the wise and knowledge to those who have understanding" (Dan. 2:21 ESV).

"With the merciful you show yourself merciful; with the blameless man you show yourself blameless" (Ps. 18:25 ESV).

"With the purified you show yourself pure; and the crooked you make yourself seem tortuous" (Ps. 18:26 ESV).

"For you save a humble people, but the haughty eyes you bring down" (Ps. 18:27 ESV).

"For it is you who light my lamp; the LORD my God lightens my darkness" (Ps. 18:28 ESV).

"He reveals deep and hidden things; he knows what is in the darkness, and the light dwells with him" (Dan. 2:22 ESV).

"How great are his signs, how mighty his wonders! His kingdom is an everlasting kingdom, and his dominion endures from generation to generation" (Dan. 4:3 ESV).

"All the inhabitants of the earth are accounted as nothing, and he does according to his will among the inhabitants of the earth; and none can stay his hand or say to him, "What have you done?" (Dan. 4:35 ESV).

"Thus says the LORD, the King of Israel and his Redeemer, the LORD of hosts: "I am the first and I am the last; besides me there is no god" (Isa. 44:6 ESV).

"Who is like me? Let him proclaim it. Let him declare and set it before me, since I appointed an ancient people. Let them declare what is to come, and what will happen" (Isa. 44:7 ESV).

"Am I a God at hand, declares the LORD, and not a God far away?" (Jer. 23:23 ESV).

"Can a man hide himself in secret places so that I cannot see him? Declares the LORD. Do I not fill heaven and earth? Declares the LORD" (Jer. 23:24 ESV).

"Shall a faultfinder contend with the Almighty? He who argues with God, let him answer it." (Job 40:2 ESV).

"Have the gates of death been revealed to you or have you seen the gates of deep darkness?" (Job 38:17 ESV).

"Do you know the ordinances of the heavens? Can you establish their rule on the earth?" (Job 38:33 ESV).

"Who has put wisdom in the inward parts or given understanding to the mind?" (Job 38:36 ESV).

"God is a righteous judge, and a God who feels indignation every day" (Ps. 7:11 ESV).

"If a man does not repent, God will whet his sword; he has bent and readied his bow" (Ps. 7:12 ESV).

"Behold, the wicked man conceives evil and is pregnant with mischief and gives birth to lies" (Ps. 7:14 ESV).

"His mischief returns upon his own head, and on his own skull his violence descends" (Ps. 7:16 ESV).

"Great peace have those who love your law; nothing can make them stumble" (Ps. 119:165 ESV).

"Your testimonies are wonderful; therefore my soul keeps them" (Ps. 119:129 ESV).

"I give thanks to you, O Lord my God, with my whole heart, and I will glorify your name forever" (Ps. 86:12 ESV).

"I will extol you, my God and King, and bless your name forever and ever" (Ps. 145:1 ESV).

"Every day I will bless you and praise your name forever and ever" (Ps. 145:2 ESV).

"On the glorious splendor of your majesty, and on your wondrous works, I will meditate" (Ps. 145:5 ESV).

"For who in the skies can be compared to the Lord? Who among the heavenly beings is like the Lord" (Ps. 89:6 ESV).

"A God greatly to be feared in the council of the holy ones, and awesome above all who are around him?" (Ps. 89:7 ESV).

"The heavens are yours; the earth also is yours; the world and all that is in it, you have found them" (Ps. 89:11 ESV).

"You rule the raging of the sea; when its waves rise, you still them" (Ps. 89:9 ESV).

"You have a mighty arm; strong is your hand, high your right hand" (Ps. 89:13 ESV).

"Righteousness and justice are the foundation of your throne; steadfast love and faithfulness go before you" (Ps. 89:14 ESV).

"For he delivers the needy when he calls, the poor and him who has no helper" (Ps. 72:12 ESV).

"He has pity on the weak and the needy, and saves the lives of the needy" (Ps. 72:13 ESV).

"Who forgives all your iniquity, who heals all your diseases" (Ps. 103:3 ESV).

"Who redeems your life from the pit, who crowns you with steadfast love and mercy" (Ps. 103:4 ESV).

"You crown the year with your bounty; your wagon tracks overflow with abundance" (Ps. 65:11 ESV).

"The Lord is near to the brokenhearted and saves the crush in spirit" (Ps. 34:18 ESV).

"The Lord redeems the life of his servants; none of those who take refuge in him will be condemned" (Ps. 34:22 ESV).

"Glorious are you, more majestic than the mountains full of prey" (Ps. 76:4 ESV).

"So I will bless you as long as I live; in your name I will lift up my hands" (Ps. 63:4 ESV).

"My soul will be satisfied as with fat and rich food, and my mouth will praise you with joyful lips" (Ps. 63:5 ESV).

"For you have been my help, and in the shadow of your wings I will sing for joy" (Ps. 63:7 ESV).

"Sing aloud to God our strength; shout for joy to the God of Jacob!" (Ps. 81:1 ESV).

"Make a joyful noise to the Lord all the earth; break into joyous song and sing praises!" (Ps. 98:4 ESV).

"Exalt the Lord our God; worship at his footstool! Holy is he!" (Ps. 99:5 ESV).

"My soul clings to you; your right hand upholds me" (Ps. 63:8 ESV).

"On the day I called, you answered me; my strength of my soul you increased" (Ps. 138:3 ESV).

"You are a hiding place for me; you preserve me from trouble; you surround me with shouts of deliverance" (Ps. 32:7 ESV). *Selah*.

"The Lord is good unto them that wait for him, To the soul that seeketh him" (Lam. 3:25 KJV).

"The Lord is my portion, saith my soul; Therefore will I hope in him" (Lam. 3:24 KJV).

"Father of the fatherless and protector of widows is God in his holy habitation" (Ps. 68:5 ESV).

"Splendor and majesty are before him; strength and beauty are in his sanctuary" (Ps. 96:6 ESV).

"Say to God, 'How awesome are your deeds! So great is your power that your enemies come cringing to you'" (Ps. 66:3 ESV).

"For the LORD, the Most High, is to be feared, a great king over all the earth" (Ps. 47:2 ESV).

"Bless be the LORD forever! Amen and Amen" (Ps. 89:52 ESV).

*In Jesus name, amen.*

## Notes

_____
_____
_____

# Lord, Remember Me in Mine Affliction

## (Prayer)

"To you, O Lord, I call; my rock, be not deaf to me, lest, if you be silent to me, I become like those who go down to the pit" (Ps. 28:1 ESV).

"I am severely afflicted; give me life, O Lord, according to your word!" (Ps. 119:107 ESV).

"My soul melts away for sorrow; strengthen me according to your word!" (Ps. 119:28 ESV).

"Preserve me, O God, for in you I take refuge" (Ps. 16:1 ESV).

"I say to the Lord, "You are my Lord; I have no good apart from you." (Ps. 16:2 ESV).

"Oh, that I knew where I might find him, that I might come even to his seat!" (Job 23:3 ESV).

"God has made my heart faint; the Almighty has terrified me" (Job 23:16 ESV).

"I was at ease, and he broke me apart; he seized me by the neck and dashed me to pieces; he set me up as his target" (Job 16:12 ESV).

"He hath fenced up my way that I cannot pass, And he hath set darkness in my paths" (Job 19:8 KJV).

"And has shriveled me up, which is a witness against me, and my leanness has risen up against me; it testifies to my face" (Job 16:8 ESV).

"He has stripped from me my glory and taken the crown from my head" (Job 19:9 ESV).

"He breaks me down on every side, and I am gone, and my hope has he pulled up like a tree" (Job 19:10 ESV).

"He has kindled his wrath against me and counts me his adversary" (Job 19:11 ESV).

"He has torn me in his wrath and hated me; he has gnashed his teeth at me; my adversary sharpens his eyes against me" (Job 16:9 ESV).

"My relatives have failed me, my close friends have forgotten me" (Job 19:14 ESV).

"All my intimate friends abhor me, and those whom I loved have turned against me" (Job 19:19 ESV).

"Reproaches have broken my heart, so that I am in despair. I looked for pity, but there was none, and for comforters, but I found none" (Ps. 69:20 ESV).

"He has made me a byword of the peoples, and I am one before whom men spit" (Job 17:6 ESV).

"He breaks me with breach upon breach; he runs upon me like a warrior" (Job 16:14 ESV).

"My face is red with weeping, and on my eyelids is deep darkness" (Job 16:16 ESV).

"Yet I am not silence because of the darkness, nor because thick darkness covers my face" (Job 23:17 ESV).

"My foot has held fast to his steps; I have kept his way and not turned aside" (Job 23:11 ESV).

"I have not departed from the commandment of his lips; I have treasured the words of his mouth more than my portion of food" (Job 23:12 ESV).

"But I am a worm and not a man, scorned by mankind and despised by the people" (Ps. 22:6 ESV).

"Behold, I go forward, but he is not there, and backward, but I do not perceive him" (Job 23:8 ESV).

"On the left hand when he is working, I do not behold him; he turns to the right hand, but I do not see him" (Job 23:9 ESV).

"But you, O Lord, do not be far off! O you my help, come quickly to my aid!" (Ps. 22:19 ESV).

"Has not man a hard service on earth, and are not his days like the days of a hired hand?" (Job 7:1 ESV).

"Like a slave who longs for the shadow, and like a hired hand who looks for his wages" (Job 7:2 ESV).

"So I am allotted months of emptiness, and nights of misery are apportioned to me" (Job 7:3 ESV).

"When I lie down I say, 'When shall I arise?' But I am full of tossing till the dawn" (Job 7:4 ESV).

""Lay down a pledge for me with you; who is there who will put up security for me?" (Job 17:3 ESV).

"O God, do not keep silence; do not hold your peace or be still, O God!" (Ps. 83:1 ESV).

"Hope deferred makes the heart sick, but a desire fulfilled is a tree of life" (Prov. 13:12 ESV).

"Heal me, O Lord, and I shall be healed; save me, and I shall be saved, for you are my praise" (Jer. 17:14 ESV).

"Remember my affliction and my wanderings, the wormwood and the gall!" (Lam. 3:19 ESV).

"My soul continually remembers it and is bowed down within me" (Lam. 3:20 ESV).

"My tears have been my food day and night, while they say to me all the day long, "Where is your God?"" (Ps. 42:3 ESV).

"All day long they injure my cause; all their thoughts are against me for evil" (Ps. 56:5 ESV).

"But I am afflicted and in pain; let your salvation, O God, set me on high!" (Ps. 69:29 ESV).

"The troubles of my heart are enlarged; bring me out of my distresses" (Ps. 25:17 ESV).

"O Lord of hosts, who tests the righteous, who sees the heart and mind, let me see your vengeance upon them, for to you have I committed my cause" (Jer. 20:12 ESV).

"Attend to me, and answer me; I am restless in my complaint and I moan" (Ps. 55:2 ESV).

"Many are saying of my soul, 'There is no salvation for him in God'" (Ps. 3:2 ESV).

"I am the Lord; that is my name; my glory I give to no other, nor my praise to carved idols" (Isa. 42:8 ESV).

"Hear, you deaf, and look, you blind, that you may see!" (Isa. 42:18 ESV).

"When the poor and needy seek water, and there is none, and their tongue is parched with thirst, I the Lord will answer them; I the God of Israel will not forsake them" (Isa. 41:17 ESV).

"I will open rivers on the bare heights, and fountains in the midst of the valleys. I will make the wilderness a pool of water, and the dry land springs of water" (Isa. 41:18 ESV).

"I will put in the wilderness the cedar, the acacia, the myrtle, and the olive. I will set in the desert the cypress, the plane and the pine together" (Isa. 41:19 ESV).

"That they may see and know, may consider and understand together, that the hand of the Lord has done this, the Holy One of Israel has created it" (Isa. 41:20 ESV).

"For I, the Lord your God, hold your right hand; it is I who say to you. 'Fear not, I am the one who helps you'" (Isa. 41:13 ESV).

"How sweet are your words to my taste, sweeter than honey to my mouth!" (Ps. 119:103 ESV).

"'Who is this that hides counsel without knowledge?' Therefore I have uttered what I did not understand, things too wonderful for me, which I did not know" (Job 42:3 ESV).

"For the word of the Lord is upright, and all his work is done in faithfulness" (Ps. 33:4 ESV).

"Your righteousness is righteous forever, and your law is true" (Ps. 119:142 ESV).

"He loves righteousness and justice; the earth is full of the steadfast love of the Lord" (Ps. 33:5 ESV).

"Hear my voice according to your steadfast love; O Lord, according to your justice give me life" (Ps. 119:149 ESV).

"I will meditate on your precepts and fix my eyes on your ways" (Ps. 119:15 ESV).

"I will delight in your statutes; I will not forget your word" (Ps. 119:16 ESV).

## PRAY IN GOD'S WORD FOR ENCOURAGEMENT AND CHANGE

"By the word of the Lord the heavens were made, and by the breath of his mouth all their host" (Ps. 33:6 ESV).

"He gathers the water of the sea as a heap; he puts the deeps in storehouses" (Ps. 33:7 ESV).

"Let all the earth fear the Lord; let all the inhabitants of the world stand in awe of him!" (Ps. 33:8 ESV).

"For he spoke, and it came to be; he commanded, and it stood firm" (Ps. 33:9 ESV).

"O Lord, our Lord, how majestic is your name in all the earth! You have set glory above the heavens" (Ps. 8:1 ESV).

"I had heard of you by the hearing of the ear, but now my eye sees you" (Job 42:5 ESV).

"Therefore I despise myself, and repent in dust and ashes." (Job 42:6 ESV).

"The Mighty One, God the Lord, speaks and summons the earth from the rising of the sun to its setting" (Ps. 50:1 ESV).

"Out of Zion, the perfection of beauty, God shines forth" (Ps. 50:2 ESV).

"He calls to the heavens above and to the earth, that he may judge his people" (Ps. 50:4 ESV).

"As your name, O God, so your praise reaches to the ends of the earth. Your right hand is filled with righteousness" (Ps. 48:10 ESV).

"The heavens declare his righteousness, for God himself is judge!" (Ps. 50:6 ESV). *Selah.*

"I will give thanks to the Lord with my whole heart; I will recount all of your wonderful deeds" (Ps. 9:1 ESV).

"I will be glad and exult in you; I will sing praise to your name, O Most High" (Ps. 9:2 ESV).

"In God, whose word I praise, in the Lord, whose word I praise" (Ps. 56:10 ESV).

"Let the redeemed of the Lord say so, whom he has redeemed from trouble" (Ps. 107:2 ESV).

"I have called upon thee, for thou wilt hear me, O God: incline thine ear unto me, and hear my speech" (Ps. 17:6 KJV).

"Wondrously show your steadfast love, O Savior of those who seek refuge from their adversaries at your right hand" (Ps. 17:7 ESV).

"For by you I can run against a troop, and by my God I can leap over a wall" (Ps. 18:29 ESV).

"When my enemies turn back, they stumble and perish before your presence" (Ps. 9:3 ESV).

"For thou hast maintained my right and my cause; Thou satest in the throne judging right" (Ps. 9:4 KJV).

"May all who seek you rejoice and be glad in you! May those who love salvation say evermore, "God is great!"" (Ps. 70:4 ESV).

"For your steadfast love is great to the heavens, your faithfulness to the clouds" (Ps. 57:10 ESV).

"Be exalted, O God, above the heavens! Let your glory be over all the earth!" (Ps. 57:11 ESV).

"Let thy mercies come also unto me, O Lord, Even thy salvation, according to thy word" (Ps. 119:41 KJV).

"This is my comfort in my affliction, that your promise gives me life" (Ps. 119:50 ESV).

*In Jesus name, amen.*

## Notes

_____
_____
_____

# The God Who Answers Prayers

## (Prayer)

"I give you thanks, O Lord, with my whole heart; before the gods I sing your praise" (Ps. 138:1 ESV).

"For the Lord is a great God, and a great King above all gods" (Ps. 95:3 ESV).

"My mouth is filled with your praise, and with your glory all the day" (Ps. 71:8 ESV).

"Do not cast me off in the time of old age; forsake me not when my strength is spent" (Ps. 71:9 ESV).

"For you, O Lord, are my hope, my trust, O Lord, from my youth" (Ps. 71:5 ESV).

"You who have made me see many troubles and calamities will revive me again; from the depths of the earth you will bring me up again" (Ps. 71:20 ESV).

"My lips shall greatly rejoice when I sing unto thee; And my soul, which thou hast redeemed" (Ps. 71:23 KJV).

"Sing praises to God, sing praises: Sing praises unto our King, sing praises" (Ps. 47:6 KJV).

"For God is the King of all the earth; sing praises with a psalm!" (Ps. 47:7 ESV).

"O you who hear prayer, to you shall all flesh come" (Ps. 65:2 ESV).

"Hear my cry, O God, listen to my prayer" (Ps. 61:1 ESV).

"Answer me, O Lord, for your steadfast love is good; according to your abundant mercy, turn to me" (Ps. 69:16 ESV).

"Hide me from the secret plots of the wicked, from the throng of evildoers" (Ps. 64:2 ESV).

"I love you, O Lord, my strength" (Ps. 18:1 ESV).

"Oh that my ways may be steadfast in keeping your statutes!" (Ps. 119:5 ESV).

"Thus says God, the Lord, who created the heavens and stretched them out, who spread out the earth and what comes from it, who gives breath to the people on it and spirit to those who walk in it" (Isa. 42:5 ESV).

"Hear, you who are far off, what I have done; and you who are near, acknowledge my might" (Isa. 33:13 ESV).

"When I shut up the heavens so that there is no rain, or command the locust to devour the land, or send pestilence among my people" (2 Chron. 7:13 ESV).

"If my people who are called by my name humble themselves, and pray and seek my face and turn from their wicked ways, then I will hear from heaven and will forgive their sin and heal their land" (2 Chron. 7:14 ESV).

"For he satisfies the longing soul, and the hungry soul he fills with good things" (Ps. 107:9 ESV).

"The Lord is merciful and gracious, slow to anger and abounding in steadfast love" (Ps. 103:8 ESV).

"Righteous are you, O Lord, and right are your rules" (Ps. 119:137 ESV).

"By awesome and wonderful things You answer us in righteousness, O God of our salvation, You who are the trust and hope of all the ends of the earth and of the farthest sea" (Ps. 65:5 AMP).

"All the earth worships you and sing praises to you; they sing praises to your name" (Ps. 66:4 ESV). *Selah.*

"The Lord of hosts is with us; the God of Jacob is our fortress" (Ps. 46:11 ESV).

"The Lord preserves the simple; when I was brought low, he saved me" (Ps. 116:6 ESV).

## PRAY IN GOD'S WORD FOR ENCOURAGEMENT AND CHANGE

"Return, O my soul, to your rest; for the LORD has dealt bountifully with you" (Ps. 116:7 ESV).

"What shall I render to the LORD for all his benefits to me?" (Ps. 116:12 ESV).

"I will never forget Your precepts, For by them You have revived me and given me life" (Ps. 119:93 AMP).

"I will run the way of Your commandments [with purpose], For You will give me a heart that is willing" (Ps. 119:32 AMP).

"I will praise the LORD as long as I live; I will sing praises to my God while I have my being" (Ps. 146:2 ESV).

"I will lift up the cup of salvation and call on the name of the LORD" (Ps. 116:13 ESV).

"O LORD, I am your servant; I am your servant, the son of your maidservant. You have loosed my bonds" (Ps. 116:16 ESV).

"You have turned for me my mourning into dancing; you have loosed my sackcloth and clothed me with gladness" (Ps. 30:11 ESV).

"I thank you that you have answered me and have become my salvation" (Ps. 118:21 ESV).

"Oh, how abundant is your goodness, which you have stored up for those who fear you and worked for those who take refuge in you, in the sight of the children of mankind!" (Ps. 31:19 ESV).

"I will offer to you the sacrifice of thanksgiving and call on the name of the LORD" (Ps. 116:17 ESV).

"I will remember the works of the LORD: Surely I will remember thy wonders of old" (Ps. 77:11 ESV).

"He set the earth on its foundations, so that it should never be moved" (Ps. 104:5 ESV).

"You visit the earth and water it; you greatly enrich it; the river of God is full of water; you provide their grain, for so you have prepared it" (Ps. 65:9 ESV).

"Yes, the LORD will give what is good, and our land will yield its increase" (Ps. 85:12 ESV).

"From your lofty abode you water the mountains; the earth is satisfied with the fruit of your work" (Ps. 104:13 ESV).

"You cause the grass to grow for the livestock and plants for man to cultivate, that he may bring forth from the earth" (Ps. 104:14 ESV).

"And wine to gladden the heart of man, oil to make his face shine and bread to strengthen man's heart" (Ps. 104:15 ESV).

"The earth has yielded its increase; God, our God, shall bless us" (Ps. 67:6 ESV).

"God shall bless us; And all the ends of the earth shall fear him" (Ps. 67:7 KJV).

*In Jesus name, amen.*

## Notes

_____
_____
_____

# Lord, My Soul Is Discouraged and Turmoiled

## (Prayer)

"To you, O Lord, I lift up my soul" (Ps. 25:1 ESV).

"For God alone, O my soul, wait in silence, for my hope is from him" (Ps. 62:5 ESV).

"As God lives, who has taken away my right, and the Almighty, who has made my soul bitter" (Job 27:2 ESV).

"As long as my breath is in me, and the spirit of God is in my nostrils" (Job 27:3 ESV).

"My lips will not speak falsehood, and my tongue will not utter deceit" (Job 27:4 ESV).

"For God alone my soul waits in silence; from him comes my salvation" (Ps. 62:1 ESV).

"Whoever walks in uprightness fears the Lord, but he who is devious in his ways despises him" (Prov. 14:2 ESV).

"The fool says in his heart, "There is no God." They are corrupt, they do abominable deeds; there is none who does good" (Ps. 14:1 ESV).

"But I have trusted in your steadfast love; my heart shall rejoice in your salvation" (Ps. 13:5 ESV).

"With regard to the works of man, by the word of your lips I have avoided the ways of the violent" (Ps. 17:4 ESV).

"I love you, O Lord, my strength" (Ps. 18:1 ESV).

"Be not far from me, for trouble is near, and there is none to help" (Ps. 22:11 ESV).

"To you, O Lord, I lift up my soul" (Ps. 25:1 ESV).

"Hear, O Lord, when I cry aloud; be gracious to me and answer me!" (Ps. 27:7 ESV).

"Be gracious to me, O Lord, for I am in distress; my eyes is wasted from grief; my soul and my body also" (Ps. 31:9 ESV).

"Because of all my adversaries I have become a reproach, especially to my neighbors, and an object of dread to my acquaintances; those who see me in the street flee from me" (Ps. 31:11 ESV).

"I have been forgotten like one who is dead; I have become like a broken vessel" (Ps. 31:12 ESV).

"As with a deadly wound in my bones, my adversaries taunt me, while they say to me all day long, "where is your God?" (Ps. 42:10 ESV).

"Even my close friends in whom I trusted, who ate my bread, has lifted his heel against me" (Ps. 41:9 ESV).

"You have caused my beloved and my friend to shun me; my companions have become darkness" (Ps. 88:18 ESV).

"Why are you cast down, O my soul, and why are you in turmoil within me? Hope in God; for I shall again praise him, my salvation" (Ps. 42:5 ESV).

"Behold, the eye of the Lord is on those who fear him, on those who hope in his steadfast love" (Ps. 33:18 ESV).

"That he may deliver their soul from death and keep them alive in famine" (Ps. 33:19 ESV).

"Blessed is the one whose transgression is forgiven, whose sin is covered" (Ps. 32:1 ESV).

"Blessed is the man against whom the Lord counts no iniquity, and in whose spirit there is no deceit" (Ps. 32:2 ESV).

"For when I kept silent, my bones wasted away through my groaning all day long" (Ps. 32:3 ESV).

"For day and night your hand was heavy upon me; my strength was dried up as by the heat of summer" (Ps. 32:4 ESV).

"Then I said, 'I will appeal to this, to the years of the right hand of the Most High'" (Ps. 77:10 ESV).

"I acknowledged my sin to you, and I did not cover my iniquity; I said, "I will confess my transgressions to the Lord," and you forgave the iniquity of my sin" (Ps. 32:5 ESV).

"You have kept count of my tossings; put my tears in your bottle. Are they not in your book?" (Ps. 56:8 ESV).

"Give ear, O Lord, to my prayer; listen to my plea for grace" (Ps. 86:6 ESV).

"O Lord, hear my voice! Let your ears be attentive to the voice of my pleas for mercy!" (Ps. 130:2 ESV).

"I counted among those who go down to the pit; I am a man who has no strength" (Ps. 88:4 ESV).

"Like one set loose among the dead, like the slain that lie in the grave, like those whom you have remember no more, for they are cut off from your hand" (Ps. 88:5 ESV).

"You have put me in the depths of the pit, in the regions dark and deep" (Ps. 88:6 ESV).

"As it is written, "For your sake we are being killed all the day long; we are regarded as sheep to be slaughtered." (Rom. 8:36 ESV).

"For my days pass away like smoke, and my bones burn like a furnace" (Ps. 102:3 ESV).

"My heart is struck down like grass and has withered; I forgot to eat my bread" (Ps. 102:4 ESV).

"Because of my loud groaning my bones cling to my flesh" (Ps. 102:5 ESV).

"I lie awake; I am like a lonely sparrow on the housetop" (Ps. 102:7 ESV).

"But you, O Lord, are enthroned forever; you are remembered throughout all generations" (Ps. 102:12 ESV).

"Let this be recorded for all generation to come, so that a people yet to be created may praise the Lord" (Ps. 102:18 ESV).

"He regards the prayer of the destitute and does not despise their prayer" (Ps. 102:17 ESV).

"For he said, 'Surely they are my people, children who will not deal falsely.' And he became their Savior" (Isa. 63:8 ESV).

"Blessed are those who keep his testimonies, who seek him with their whole heart" (Ps. 119:2 ESV).

"Bless the Lord, O my soul, and that all that is within me, bless his holy name!" (Ps. 103:1 ESV).

"I rejoice at your word like one who finds great spoil" (Ps. 119:162 ESV).

"Bless the Lord, O my soul, and forget not all his benefits" (Ps. 103:2 ESV).

"The Lord works righteousness and justice for all who are oppressed" (Ps. 103:6 ESV).

"He will not always chide, nor will he keep his anger forever" (Ps. 103:9 ESV).

"He does not deal with us according to our sins, nor repay us according to our iniquities" (Ps. 103:10 ESV).

"For as high as the heavens are above the earth, so great is his steadfast love toward those who fear him" (Ps. 103:11 ESV).

"As far as the east is from the west, so far does the he remove our transgressions from us" (Ps. 103:12 ESV).

"As a father shows compassion to his children, so the Lord shows compassion to those who fear him" (Ps. 103:13 ESV).

"For he knows our frame; he remembers that we are dust" (Ps. 103:14 ESV).

"The Lord records as he registers the peoples, "This one was born there." (Ps. 87:6 ESV).

"Behold, the Lord will empty the earth and make it desolate, and he will twist its surface and scatter its inhabitants" (Isa. 24:1 ESV).

"But the steadfast love of the Lord is from everlasting to everlasting on those who fear him, and his righteousness to children's children" (Ps. 103:17 ESV).

"I was pushed hard, so that I was falling, but the Lord helped me" (Ps. 118:13 ESV).

"The Lord is my strength and my song; he has become my salvation" (Ps. 118:14 ESV).

"Glad songs of salvation are in the tents of the righteous: "The right hand of the Lord does valiantly" (Ps. 118:15 ESV).

"The right hand of the Lord exalts, the right hand of the Lord does valiantly!" (Ps. 118:16 ESV).

"Keep me as the apple of your eye; hide me in the shadow of your wings" (Ps. 17:8 ESV).

"O Lord, you hear the desire of the afflicted; you will strengthen their heart; you will incline your ear" (Ps. 10:17 ESV).

"It was good for me that I was afflicted, that I might learn your statutes" (Ps. 119:71 ESV).

"For you have delivered my soul from death, yes, my feet from falling, that I may walk before God in the light of life" (Ps. 56:13 ESV).

"Therefore I will look unto the Lord; I will wait for the God of my salvation: my God will hear me" (Mic. 7:7 ESV).

*In Jesus name, amen.*

## Notes

_____

_____

_____

# Thanking Abba for My Covenant Blessings

## (Prayer)

"With my voice I cry out to the LORD; with my voice I plead for mercy to the LORD" (Ps. 142:1 ESV).

"And I said, 'O LORD God of heaven, the great and awesome God who keeps covenant and steadfast love with those who love him and keep his commandments'" (Neh. 1:5 ESV).

"Blessed is the man who walks not in the counsel of the wicked, nor stands in the way of sinners, nor sits in the seat of scoffers" (Ps. 1:1 ESV).

"For you are not a God who delights in wickedness; evil may not dwell with you" (Ps. 5:4 ESV).

"Turn, O LORD, deliver my life; save me for the sake of your steadfast love" (Ps. 6:4 ESV).

"I am weary with my moaning; every night I flood my bed with tears; I drench my couch with my weeping" (Ps. 6:6 ESV).

"My eye wastes away because of grief; it grows weak because of all my foes" (Ps. 6:7 ESV).

"For my sighing comes instead of my bread, and my groanings are poured out like water" (Job 3:24 ESV).

"For the thing that I fear comes upon me, and what I dread befalls me" (Jobs 3:25 ESV).

"I am not at ease, nor am I quiet; I have no rest, but trouble comes." (Job 3:26 ESV).

"Oh that I might have my request, and that God would fulfill my hope" (Job 6:8 ESV).

"Have I any help in me, when resource is driven from me?" (Job 6:13 ESV).

"Therefore I will not restrain my mouth; I will speak in the anguish of my spirit; I will complain in the bitterness of my soul" (Job 7:11 ESV).

"For you will not abandon my soul to Sheol, or let your holy one see corruption" (Ps. 16:10 ESV).

"From the wicked who do me violence, my deadly enemies who surround me" (Ps. 17:9 ESV).

"They close their hearts to pity; with their mouths they speak arrogantly" (Ps. 17:10 ESV).

"The LORD is my portion; I promise to keep your words" (Ps. 119:57 ESV).

"O LORD, you are my God; I will exalt you; I will praise your name, for you have done wonderful things, plans formed of old, faithful and sure" (Isa. 25:1 ESV).

"All the paths of the LORD are steadfast love and faithfulness, for those who keeps his covenant and his testimonies" (Ps. 25:10 ESV).

"The friendship of the LORD is for those who fear him, and he makes known to them his covenant" (Ps. 25:14 ESV).

"O LORD of hosts, blessed is the one who trusts in you!" (Ps. 84:12 ESV).

"I give you thanks, O LORD, with my whole heart; before the gods I sing your praise" (Ps. 138:1 ESV).

"Behold, the LORD's hand is not shortened, that it cannot save; neither his ear heavy, that it cannot hear" (Isa. 59:1 ESV).

"Give thanks to the LORD, for he is good, for his steadfast love endures forever" (Ps. 136:1 ESV).

"Give thanks to the God of gods, for his steadfast love endures forever" (Ps. 136:2 ESV).

"Give thanks to the Lord of lords, for his steadfast love endures forever" (Ps. 136:3 ESV).

"He sent redemption to his people; he has commanded his covenant forever. Holy and awesome is his name!" (Ps. 111:9 ESV).

"Praise the Lord! I will give thanks to the Lord with my whole heart, in the company of the upright, in the congregation" (Ps. 111:1 ESV).

"I will lift up mine eyes unto the hills, from whence cometh my help" (Ps. 121:1 KJV).

"My help cometh from the Lord, Which made heaven and earth" (Ps. 121:2 KJV).

"He brings the clouds from the other side of the earth. He sends the lightning and the rain, and he opens the doors to release the winds" (Ps. 135:7 ERV).

"Lord, your name will be famous forever! Lord, people will remember you forever and ever" (Ps. 135:13 ERV).

"The Lord defends his people; he is kind to his servants" (Ps. 135:14 ERV).

"Hear my prayer, O Lord; let my cry come to you!" (Ps. 102:1 ESV).

"Do not hide your face from me in the day of my distress! Incline your ear to me; answer me speedily in the day when I call!" (Ps. 102:2 ESV).

"Have regard for the covenant, for the dark places of the land are full of the habitations of violence" (Ps. 74:20 ESV).

"Look down from heaven and see, from your holy and beautiful habitation. Where are your zeal and your might? The stirring of your inner parts and your compassion are held back from me" (Isa. 63:15 ESV).

"Oh that you would rend the heavens and come down, that the mountains might quake at your presence—" (Isa. 64:1 ESV).

"For the enemy has pursued my soul; he has crushed my life to the ground; he has made me sit in darkness like those long dead" (Ps. 143:3 ESV).

"Therefore my spirit faints within me; my heart within me is appalled" (Ps. 143:4 ESV).

"But you, O God my Lord, deal on my behalf for your name's sake; because your steadfast love is good, deliver me!" (Ps. 109:21 ESV).

## PRAY IN GOD'S WORD FOR ENCOURAGEMENT AND CHANGE

"Be not silent, O God of my praise!" (Ps. 109:1 ESV).

"There is no speech, nor are there words, whose voice is not heard" (Ps. 19:3 ESV).

"Even before a word is on my tongue, behold, O Lord, you know it altogether" (Ps. 139:4 ESV).

"Let my cry come near before thee, O Lord: Give me understanding according to thy word" (Ps. 11:169 KJV).

"Let my plea come before you; deliver me according to your word" (Ps. 119:170 ESV).

"The law of the Lord is perfect reviving the soul; the testimony of the Lord is sure, making wise the simple" (Ps. 19:7 ESV).

"The precepts of the Lord are right, rejoicing the heart; the commandment of the Lord is pure, enlightening the eyes" (Ps. 19:8 ESV).

"The fear of the Lord is clean, enduring forever; the rules of the Lord are true, and righteous altogether" (Ps. 19:9 ESV).

"More to be desired are they than gold, even much fine gold; sweeter also than honey and drippings of the honeycomb" (Ps. 19:10 ESV).

"They are established forever and ever, to be performed with faithfulness and uprightness" (Ps. 111.8 ESV).

"I have chosen the way of faithfulness; I set your rules before me" (Ps. 119:30 ESV).

"He hath made his wonderful works to be remembered: The Lord is gracious and full of compassion" (Ps. 111:4 ESV).

"Remember the word unto thy servant, Upon which thou hast caused me to hope" (Ps. 119:49 KJV).

"May God give you of the dew of heaven and of the fatness of the earth and plenty of grain and wine" (Gen. 27:28 ESV).

"Let peoples serve you, and nations bow down to you. Be lord over your brothers, and may your mother's sons bow down to you. Cursed be everyone who curses you, and blessed be everyone who blesses you!" (Gen. 27:29 ESV).

"This blessing has fallen to me, that I have kept your precepts" (Ps. 119:56 ESV).

"He sent redemption to his people; he has commanded his covenant forever. Holy and awesome is his name!" (Ps. 111:9 ESV).

"For in Christ Jesus you are all sons God, through faith" (Gal. 3:26 ESV).

"For as many of you as were baptized into Christ have put on Christ" (Gal. 3:27 ESV).

"And Christ's, then you are Abraham's offspring, heirs according to promise" (Gal. 3:29 ESV).

"My eyes long for your salvation and for the fulfillment of your righteous promise" (Ps. 119:123 ESV).

"I am your servant; give me understanding, that I may know your testimonies!" (Ps. 119:125 ESV).

"Thus says the Lord: 'As the new wine is found in the cluster, and they say, "Do not destroy it, for there is a blessing in it," so I will do for my servants' sake, and not destroy them all'" (Isa. 65:8 ESV).

"Because the poor are plundered, because the needy groan, I will now arise, "says the Lord; "I will place him in the safety for which he longs" (Ps. 12:5 ESV).

"For as the new heavens and the new earth that I make shall remain before me, says the Lord, so shall your offspring and your name remain" (Isa. 66:22 ESV).

"From new moon to new moon, and from Sabbath to Sabbath, all flesh shall come to worship before me, declares the Lord" (Isa. 66:23 ESV).

"But now in Christ Jesus you who once were far off have been brought near by the blood of Christ" (Eph. 2:13 ESV).

"I will give to the Lord the thanks due to his righteousness, and I will sing praise to the name of the Lord, the Most High" (Ps. 7:17 ESV).

"My shield and my defense depend on God, Who saves the upright in heart" (Ps. 7:10 ESV).

"He reached from on high, He took me; He drew me out of many waters" (Ps. 18:16 AMP).

"Therefore my heart is glad, and my whole being rejoices; my flesh also dwells secure" (Ps. 16:9 ESV).

"He rescued me from my strong enemy and from those who hated me, for they were too mighty for me" (Ps. 18:17 ESV).

"You have dealt well with your servant, O Lord, according to your word" (Ps. 119:65 ESV).

"You have granted me life and steadfast love, and your care has preserved my spirit" (Job 10:12 ESV).

"That my glory may sing your praise and not be silent. O Lord my God, I will give thanks to you forever!" (Ps. 30:12 ESV).

"For great is his steadfast love toward us, and the faithfulness of the Lord endures forever. Praise the Lord!" (Ps. 117:2 ESV).

"The lines have fallen for me in pleasant places; indeed, I have a beautiful inheritance" (Ps. 16:6 ESV).

"Blessed be the Lord, the God of Israel, who alone does wondrous things" (Ps. 72:18 ESV).

"Blessed be his glorious name forever; may the whole earth be filled with his glory! Amen and Amen!" (Ps. 72:19 ESV).

"To the only wise God be glory forever through Jesus Christ! Amen" (Rom. 16:27 ESV).

## Notes

_____
_____
_____

# Lord, I Am Trapped, When Will You Come?

## (Prayer)

"I called on your name, O Lord, from the depths of the pit" (Lam. 3:55 ESV).

"You have seen the wrong done to me, O Lord; judge my cause" (Lam. 3:59 ESV).

"You have seen all their vengeance, all their plots against me" (Lam. 3:60 ESV).

"You have heard their taunts, O Lord, all their plots against me" (Lam. 3:61 ESV).

"How long, O Lord, will you look on? Rescue me from their destruction, my precious life from the lions!" (Ps. 35:17 ESV).

"How long must your servant endure? When will you judge those who persecute me?" (Ps. 119:84 ESV).

"How long will all of you attack a man to batter him, like a leaning wall, a tottering fence?" (Ps. 62:3 ESV).

"Those who seek my life lay their snares; those who seek my hurt speak of ruin and meditate treachery all day long" (Ps. 38:12 ESV).

"But for you, O Lord, do I wait; it is you, O Lord my God, who will answer" (Ps. 38:15 ESV).

"Hear my prayer, O Lord; give ear to my please for mercy! In your faithfulness answer me, in your righteousness!" (Ps. 143:1 ESV).

## PRAY IN GOD'S WORD FOR ENCOURAGEMENT AND CHANGE

"My soul, wait thou only upon God; For my expectation is from him" (Ps. 62:5 ESV).

"My eyes long for your promise; I ask, "When will you comfort me?" (Ps. 119:82 ESV).

"My soul thirst for God, for the living God. When shall I come and appear before God?" (Ps. 42:2 ESV).

"I remember the days of old; I meditate on all that you have done; I ponder the work of your hands" (Ps. 143:5 ESV).

"He turns rivers into a desert, springs of water into thirsty ground" (Ps. 107:33 ESV).

"He turns a desert into pools of water, a parched land into springs of water" (Ps. 107:35 ESV).

"And there he lets the hungry dwell, and they establish a city to live in" (Ps. 107:36 ESV).

"They sow fields and plant vineyards and get a fruitful yield" (Ps. 107:37 ESV).

"By his blessing they multiply greatly, and he does not let their livestock diminish" (Ps. 107:38 ESV).

"For the Lord takes pleasure in his people; he adorns the humble with salvation" (Ps. 149:4 ESV).

"He sent Moses, his servant, and Aaron, whom he had chosen" (Ps. 105:26 ESV).

"They performed his signs among them and miracles in the land of Ham" (Ps. 105:27 ESV).

"Then he brought out Israel with silver and gold, and there was none among his tribes who stumbled" (Ps. 105:37 ESV).

"Egypt was glad when they departed, for dread of them had fallen upon it" (Ps. 105:38 ESV).

"He spread a cloud for a covering, and fire to give light by night" (Ps. 105:39 ESV).

"They asked, and he brought quail, and gave them bread from the heaven in abundance" (Ps. 105:40 ESV).

"He opened the rock, and water gushed out; it flowed through the desert like a river" (Ps. 105:41 ESV).

"By day the Lord commands his steadfast love, and at night his song is with me, a prayer to the God of my life" (Ps. 42:8 ESV).

"Draw near to my soul, redeem me; ransom me because of my enemies!" (Ps. 69:18 ESV).

"When I wept and humbled my soul with fasting, it became my reproach" (Ps. 69:10 ESV).

"For the zeal for your house has consumed me, and the reproaches of those who reproach you have fallen on me" (Ps. 69:9 ESV).

"But as for me, my prayer is to you, O Lord. At an acceptable time, O God, in the abundance of your steadfast love answer me in your saving faithfulness" (Ps. 69:13 ESV).

"Deliver me from sinking in the mire; let me be delivered from my enemies and from the deep waters" (Ps. 69:14 ESV).

"From the end of the earth I call to you when my heart is faint. Lead me to the rock that is higher than I" (Ps. 61:2 ESV).

"For you have been my refuge, a strong tower against the enemy" (Ps. 61:3 ESV).

"O my strength, I will watch for you, for you, O God, are my fortress" (Ps. 59:9 ESV).

"My God in his steadfast love will meet me; God will let me look in triumph on my enemies" (Ps. 59:10 ESV).

"They all shall be given over to the power of the sword; they shall be portion for jackals" (Ps. 63:10 ESV).

"Blessed be the Lord, who daily bears us up; God is our salvation" (Ps. 68:19 ESV). *Selah.*

"For behold, those who are far from you shall perish; you put an end to everyone who is unfaithful to you" (Ps. 73:27 ESV).

"But for me it is good to be near God; I have made the Lord God my refuge, that I may tell of all your works" (Ps. 73:28 ESV).

"May my meditation be pleasing to him, for I rejoice in the Lord" (Ps. 104:34 ESV).

"For God alone my soul waits in silence; from him comes my salvation" (Ps. 62:1 ESV).

*In Jesus name, amen.*

PRAY IN GOD'S WORD FOR ENCOURAGEMENT AND CHANGE

## Notes

# A Declaration of Praise

## (Prayer)

"The Lord is gracious and merciful, slow to anger and abounding in steadfast love" (Ps. 145:8 ESV).

"The Lord is good to all, and his mercy is over all that he has made" (Ps. 145:9 ESV).

"How you have helped him who has no power! How you have saved the arm that has no strength!" (Job 26:2 ESV).

"How you have counseled him who has no wisdom, and plentifully declared sound knowledge!" (Job 26:3 ESV).

"They that are deceased trembled Beneath the waters and the inhabitants thereof" (Job 26:5 ESV).

"Sheol is naked before God, and Abaddon has no covering" (Job 26:6 ESV).

"The pillars of heaven tremble and are astounded at his rebuke" (Job 26:11 ESV).

"By his power he stilled the sea; by his understanding he shattered Rahab" (Job 26:12 ESV).

"Behold, these are but the outskirts of his ways, and how the thunder of his power who can understand?" (Job 26:14 ESV).

"O Lord God of hosts, who is mighty as you are, O Lord, with your faithfulness all around you?" (Ps. 89:8 ESV).

"Blessed are the people who know the festal shout, who walk, O Lord, in the light of your face" (Ps. 89:15 ESV).

"Make your face shine upon your servant, and teach me your states" (Ps. 119:135 ESV).

"The unfolding of your words gives me light; it imparts understanding to the simple" (Ps. 119:130 ESV).

"Therefore I consider all your precepts to be right; I hate every false way" (Ps. 119:128 ESV).

"For he will complete what he appoints for me, and many such things are in his mind" (Job 23:14 ESV).

"But he is unchangeable, and who can turn him back? What he desires, that he does" (Job 23:13 ESV).

"With God are wisdom and might; he has counsel and understanding" (Job 12:13 ESV).

"There is no wisdom nor understanding Nor counsel against the LORD" (Prov. 21:30 KJV).

"The counsel of the LORD stands forever, the plans of his heart to all generations" (Ps. 33:11 ESV).

"O LORD, our Lord, How majestic and glorious and excellent is Your name in all the earth! You have displayed Your splendor above the heavens" (Ps. 8:1 AMP).

"I will give thanks and praise the LORD, with all my heart; I will tell aloud all Your wonders and marvelous deeds" (Ps. 9:1 AMP).

"I will rejoice and exult in you; I will sing praise to Your name, O Most High" (Ps. 9:1 AMP).

"This God—his way is perfect; the word of the LORD proves true; he is a shield for all those who take refuge in him" (Ps. 18:30 ESV).

"And he judges the world with righteousness; he judges the peoples with uprightness" (Ps. 9:8 ESV).

"The LORD is a stronghold for the oppressed, a stronghold in times of trouble" (Ps. 9:9 ESV).

"God is our refuge and strength, a very present help in trouble" (Ps. 46:1 ESV).

"And those who know your name put their trust in you, for you, O LORD, have not forsaken those who seek you" (Ps. 9:10 ESV).

"Blessed are those whose way is blameless, who walk in the law of the LORD!" (Ps. 119:1 ESV).

"Blessed is the man whom you discipline, O Lord, and whom you teach out of your law" (Ps. 94:12 ESV).

"To give him rest from days of trouble, until a pit is dug for the wicked" (Ps. 94:13 ESV).

"For justice will return to the righteous, and all the upright in heart will follow it" (Ps. 94:15 ESV).

"Who rises up for me against the wicked? Who stands up for me against evildoers?" (Ps. 94:16 ESV).

"If the Lord had not been my help, my soul would soon have lived in the land of silence" (Ps. 94:17 ESV).

"When I thought, 'My foot slips,' your steadfast love, O Lord, held me up" (Ps. 94:18 ESV).

"In the multitude of my thoughts within me Thy comforts delights my soul" (Ps. 94:19 ESV).

"For the Lord is a great God And a great King above all gods" (Ps. 95:3 AMP).

"In his hand are the depths of the earth; the heights of the mountains are his also" (Ps. 95:4 ESV).

"The sea is his, for he made it, and his hands formed the dry land" (Ps. 95:5 ESV).

"Make a joyful noise to the Lord, all the earth!" (Ps. 100:1 ESV).

"Serve the Lord with gladness! Come into his presence with singing!" (Ps. 100:2 ESV).

"Know that the Lord, he is God! It is he who made us, and we are his; we are his people, and the sheep of his pasture" (Ps. 100:3 ESV).

"For the Lord is good; his steadfast love endures forever, and his faithfulness to all generations" (Ps. 100:5 ESV).

"Blessed are those whose strength is in you, in whose heart are the highways to Zion" (Ps. 84:5 ESV).

"Bless the Lord, O you his angels, you mighty ones who do his word, obeying the voice of his word!" (Ps. 103:20 ESV).

"Bless the Lord, O you his angels, you mighty ones who do his word, obeying the voice of his word!" (Ps. 103:21 ESV).

## PRAY IN GOD'S WORD FOR ENCOURAGEMENT AND CHANGE

"Bless the Lord, O my soul! O Lord my God, you are very great! You are clothed with splendor and majesty" (Ps. 104:1 ESV).

"O Lord, how many and varied are Your works! In wisdom You have made them all; The earth is full of Your riches and Your creatures" (Ps. 104:24 AMP).

"Here is the sea, great and wide, which teems with creatures innumerable, living things both small and great" (Ps. 104:25 ESV).

"These all look to you, to give them their food in due season" (Ps. 104:27 ESV).

"You give it to them, they gather it up; You open Your hand, they are filled and satisfied with good [things]" (Ps. 104:28 ESV).

"You hide Your face, they are dismayed; You take away their breath, they die And return to their dust" (Ps. 104:29 ESV).

"May the glory of the Lord endure forever; May the Lord rejoice and be glad in His works—" (Ps. 104:31 AMP).

"Praise the Lord, all nations! Extol him, all peoples!" (Ps. 117:1 ESV).

"Seek the Lord and his strength; seek his presence continually!" (Ps. 105:4 ESV).

"Praise the Lord! (Hallelujah!) Blessed [fortunate, prosperous, and favored by God] is the man who fears the Lord [with awe-inspired reverence and worships Him with obedience], Who delights greatly in His commandments" (Ps. 112:1 AMP).

"Oh give thanks unto Jehovah, call upon his name; Make known among the peoples his doings" (Ps. 105:1 ASV).

"Remember the wondrous works that he has done, his miracles, and the judgments he uttered" (Ps. 105:5 ESV).

"My eyes will be on the faithful (honorable) of the land, that they may dwell with me; He who walks blamelessly is the one who will minister to and serve me" (Ps. 101:6 ESV).

"He remembers his covenant forever, the word that he commanded, for a thousand generations" (Ps. 105:8 ESV).

"The covenant that he made with Abraham, his sworn promise to Isaac" (Ps. 105:9 ESV).

"Behold, my covenant is with you, and you shall be the father of a multitude of nations" (Gen. 17:4 ESV).

"He allowed no one to oppress them; he rebuked kings on their behalf" (Ps. 105:14 ESV).

"Saying, 'Touch not my anointed ones, do my prophets no harm!'" (Ps. 105:15 ESV).

"Whoever is wise, let him attend to these things; let them consider the steadfast love of the Lord" (Ps. 107:43 ESV).

"He will not let your foot ne moved; he who keeps you will not slumber" (Ps. 121:3 ESV).

"Behold, he who keeps Israel will neither slumber nor sleep" (Ps. 121:4 ESV).

"Blessed and favored by God are those who keeps His testimonies, And who [consistently] seek Him and long for Him with all their heart" (Ps. 119:2 AMP).

"I will praise thee, O Lord, with my whole heart; I will shew forth all thy marvelous works" (Ps. 9:1 KJV).

"I delight to do your will. O my God, your law is within my heart" (Ps. 40:8 ESV).

"May integrity and uprightness preserve me, for I wait for you" (Ps. 25:21 ESV).

"I wait for the Lord, my soul waits, and in his word I hope" (Ps. 130:5 ESV).

"My soul waits for the Lord more than watchmen for the morning, more than watchmen for the morning" (Ps. 130:6 ESV).

"For though the Lord is high, he regards the lowly, but the haughty he knows from afar" (Ps. 138:6 ESV).

"He will have compassion on the poor and needy, And he will save the lives of the needy" (Ps. 72:13 AMP).

"From oppression and violence he redeems their life, and precious is their blood in his sight" (Ps. 72:14 ESV).

"For the Lord will not forsake his people; he will not abandon his heritage" (Ps. 94:14 ESV).

"The Lord has made known his salvation; he has revealed his righteousness in the sight of the nations" (Ps. 98:2 ESV).

"He has remembered his steadfast love and faithfulness to the house of Israel. All the ends of the earth have seen the salvation of our God" (Ps. 98:3 ESV).

"Oh sing to the LORD a new song, for he has done marvelous things! His right hand and his holy arm have worked salvation for him" (Ps. 98:1 ESV).

"Blessed be the LORD, the God of Israel, from everlasting to everlasting! And let all the people say, 'Amen!' Praise the LORD!" (Ps. 106:48 ESV).

*In Jesus name, amen.*

## Notes

_____
_____
_____

# God Cares for the Backslider

## (Prayer)

"The Lord is my shepherd; I shall want" (Ps. 23:1 ESV).

"He makes me lie down in green pastures. He leads me besides still waters" (Ps. 23:2 ESV).

"He restores my soul. He leads me in paths of righteousness for his name's sake" (Ps. 23:3 ESV).

"For us a child is born, to us a son is given; and the government shall be upon his shoulder, and his name shall be called Wonderful Counselor, Mighty God, Everlasting Father, Prince of Peace" (Isa. 9:6 ESV).

"The Lord is in his holy temple; the Lord throne is in heaven; his eyes see, his eyelids test the children of man" (Ps. 11:4 ESV).

"The Lord tests the righteous, but his soul hates the wicked and the one who loves violence" (Ps. 11:5 ESV).

"For the Lord is righteous; he loves righteous deeds; the upright shall behold his face" (Ps. 11:7 ESV).

"This is what the Sovereign Lord the Holy One of Israel, says: "Only in returning to me and resting in me will you be saved, In quietness and confidence is your strength. But you would have none of it" (Isa. 30:15 NLT).

"Only acknowledge your guilt—you have rebelled against the Lord your God, you have scattered your favors to foreign gods under every spreading tree, and have not obeyed me,'" declares the Lord" (Jer. 3:13 NIV).

## PRAY IN GOD'S WORD FOR ENCOURAGEMENT AND CHANGE

"Turn, O backsliding children, saith the LORD; for I am married unto you: and I will take you one of a city, and two of a family, and I will bring you to Zion" (Jer. 3:14 KJV).

"If my people, who are called by my name, will humble themselves and pray and seek my face and turn from their wicked ways, then I will hear from heaven, and I will forgive their sin and will heal their land" (2 Chron. 7:14 NIV).

"And I will give you pastors according to mine heart, which shall feed you with knowledge and understanding" (Jer. 3:15 KJV).

"If a man has a hundred sheep and one of them wanders away, what will he do? Won't he leave the ninety-nine others on the hills and go out to search for the one that is lost?" (Matt. 18:12 NLT).

"And if he finds it, I tell you the truth, he will rejoice over it more than over the ninety-nine that didn't wander away!" (Matt. 18:13 NLT).

"In the same way, there is more joy in heaven over one lost sinner who repents and returns to God than over ninety-nine others who are righteous and haven't strayed away!" (Luke 15:7 NLT).

"In the same way, it is not my heavenly Father's will that even one of these little ones should perish" (Matt. 18:14 NLT).

"I am faint and sorely bruised [deadly cold and quite worn out]; I groan by reason of the disquiet and moaning of my heart" (Ps. 38:8 AMPC).

"As for me, I look to the LORD for help. I waited confidently for God to save me, and my God will certainly hear me" (Mic. 7:7 NLT).

"Yes, you have been with me from birth; from my mother's womb you have cared for me. No wonder I am always praising you!" (Ps. 71:6 NLT).

"Be my rock of safety where I can always hide. Give the order to save me, for you are my rock and fortress" (Ps. 71:3 NLT).

"Then this message came to me from the LORD" (Ezek. 28:1 NLT).

"My people will live in safety, quietly at home. They will be at rest" (Isa. 32:18 NLT).

"Work hard so you can present yourself to God and receive his approval. Be a good worker, one who does not need to be ashamed and who correctly explains the word of truth" (2 Tim. 2:15 NLT).

"Avoid worthless, foolish talk that only leads to more godless behavior" (2 Tim. 2:16 NLT).

"This is what the Lord says: 'What fault did your ancestors find in me, that they strayed so far from me? They followed worthless idols and became worthless themselves'" (Jer. 2:5 NIV).

"You have rejected me, "declares the Lord. "You keep on backsliding. So I will reach out and destroy you; I am tired of holding back" (Jer. 15:6 NIV).

"Those whom I love I rebuke and discipline. So be earnest and repent" (Rev. 3:19 NIV).

"Godly sorrow brings repentance that leads to salvation and leaves no regret, but worldly sorrow brings death" (2 Cor. 7:10 NIV).

"I have strayed like a lost sheep. Seek your servant, for I have not forgotten your commands" (Ps. 119:176 NIV).

"I long for your salvation, Lord, and your law gives me delight" (Ps. 119:174 NIV).

"May my cry come before you, Lord; give me understanding according to your word" (Ps. 119:169 NIV).

"And he said, 'There was a man who had two sons'" (Luke 15:11 ESV).

"The younger son told his father, 'I want my share of your estate now before you die.' So his father agreed to divide his wealth between his sons" (Luke 15:12 NLT).

"A few days later this younger son packed all his belongings and moved to a distant land, and there wasted all his money in wild living" (Luke 15:13 NLT).

"About the time his money ran out, a great famine swept over the land, and he began to starve" (Luke 15:14 NLT).

"The young man became so hungry that even the pods he was feeding the pigs looked good to him. But no one gave him anything" (Luke 15:16 NLT).

"When he finally came to his senses, he said to himself, 'At home even the hired servants have food enough to spare, and here I am dying of hunger!'" (Luke 15:17 NLT).

"I will go home to my father and say, 'Father, I have sinned against both heaven and you'" (Luke 15:18 NLT).

"And I am no longer worthy of being called your son. Please take me on as a hired servant.'" (Luke 15:19 NLT).

"But his father said to the servants, 'Quick! Bring the finest robe in the house and put it on him. Get a ring for his finger and sandals for his feet'" (Luke 15:22 NLT).

"And kill the calf we have been fattening. We must celebrate with a feast" (Luke 15:23 NLT).

"'For this son of mine was dead and his now returned to life. He was lost, but now he is found.' So the party began" (Luke 15:24 NLT).

"Look! I stand at the door and knock. If you hear my voice and open the door, I will come in, and we will share a meal together as friends" (Rev. 3:20 NLT).

"Those who are victorious will sit with me on my throne, just as I was victorious and sat with my Father on his throne" (Rev. 3:21 NLT).

"Anyone with ears to hear must listen to the Spirit and understand what he is saying to the churches" (Rev. 3:22 NLT).

"I correct and discipline everyone I love. So be diligent and turn from your indifference" (Rev. 3:19 NLT).

"I will be glad and rejoice in your unfailing love, for you have seen my troubles, and you care about the anguish of my soul" (Ps. 31:7 NLT).

"The LORD gives his people strength. The LORD blesses them with peace" (Ps. 29:11 NLT).

"Oh, what joy for those whose disobedience is forgiven, whose sin is put out of sight!" (Ps. 32:1 NLT).

"Yes, what joy for those whose record the LORD has cleared of guilt, whose lives are lived in complete honesty!" (Ps. 32:2 NLT).

"The LORD says, 'I will guide you along the best pathway for your life. I will advise you and watch over you'" (Ps. 32:8 NLT).

"Do not be like a senseless horse or mule that needs a bit and bridle to keep it under control." (Ps. 32:9 NLT).

"I have chosen to be faithful; I have determined to live by your regulations" (Ps. 119:30 NLT).

"Lord, I have given up my pride and turned away from my arrogance. I am not concerned with great matters or with subjects too difficult for me" (Ps. 131:1 GNT).

"Instead, I am content and at peace. As a child lies quietly in its mother's arms, so my heart is quiet within me" (Ps. 131:2 GNT).

"You will do everything you have promised; Lord, your love is eternal. Complete the work that you have begun" (Ps. 138:8 GNT).

*In Jesus name, amen.*

## Notes

_____
_____

## Repentance Prayer List

# Be Encouraged

The father of this fallen world (Satan) has given you (those who have not yet accepted Jesus Christ as your Lord and Savior) an identity. He has deceived you, to think and believe you can't count on anyone but yourself or to always with all malice, seek selfish desires. To continue his control over you, he will tell you that God doesn't want or care about you because of all the bad things you have done. He will convince you to always try and impress people for them to accept you. He may place people in your life whom you trust to verbally abuse you, telling you your nothing, you're worthless, or you will never amount to anything worthy. All of which is another layer of perpetual bondage designed to keep you from truly knowing who you are in Christ Jesus and knowing the deep love and care He has for you (us).

Satan want to be Lord in your life and in mine. He was booted out of heaven when he tried to dethrone God. He was called Lucifer then, and he was created by God. So he is not all powerful. He is not all knowing. So why do we allow him to take up such large territories in our life? Why do we take what he says about us as absolute truth? He is a liar. In fact, he is called the father of lies and anyone who indulges in lying, he is their father.

> For you are the children of your father the devil, and you love to do the evil things he does. He was a murderer from the beginning. He has always hated the truth, because there is no truth in him. When he lies, it is consistent with his

character; for he is a liar and the father of lies. (John 8:44 NLT)

Only God is absolute. "Remember the former things of old: for I am God, and there is none else; I am God, and there is none like me" (Isa. 46:9 KJV). "I am Alpha and Omega, the beginning and the end, the first and the last" (Rev. 22:13 KJV). "And fear not them which kill the body, but are not able to kill the soul: but rather fear him which is able to destroy both soul and body in hell" (Matt. 10:28 KJV). Only God is complete. By these scriptures alone give us freedom from the lies of the devil and run toward the loving arms of Jesus Christ, who is the author and finisher of our faith. "Looking unto Jesus the author and finisher of our faith; who for the joy that was set before him endured the cross, despising the shame, and is set down at the right hand of the throne of God" (Heb. 12:2). When we receive Jesus Christ as our Lord and savior into our hearts, meaning we give him permission to rule every part of our life. God is now our heavenly father, and we are His child. "Ye are of God, little children, and have overcome them: because greater is he that is in you, than he that is in the world" (1 John 4:4 KJV). We now have power over the devil. God loves us dearly. He only wants our good.

When the world says you're ugly, God says we are made in his image: "So God created man in his own image, in the image of God created he him; male and female created he them" (Gen. 1:27 KJV).

When the world says you're not good enough, God says you're the chosen of God: "But you are a chosen people, a royal priesthood, a holy nation, God's special possession, that you may declare the praise of him who called you out of darkness into his wonderful light" (1 Pet. 2:9 NIV).

"I am the vine; you are the branches. If you remain in me and I in you, you will bear much fruit; apart from me you can do nothing" (John 15:5 NIV).

"If you remain in me and my words remain in you, ask whatever you wish, and it will be done for you" (John 15:7 NIV).

## PRAY IN GOD'S WORD FOR ENCOURAGEMENT AND CHANGE

When the world says there is nothing special about you, God says you're the light in the darkness. "You are the light of the world. A town built on a hill cannot be hidden" (Matt. 5:14 NIV).

When the world says you will never succeed, stop trying, God says you're a winner. "Nay, in all these things we are more than conquerors through him that loved us" (Rom. 8:37 KJV).

When the world says you're not strong or mentally tough. God says He will give us what we need to overcome. "He giveth power to the faint; and to them that have no might he increaseth strength" (Isa. 40:29 KJV).

This world is dying, and all it can offer you is death. In the final judgment, Satan and all who follow after him, will be thrown in the lake of fire.

> And the devil that deceived them was cast into the lake of fire and brimstone, where the beast and the false prophet are, and shall be tormented day and night for ever and ever...And whoever was not found written in the book of life was cast into the lake of fire. (Rev. 20:10, 15).

God loves us dearly and does not want any harm to come to us. "Beloved, I pray that in every way you may succeed and prosper and be in good health [physically], just as [I know] your soul prospers [spiritually]." It is wise to choose Christ always because our existence in this life and the next depends on it.

*Be blessed.*

# Love

And if I have the gift of prophecy [and speak a new message from God to the people], and understand all mysteries, and [possess] all knowledge; and if I have all [sufficient] faith so that I can remove mountains, but do not have love [reaching out to others], I am nothing. (1 Cor. 13:2 AMP)

# God's Love

## The Greatest Love
## (A Word from God in Prayer)

"I have yet many things to say unto you, but ye cannot bear them now" (John 16:12 KJV).

"If ye love me, keep My commandments" (John 14:15 KJV).

"This is my commandment, that ye love one another, as I have loved you" (John 15:13 KJV).

"Greater love hath no man than this, that a man lay down his life for his friends" (John 15:13 KJV).

"For God so love the world, that he gave His only begotten Son, that whosoever believeth in him should not perish, but have everlasting life" (John 3:16KJV).

"For God sent not his Son into the world to condemn the world, but that the world through him might be saved" (John 3:17 KJV).

"Remember the word that I said unto you, The servant is not greater than his lord. If they persecuted me, they will persecute you; if they have kept my saying, they will keep yours also" (John 15:20 KJV).

"Ye are my friend, if ye do whatsoever I command you" (John 15:14 KJV).

"Henceforth I call you not servants; for the servant knoweth not what his lord doeth: but I have called you friends; for all things that I have heard of my father I have made known unto you" (John 15:15 KJV).

"Let all your things be done with charity" (1 Cor. 16:14 KJV).

"Charity suffereth long, and is kind; charity envieth not; charity vaunteth not itself, is not puffed up" (1 Cor. 13:4 KJV).

"Doth not behave itself unseemly, seeketh not her own, is not easily provoked, thinketh no evil" (1 Cor. 13:5 KJV).

"Rejoiceth not in iniquity, but rejoiceth in truth" (1 Cor. 13:6 KJV).

"Beareth all things, believeth all things, hopeth all things, endureth all things" (1 Cor. 13:7 KJV).

"With all lowliness and meekness, with longsuffering, forbearing one another in love" (Eph. 4:2 KJV).

"And above all things have fervent charity among yourselves: for charity shall cover the multitude of sins" (1 Pet. 4:8 KJV).

"Then this message came to me from the LORD" (Ezek. 34:1 NLT).

"Beloved, let us love one another: for love is of God; and every one that loveth is born of God, and knoweth God" (1 John 4:7 KJV).

"Beloved, if God so loved us, we ought also to love one another" (1 John 4:11 KJV).

"Herein is love, not that we loved God, but that he loved us, and sent his Son to be the propitiation for our sins" (1 John 4:10 KJV).

"And we have known and believed the love that God hath to us. God is love; and he that dwelleth in love dwelleth in God, and God in him" (1 John 4:16 KJV).

"Unto thee, O Lord, do I lift up my soul" (Ps. 25:1 KJV).

"I will love thee, O Lord, my strength" (Ps. 18:1 KJV).

"O my strength, to you I sing praises, for you, O God, are my refuge, the God who shows me unfailing love" (Ps. 59:17 NLT).

*In Jesus name, amen.*

## Notes

_____

_____

_____

# Adoration to God

## (Prayer)

"The comforting word of the Lord came to me saying; Rejoice in the Lord, O ye righteous: for praise is comely for the upright" (Ps. 33:1 KJV).

"Great is the Lord! He is most worthy of praise! He is to be feared above all gods" (Ps. 96:4 NLT).

"The Lord looks down from heaven; he sees all the children of man" (Ps. 33:13 ESV).

"What is man, that thou art mindful of him? and the son of man, that thou visitest him?" (Ps. 8:4).

"For thou hast made him a little lower than the angels, and hast crowned him with glory and honour" (Ps. 8:5 KJV).

"My soul makes its boast in the Lord; let the humble hear and be glad" (Ps. 34:2 ESV).

"Oh, magnify the Lord with me, and let us exalt his name together!" (Ps. 34:3 ESV).

"My enemies taunt me day after day. They mock and curse me" (Ps. 102:8 NLT).

"The Lord is my light and my salvation; whom shall I fear? the Lord is the strength of my life; of whom shall I be afraid" (Ps. 27:1 KJV).

"The Lord is nigh unto all them that call upon him, to all that call upon him in truth" (Ps. 145:18 KJV).

"The righteousness of God through faith in Jesus Christ for all who believe. For there is no distinction" (Rom. 3:22 KJV).

"The Lord will give strength unto his people; the Lord will bless his people with peace" (Ps. 29:11 KJV).

"He will fulfill the desire of them that fear him: he also will hear their cry, and will save them" (Ps. 145:19 KJV).

"He rescued me from my powerful enemy, from my foes, who were too strong for me" (Ps. 18:17 NIV).

"They confronted me in the day of my disaster, but the Lord was my support" (Ps. 18:18 NIV).

"The Lord thundered from heaven; the voice of the Most High resounded amid the hail and burning coals" (Ps. 18:13 NLT).

"For the righteous will never be moved; he will be remembered forever" (Ps. 112:6 ESV).

"Blessed be the name of the LORD from this time forth and forevermore!" (Ps. 113:2 ESV).

"From the rising of the sun to its setting, the name of the LORD is to be praised!" (Ps. 113:3 ESV).

> HE is my *Adonai*. (Lord, Master)
> HE is my *El Ohim*. (God)
> HE is my *El Elyon*. (The Most High God)
> HE is my *El Olam*. (The Lord Everlasting)
> HE is my *El Shaddi*. (Lord God Almighty)
> HE is my *Ebenezer*. (Hitherto hath the Lord helped us)
> HE is my *Jehovah Mekaddishkem*. (The Lord who sanctifies)
> HE is my *Jehovah Nissi*. (The Lord my banner)
> HE is my *Jehovah Raah*. (The Lord my shepherd)
> HE is my *Jehovah Rapha*. (The Lord that heals)
> HE is my *Jehovah Jireh*. (The Lord will provide)
> HE is my *Jehovah Tsidkenu*. (The Lord our righteousness)
> HE is my *Jehovah Shalom*. (The Lord is peace)
> HE is my *Jehovah Shammah*. (The Lord is there)
> HE is my *Yahweh*. (Lord, Jehovah)
> HE is my *Yahweh Rohi*. (The Lord our Shepherd)

"O Lord our Lord, how excellent is thy name in all the earth! who hast set thy glory above the heavens" (Ps. 8:1 KJV).

"The mighty God, even the Lord, hath spoken, and called the earth from the rising of the sun unto the going down thereof" (Ps. 50:1 KJV).

"Praise waiteth for thee, O God, in Zion: and unto thee shall the vow be performed" (Ps. 65:1 KJV).

"Make a joyful noise unto God, all ye lands" (Ps. 100:1 KJV).

"For thou Lord, art high above all the earth: thou art exalted far above all gods" (Ps. 97:9 KJV).

"Sing forth the honour of his name: make his praise glorious" (Ps. 66:2 KJV).

"Say unto God, how terrible art thou in thy works! through the greatness of thy power shall thine enemies submit themselves unto thee" (Ps. 66:3 KJV).

"For since the beginning of the world men have not heard, nor perceived by the ear, neither hath the eye seen, O God, beside thee, what he hath prepared for him that waiteth for him" (Isa. 64:4 KJV).

"Sing unto the Lord, bless his name; shew forth his salvation from day to day" (Ps. 96:2 KJV).

"For thou, Lord hast made me glad through thy work: I will triumph in the works of thy hands" (Ps. 92:4 KJV).

"O Lord, how great are thy works! and thy thoughts are very deep" (Ps. 92:5 KJV).

"Thy testimonies are very sure: holiness becometh thine house, O Lord, for ever" (Ps. 93:5 KJV).

"It is a good thing to give thanks unto the Lord, and to sing praises unto thy name, O most High" (Ps. 92:1 KJV).

"For the Lord is a great God, and a great king above all gods" (Ps. 95:5 KJV).

"Honour and majesty are before him: strength and beauty are in his sanctuary" (Ps. 96:6 KJV).

"Sing unto the Lord, praise ye the Lord: for he hath delivered the soul of the poor from the hand of evildoers" (Jer. 20:13 KJV).

"He leads the humble in what is right, and teaches the humble his way" (Ps. 25:9 ESV).

"That is why I can never stop praising you; I declare your glory all day long" (Ps. 71:8 NLT).

"The Lord hath done great things for us; whereof we are glad" (Ps. 126:3 KJV).

*In Jesus name, amen.*

## Notes

_____
_____
_____

# God Saves the Righteous

## (Prayer)

Lord I call upon your name to help me! I know you are a faithful God who saves, as your word says: "You can be sure of this: The Lord set apart the godly for himself. The Lord will answer when I call to him" (Ps. 4:3 NLT).

"In my panic I cried out, 'I am cut off from the Lord!' But you heard my cry for mercy and answered my call for help" (Ps. 31:22 NLT).

"This I recall to my mind, therefore have I hope" (Lam. 3:21 KJV).

"The eyes of the Lord watch over those who do right; his ears are open to their cries for help" (Ps. 34:15 NLT).

"Moreover the comforting word of God, says; Love the Lord, all you godly ones! For the Lord protects those who are loyal to him, but he harshly punishes the arrogant" (Ps. 31:23 NLT).

"Calamity will surely destroy the wicked, and those who hate the righteous will be punished" (Ps. 34:21 NLT).

"He that followeth after righteousness and mercy findeth life, righteousness, and honour" (Prov. 21:21 KJV).

"So now there is no condemnation for those who belong to Christ Jesus" (Rom. 8:1 NLT).

"How great is the goodness you have stored up for those who fear you. You lavish it on those who come to you for protection, blessing them before the watching world" (Ps. 31:19 NLT).

"You hide them in the shelter of your presence, safe from those who conspire against them. You shelter them in your presence, far from accusing tongues" (Ps. 31:20 NLT).

"Blessed is he whose transgression is forgiven, whose sin is covered" (Ps. 32:1 KJV).

"So be strong and courageous, all you who put your hope in the Lord!" (Ps. 31:24 NLT).

"Sow to yourselves in righteousness, reap in mercy; break up your fallow ground: for it is time to seek the Lord, till he come and rain righteousness upon you" (Hosea 10:12 KJV).

"Preserved me, O God; for in thee do I put my trust" (Ps. 16:1 KJV).

"Hear me when I call, O God of my righteousness: thou hast enlarged me when I was in distress" (Ps. 4:1 KJV).

"I am severely afflicted; give me life, O Lord, according to your word!" (Ps. 119:107 ESV).

"You who have made me see many troubles and calamities will revive me again; from the depths of the earth you will bring me up again" (Ps. 71:20 ESV).

"For I recon that the sufferings of this present time are not worthy to be compared with the glory which shall be revealed in us" (Rom. 8:18 KJV).

"Thou art good, and doest good; teach me thy statues" (Ps. 119:68 KJV).

And the comforting word of God says, "There is no wisdom, no insight, no plan that can succeed against the Lord" (Prov. 21:30 NIV).

"For what is the hope of the godless, when God cuts him off, when God takes away his life?" (Job 27:8 ESV).

"Will God hear his cry when distress comes upon him?" (Job 27:9 ESV).

"Leave your simple ways behind, and begin to live; learn to use good judgment" (Prov. 9:6 NLT).

"A senseless man [in his crude and uncultivated state] knows nothing, Nor does a [self-righteous] fool understand this" (Ps. 92:6 AMP).

"That though the wicked sprout up like grass and evildoers flourish, They will be destroyed forever" (Ps. 92:7 AMP).

"Though he heap up silver like dust, and pile up clothing like clay" (Job 27:16 ESV).

"He may pile it up, but the righteous will wear it, and the innocent will divide the silver" (Job 27:17 ESV).

"He goes to bed rich, but will do so no more; he opens his eyes, and his wealth is gone" (Job 27:19 ESV).

"If his children are multiplied, it is for the sword, and his descendants have not enough bread" (Job 27:14 ESV).

"Terrors overtake him like a flood; in the night a whirlwind carries him off" (Job 27:20 ESV).

"The east wind lifts him up and he is gone; it sweeps him out of his place" (Job 27:21 ESV).

"This is the portion of the wicked man with God, and the heritage that oppressors receive from the Almighty" (Job 27:13 ESV).

"The enemy is finished, in endless ruins; the cities you uprooted are now forgotten" (Ps. 9:6 NLT).

"But the Lord reigns forever, executing judgment from his throne" (Ps. 9:7 NLT).

"The Lord detests evil plans, but he delights in pure words" (Prov. 15:26 NAS).

"Be thou exalted, O God, above the heavens, and thy glory above all the earth" (Ps. 108:5 KJV).

"In peace I will both lie down and sleep; for you alone, O Lord, make me dwell in safety" (Ps. 4:8 ESV).

"You have given me your shield of victory. Your right hand supports me; your help has made me great" (Ps. 18:35 NLT).

"Who is a God like unto thee, that pardoneth iniquity, and passeth by the transgression of the remnant of his heritage? he retaineth not his anger for ever, because he delights in mercy" (Mic. 7:18 KJV).

"Arise, O Lord; O God, lift up thine hand: forget not the humble" (Ps. 10:12 KJV).

"By humility and the fear of the Lord are riches, and honour, and life" (Prov. 22:4 KJV).

"The just man walketh in his integrity: his children are blessed after him" (Prov. 20:7 KJV).

"And a harvest of righteousness is sown in peace by those who make peace" (James 3:18 ESV).

"'There is no peace,' says my God, 'for the wicked'" (Isa. 57:21 ESV).

"If anyone, then, knows the good they ought to do and doesn't do it, it is sin for them" (James 4:17 NIV).

"I have set the Lord always before me: because he is at my right hand, I shall not be moved" (Ps. 16:8 KJV).

"The Lord will not suffer the soul of the righteous to famish: but he casteth away the substance of the wicked" (Prov. 10:3 KJV).

"Blessings are upon the head of the just: but violence covereth the mouth of the wicked" (Prov. 10:6 KJV).

"The memory of the just is blessed: but the name of the wicked shall rot" (Prov. 10:7 KJV).

"The fear of the wicked, it shall come upon him: but the desire of the righteous shall be granted" (Prov. 10:24 KJV).

"As the whirlwind passeth, so is the wicked no more: but the righteous is an everlasting foundation" (Prov. 10:25 KJV).

"The righteous shall never be removed: but the wicked shall not inhabit the earth" (Prov. 10:30 KJV).

"He that diligently seeketh good procureth favour: but he that seeketh mischief, it shall come unto him" (Prov. 11:27 KJV).

"Deal bountifully with thy servant, that I may live, and keep thy word" (Ps. 119:17 KJV).

"Thou hast rebuked the proud that are cursed, which do err from thy commandments" (Ps. 119:21 KJV).

"With the pure thou wilt shew thyself pure; and with the froward thou wilt shew thyself unsavoury" (2 Sam. 22:27 KJV).

"The Lord is far from the wicked: but he heareth the prayer of the righteous" (Prov. 15:29 KJV).

"For he satifieth the longing soul, and filleth hungry soul with goodness" (Ps. 107:9 KJV).

"His work is honourable and glorious: and his righteousness endureth forever" (Ps. 111:3 KJV).

"Thou art my hiding place and my shield: I hope in thy word" (Ps. 119:114 KJV).

"Uphold me according unto thy word, that I may live: and let me not be ashamed continually" (Ps. 119:116 KJV).

"I will walk before the Lord in the land of the living" (Ps. 119:9 KJV).

"The wicked shall be a ransom for the righteous, and the transgressor for the upright" (Prov. 21:18 KJV).

"For there shall be no reward to the evil man; the candle of the wicked shall be put out" (Prov. 24:20 KJV).

"But blessed are those who trust in the Lord and have made the Lord their hope and confidence" (Jer. 17:7 NLT).

"My righteousness I hold fast, and will not let it go: my heart shall not reproach me so long as I live" (Job 27:6 KJV).

"Because I am righteous, I will see you. When I awake, I will see you face to face and be satisfied" (Ps. 17:15 NLT).

*In Jesus name, amen.*

## Notes

_____
_____
_____

# Joy

Go your way, eat your bread with joy and drink your wine with a cheerful heart [If you are righteous, wise, and in the hands of God]; for God has already approved and accepted your works" (Eccles. 9:7 AMP).

# God's Joy

## Joy in the Day of Trouble
## (A Word from God in Prayer)

"O clap your hands, all ye people, shout unto God with the voice of triumph" (Ps. 47:1 KJV).

"For the Lord most high is terrible; he is a great king overall the earth" (Ps. 47:2 KJV).

"Behold, the Lord's hand is not shortened, that it cannot save; neither his ear heavy, that it cannot hear" (Isa. 59:1 KJV).

"Until now you have asked nothing in my name. Ask, and you will receive, that your joy may be full" (John 16:24 KJV).

"Violence shall no more be heard in thy land, wasting nor destruction within thy borders; but thou shalt call thy walls salvation, and thy gates praise" (Isa. 60:18KJV).

"These things I have spoken to you, that my joy may be in you, and that your joy may be full" (John 15:11 ESV).

"Blessed are you when people hate you and when they exclude you and revile you and spurn your name as evil, on account of the Son of man!" (Luke 6:22 ESV).

"Rejoice in that day, and leap for joy, for behold, your reward is great in heaven; for so their fathers did to the prophets" (Luke 6:23 ESV).

"Then the eyes of those who see will not be blinded, And the ears of those who hear will listen attentively" (Isa. 32:3 AMP).

"The heart (mind) of those who act impulsive will discern the truth, And the tongue of stammerers will hurry to speak clearly" (Isa. 32:4 AMP).

"'For I know the plans and thoughts that I have for you,' says the Lord, 'plans for peace and well-being and not for disaster, to give you a future and a hope'" (Jer. 29:11 AMP).

"Little children, you are from God and have overcome them, for he who is in you is greater than he who is in the world" (1 John 4:4 ESV).

"Strongholds in the day of trouble; he knows those who take refuge in him" (Nehum 1:7 ESV).

"You satisfy me more than the richest feast. I will praise you with songs of joy" (Ps. 63:5 NLT).

"The Lord's promises are pure, like silver refined seven times over" (Ps. 12:6 NLT).

"Restore to me the joy of your salvation, and make me willing to obey you" (Ps. 51:12 NLT).

"I will praise you as long as I live, lifting up my hands to you in prayer" (Ps. 63:4 NLT).

*In Jesus name, amen.*

## Notes

_____
_____
_____

# To Be Blessed by God

## (Prayer)

"Blessed is the man that trusteth in the Lord, and whose hope the Lord is" (Jer. 17:7 KJV).

"Lord, you alone are my inheritance, my cup of blessing. You guard all that is mine" (Ps. 16:5 NLT).

"No wonder my heart is glad, and I rejoice. My body rests in safety" (Ps. 16:9 NLT).

"I am blessed for: Thy throne, O God, is for ever and ever: the sceptre of thy kingdom is a right sceptre" (Ps. 45:6 KJV).

"I am blessed for: Thy righteousness also, O God, is very high, who hast done great things: O God, who is like unto thee!" (Ps. 71:19 KJV).

"I am blessed, for the LORD: He shall choose our inheritance for us, the excellency of Jacob whom he loved" (Ps. 47:4 KJV). *Selah*.

"I am blessed, for the LORD: Wash me thoroughly from mine iniquity, and cleanse me from my sin" (Ps. 51:2 KJV).

"I am blessed for: I will praise thee for ever, because thou hast done it: and I will wait on thy name; for it is good before thy saints" (Ps.52:9 KJV).

"I am blessed, for the LORD: He shall reward evil unto mine enemies: cut them off in thy truth" (Ps. 54:5 KJV).

"I am blessed, for the LORD said: I will go before thee, and make the crooked places straight: I will break in pieces the gates of brass, and cut in sunder the bars of iron" (Isa. 45:2 KJV).

"Drop down, ye heavens, from above, and let the skies pour down righteousness: let the earth open, and let them bring forth salvation, and let righteousness spring up together; I the LORD have created it" (Isa. 45:8 KJV).

"Blessed are the poor in spirit: for theirs is the kingdom of heaven" (Matt. 5:3 KJV).

"Blessed are they that mourn: for they shall be comforted" (Matt. 5:4 KJV).

"Blessed are the meek: for they shall inherit the earth" (Matt. 5:5 KJV).

"Blessed are they which do hunger and thirst after righteousness: for they shall be filled" (Matt. 5:6 KJV).

"Blessed are the merciful: for they shall obtain mercy" (Matt. 5:7 KJV).

"Blessed are the pure in heart: for they shall see God" (Matt. 5:8 KJV).

"Blessed are the peacemakers: for they shall be called the children of God" (Matt. 5:9 KJV).

"Blessed are they which are persecuted for righteousness sake: for theirs is the kingdom of God" (Matt. 5:10 KJV).

"Blessed are ye, when men shall revile you, and persecute you, and shall say all manner of evil against you falsely, for my sake" (Matt. 5:11 KJV).

"Be blessed, rejoice and be exceeding glad: for great is your reward in heaven: for so persecuted they the prophets which were before you" (Matt. 5:12 KJV).

"Let your light so shine before men, that they may see your good works, and glorify your Father which is in heaven" (Matt. 5:16 KJV).

"Unto thee, O my strength, will I sing: for God is my defense, and the God of my mercy" (Ps. 59:17 KJV).

"For thou hast been a shelter for me, and a strong tower from the enemy" (Ps. 61:3 KJV).

"Who shall lay any thing to the charge of God's elect? It is God that justifieth" (Rom. 8:33 KJV).

"O Lord, thou knowest: remember me, and visit me, and revenge me of my persecutors; take me not away in thy longsuffering: know that for thy sake I have suffered rebuke" (Jer. 15:15 KJV).

"God says, 'At the time I have planned, I will bring justice against the wicked'" (Ps. 75:2 NLT).

"Declare me not guilty, O Lord my God, for you give justice. Don't let my enemies laugh about me in my troubles" (Ps. 35:24 NLT).

"For God says, 'I will break the strength of the wicked, but I will increase the power of the godly'" (Ps. 75:10 NLT).

"Then this further message came to me from the Lord" (Ezek. 36:16 NLT).

"The Lord hath taken away thy judgments, he hath cast out thine enemy: the king of Israel, even the Lord, is in the midst of thee: thou shalt not see evil any more" (Zeph. 3:15 KJV).

*In Jesus name, amen.*

## Notes

_____
_____
_____

# Security in the Lord

## (Prayer)

"Bless the Lord, O my soul: and all that is within me, bless his holy name" (Ps. 103:1 KJV).

"Bless the Lord, O my soul, and forget not all his benefits" (Ps. 103:2 KJV).

"Who forgiveth all thine iniquities; who healeth all thy diseases" (Ps. 103:3 KJV).

"Who redeemeth thy life from destruction; who crowneth thee with lovingkindness and tender mercies" (Ps. 103:4 KJV).

"Have mercy on me, O God, have mercy! I look to you for protection. I will hide beneath the shadow of your wings until the danger passes by" (Ps. 57:1 NLT).

"I will call to you whenever I'm in trouble, and you will answer me" (Ps. 86:7 NLT).

"I will tell everyone about your righteousness. All day long I will proclaim your saving power, though I am not skilled with words" (Ps. 71:15 NLT).

"For he is our God; and we are the people of his pasture, and the sheep of his hand. Today if ye will hear his voice" (Ps. 95:7 KJV).

"So be strong and courageous, all you who put your hope in the Lord!" (Ps. 31:24 NLT).

"Honour and majesty are before him: strength and beauty are in his sanctuary" (Ps. 96:6 KJV).

"O worship the Lord in the beauty of holiness: fear before him, all the earth" (Ps. 96:9 KJV).

"The heavens declare his righteousness, and all the people see his glory" (Ps. 97:6 KJV).

"For thou, Lord, art high above all the earth: thou art exalted far above all gods" (Ps. 97:9 KJV).

"O taste and see that the Lord is good: blessed is the man that trusteth in him" (Ps. 34:8 KJV).

"Ye that love the Lord, hate evil: he preserveth the souls of his saints; he delivereth them out of the hand of the wicked" (Ps. 97:10 KJV).

"Light is sown for the righteous, and gladness for the upright in heart" (Ps. 97:11 KJV).

"Rejoice in the Lord, ye righteous; and give thanks at the remembrance of his holiness" (Ps. 97:12 KJV).

"Know ye that the Lord he is God: it is he that hath made us, and not we ourselves; we are his people, and the sheep of his pasture" (Ps. 100:3 KJV).

"Enter into his gates with thanksgiving, and into his courts with praise: be thankful unto him, and bless his name" (Ps. 100:4 KJV).

"For the Lord is good; his mercy is everlasting; and his truth endureth to all generations" (Ps. 100:5 KJV).

"He will listen to the prayers of the destitute. He will not reject their pleas" (Ps. 102:17 NLT).

"I said, O my God, take me not away in the midst of my days: thy years are throughout all generations" (Ps. 102:24 KJV).

"Of old hast thou laid the foundation of the earth: and the heavens are the work of thy hands" (Ps. 102:25 KJV).

"He watereth the hills from his chambers: the earth is satisfied with the fruit of thy works" (Ps. 104:13 KJV).

"And wine that maketh glad the heart of man, and oil to make his face to shine, and bread which strengtheneth man's heart" (Ps. 104:15 KJV).

"The glory of the Lord shall endure for ever: the Lord shall rejoice in his works" (Ps. 104:31 KJV).

"O ye seed of Abraham his servant, ye children of Jacob his chosen" (Ps. 105:6 KJV).

"He hath remember his covenant for ever, the word which he commanded to a thousand generations" (Ps. 105:8 KJV).

"Which covenant he made with Abraham, and his oath unto Isaac" (Ps. 105:9 KJV).

"And confirmed the same unto Jacob for a law, and to Israel for an everlasting covenant" (Ps. 105:10 KJV).

"Saying, Unto thee will I give the land of Canaan, the lot of your inheritance" (Ps. 105:11 KJV).

"He suffered no man to do them wrong: yea, he reproved kings for their sakes" (Ps. 105:14 KJV).

"Saying, Touch not mine anointed, and do my prophets no harm" (Ps. 105:15 KJV).

"Who can utter the mighty acts of the Lord? who can shew forth all his praise?" (Ps. 106:2 KJV).

"For he satisfieth the longing soul, and filleth the hungry soul with goodness" (Ps. 107:9 KJV).

"He turneth the wilderness into a standing water, and dry ground into watersprings" (Ps. 107:35 KJV).

"And there he maketh the hungry to dwell, that they may prepare a city for habitation" (Ps. 107:36 KJV).

"And sow the fields, and plant vineyards, which may yield fruits of increase" (Ps. 107:37 KJV).

"The works of the Lord are great, sought out of all them that have pleasure therein" (Ps. 111:2 KJV).

"His work is Honourable and glorious: and his righteousness endureth for ever" (Ps. 111:3 KJV).

"He hath made his wonderful works to be remembered: the Lord is gracious and full of compassion" (Ps. 111:4 KJV).

"He hath given meat unto them that fear him: he will ever be mindful of his covenant" (Ps. 111:5 KJV).

"He hath shewed his people the power of his works, that he may give them the heritage of the heathen" (Ps. 111:6 KJV).

"The works of his hands are verity and judgment; all his commandments are sure" (Ps. 111:7 KJV).

# PRAY IN GOD'S WORD FOR ENCOURAGEMENT AND CHANGE

"They stand fast for ever and ever, and are done in truth and uprightness" (Ps. 111:8 KJV).

"He sent redemption unto his people: he hath commanded his covenant for ever: holy and reverend is his name" (Ps. 111:9 KJV).

"All you who fear the Lord, trust the Lord! He is your helper and your shield" (Ps. 115:11 NLT).

"And the word of Jehovah came unto me the second time, saying" (Jer. 13:3 ASV).

"He will bless them that fear the Lord, both small and great" (Ps. 115:13 KJV).

"The LORD said to me" (Jer. 1:4 GNT).

"Ye are blessed of the Lord which made heaven and earth" (Ps. 115:14 KJV).

"The heaven, even the heavens, are the Lord's: but the earth hath he given to the children of men" (Ps. 115:16 KJV).

"Help me understand the meaning of your commandments, and I will meditate on your wonderful deeds" (Ps. 119:27 NLT).

"Let thy mercies come also unto me, O Lord, even thy salvation, according to thy word" (Ps. 119:41 KJV).

"Deal bountifully with thy servant, that I may live, and keep thy word" (Ps. 119:17 KJV).

"O Lord, truly I am thy servant; I am thy servant, and the son of thine handmaid: thou hast loosed my bonds" (Ps. 116:16 KJV).

"I will walk before the Lord in the land of the living" (Ps. 116:9 KJV).

"Thou art my God, and I will praise thee: thou art my God, I will exalt thee" (Ps. 118:28 KJV).

"O praise the Lord, all ye nations: praise him, all ye people" (Ps. 117:1 KJV).

"For his merciful kindness is great toward us: and the truth of the Lord endureth for ever. Praise ye the Lord" (Ps. 117:2 KJV).

"Blessed be the name of the Lord from this time forth and for evermore" (Ps. 113:2 KJV).

*In Jesus name, amen.*

## Notes

# Praising God for Our Children

## (Prayer)

"O Lord, you alone are my hope. I've trusted you, O Lord, from childhood" (Ps. 71:5 NLT).

"Yes, you have been with me from birth; from my mother's womb you have cared for me. No wonder I am always praising you!" (Ps. 71:6 NLT).

"I will praise your mighty deeds, O Sovereign Lord. I will tell everyone that you alone are just" (Ps. 71:16 NLT).

"Your righteousness, O God, reaches to the highest heavens. Who can compare with you, O God?" (Ps. 71:19 NLT).

"Praise ye the Lord. Praise ye the Lord from the heavens: praise him in the heights" (Ps. 148:1 KJV).

"Praise ye him, all his angels: praise ye him, all his hosts" (Ps. 148:2 KJV).

"Sing unto the Lord with thanksgiving; sing praise upon the harp unto our God" (Ps. 147:7 KJV).

"Praise the Lord; for the Lord is good: sing praises unto his name; for it is pleasant" (Ps. 135:3 KJV).

"For he has strengthened the bars of your gates and blessed your children within your walls" (Ps. 147:13 NLT).

"Let every created thing give praise to the Lord, for he issued his command, and they came into being" (Ps. 148:5 NLT).

"Let them all praise the name of the Lord. For his name is very great; his glory towers over the earth and heaven!" (Ps. 148:13 NLT).

"Praise ye the Lord. Praise ye the name of the Lord; praise him, O ye servants of the Lord" (Ps. 135:1 KJV).

"Because of the house of the Lord our God I will seek thy good" (Ps. 122:9 KJV).

"My help comes from the Lord, who made heaven and earth!" (Ps. 121:2 NLT).

"Then the word of Jehovah came unto me, saying" (Jer. 13:8 ASV).

"The faithful love of the Lord never ends! His mercies never cease" (Lam. 3:22 NLT).

"Children are a gift from the Lord; they are a reward from him" (Ps. 127:3 NLT).

"Children born to a young man are like arrows in a warrior's hands" (Ps. 127:4 NLT).

"How joyful is the man whose quiver is full of them! He will not be put to shame when he confronts his accusers at the city gates" (Ps. 127:5 NLT).

"Oh how great is thy goodness, which thou hast laid up for them that fear thee; which thou hast wrought for them that trust in thee before the sons of men!" (Ps. 31:19 KJV).

"How joyful are those who fear the Lord all who follow his ways!" (Ps. 128:1 NLT).

"You will enjoy the fruits of your labor. How joyful and prosperous you will be!" (Ps. 128:2 NLT).

"Your wife will be like a fruitful grapevine, flourishing within your home. Your children will be like vigorous young olive trees as they sit around your table" (Ps. 128:3 NLT).

"That is the Lord's blessing for those who fear him" (Ps. 128:4 NLT).

"Joyful are those who obey his laws and search for him with all their hearts" (Ps. 119:2 NLT).

"Moreover the word of Jehovah came unto me, saying" (Ezek. 7:1 ASV).

"Children, obey your parents in the Lord: for this is right" (Eph. 6:1 KJV).

"Children, obey your parents in all things: for this is well pleasing unto the Lord" (Col. 3:20 KJV).

"Honour thy father and mother; which is the first commandment with promise" (Eph. 6:2 KJV).

"That it may be well with thee, and thou mayest live long on the earth" (Eph. 6:3 KJV).

"Fathers, do not provoke your children to anger by the way you treat them. Rather, bring them up with the discipline and instruction that comes from the Lord" (Eph. 6:4 NLT).

"Fathers, provoke not your children to anger, lest they be discouraged" (Col. 3:21 KJV).

"Direct your children onto the right path, and when they are older, they will not leave it" (Prov. 22:6 NLT).

"Children's children are the crown of old men; and the glory of children are their fathers" (Prov. 17:6 KJV).

"I will never forget your commandments, for by them you give me life" (Ps. 119:93 NLT).

"Your faithfulness extends to every generation, as enduring as the earth you created" (Ps. 119:90 NLT).

"Your regulations remain true to this day, for everything serves your plans" (Ps. 119:91 NLT).

"Yes, the Lord has done amazing things for us! What joy!" (Ps. 126:3 NLT).

*In Jesus name, amen.*

## Notes

_____
_____
_____

# By God's Grace and Mercy

## (Prayer)

"Let the godly exult in glory; let them sing for joy on their beds" (Ps. 149:5 ESV).

"Arise, shine; for thy light is come, and the glory of the Lord is risen upon thee" (Isa. 60:1 KJV).

"For unto us a child is born, unto us a son is given: and the government shall be upon his shoulder: and his name shall be called Wonderful, Counsellor, The mighty God, The everlasting Father, the Prince of Peace" (Isa. 9:6 KJV).

"You have ordained Your precepts, That we should follow them with [careful] diligence" (Ps. 119:4 AMP).

"Wherefore thou art great, O Lord God: for there is none like thee, neither is there any God beside thee, according to all that we have heard with our ears" (2 Sam. 7:22 KJV).

"For thy word's sake, and according to thine own heart, hast thou done all these great things, to make thy servant know them" (2 Sam. 7:21 KJV).

"For the earth is the Lord's, and the fulness thereof" (1 Cor. 10:26 KJV).

"How precious is your unfailing love, O God! All humanity finds shelter in the shadow of your wings" (Ps. 36:7 NLT).

"If we believe not, yet he abideth faithful: he cannot deny himself" (2 Tim. 2:13 KJV).

"You feed them from the abundance of your own house, letting them drink from your river of delights" (Ps. 36:8 NLT).

"For you are the fountain of life, the light by which we see" (Ps. 36:9 NLT).

"Pour out your unfailing love on those who love you; give justice to those with honest hearts" (Ps. 36:10 NLT).

"This is a true saying: "If we have died with him, we shall also live with him" (2 Tim. 2:11 GNT).

"Thy hands have made me and fashioned me: give me understanding, that I may learn thy commandments" (Ps. 119:73 KJV).

"O how love I thy law! it is my meditation all the day" (Ps. 119:97 KJV).

"The heavens declare the glory of God; the sky displays his handiwork" (Ps. 19:1 NET).

"But I would have you know, that the head of every man is Christ; and the head of the woman is the man; and the head of Christ is God" (1 Cor. 11:3 KJV).

"Let every soul be subject unto the higher powers. For there is no power but of God: the powers that be are ordained of God" (Rom. 13:1 KJV).

"Ye cannot drink the cup of the Lord, and the cup of devils: ye cannot be partakers of the Lord's table, and of the table of devils" (1 Cor. 10:21 KJV).

"For God is not the author of confusion, but of peace, as in all churches of the saints" (1 Cor. 14:33 KJV).

"Wherefore let him that thinketh he standeth take heed lest he fall" (1 Cor. 10:12 KJV).

"Don't raise your fists in defiance at the heavens or speak with such arrogance" (Ps. 75:5 NLT).

"There hath no temptation taken you but such as is common to man: but God is faithful, who will not suffer you to be tempted above that ye are able; but will with the temptation also make a way to escape, that ye may be able to bear it" (1 Cor. 10:13 KJV).

"Lord, I wait for you; you will answer, Lord my God" (Ps. 38:15 NIV).

"Let my soul live, and it shall praise thee; And let thine ordinances help me" (Ps. 119:175 ASV).

"For God, who commanded the light to shine out of darkness, hath shined in our hearts, to give the light of the knowledge of the glory of God in the face of Jesus Christ" (2 Cor. 4:6 KJV).

"For all the promises of God in him are yea, and in him Amen, unto the glory of God by us" (2 Cor. 1:20 KJV).

"For we walk by faith, not by sight" (2 Cor. 5:7 KJV).

"For God says, 'At just the right time, I heard you. On the day of salvation, I helped you.' Indeed, the 'right time' is now. Today is the day of salvation" (2 Cor. 6:2 NLT).

"My enemies retreated; they staggered and died when you appeared" (Ps. 9:3 NLT).

"I will be filled with joy because of you. I will sing praises to your name, O Most High" (Ps. 9:2 NLT).

"I eagerly obey your commands, because you will give me more understanding" (Ps. 119:32 GNT).

"Let thy hand be ready to help me; For I have chosen thy precepts" (Ps. 119:173 ASV).

"As the mountains are round about Jerusalem, So Jehovah is round about his people From this time forth and for evermore" (Ps. 125:2 ASV).

"Now he that ministereth seed to the sower both minister bread for your food, and multiply your seed sown, and increase the fruits of your righteousness" (2 Cor. 9:10 KJV).

"For bodily exercise profiteth little: but godliness is profitable unto all things, having promise of the life that now is, and of that which is to come" (1 Tim. 4:8 KJV).

"This is a faithful saying and worthy of all acceptation" (1 Tim. 4:9 KJV).

"How precious is your steadfast love, O God!" (Ps. 36:7 ESV).

"That they do good, that they be rich in good works, ready to distribute, willing to communicate" (1 Tim. 6:18 KJV).

"Laying up in store for themselves a good foundation against the time to come, that they may lay hold on eternal life" (1 Tim. 6:19 KJV).

## PRAY IN GOD'S WORD FOR ENCOURAGEMENT AND CHANGE

"Fight the good fight of faith, lay hold on eternal life, whereunto thou art also called, and hast professed a good profession before many witnesses" (1 Tim. 6:12 KJV).

"For, At just the right time Christ will be revealed from heaven by the blessed and only almighty God, the King of all kings and Lord of lords" (1 Tim. 6:15 NLT).

"Day by day the Lord takes care of the innocent, and they will receive an inheritance that lasts forever" (Ps. 37:18 NLT).

"Thou therefore endure hardness, as a good soldier of Jesus Christ" (2 Tim. 2:3 KJV).

"Look at those who are honest and good, for a wonderful future awaits those who love peace" (Ps. 37:37 NLT).

"Deliver my soul, O Lord, from lying lips, and from a deceitful tongue" (Ps. 120:2 KJV).

"I will lift up mine eyes unto the hills, from whence cometh my help" (Ps. 120:1 KJV).

"In God I trust and am not afraid. What can man do to me?" (Ps. 56:11 NIV).

"For God hath not given us the spirit of fear; but of power, and of love, and of a sound mind" (2 Tim. 1:7 KJV).

"Let us therefore come boldly unto the throne of grace, that we may obtain mercy, and find grace to help in time of need" (Heb. 4:16 KJV).

"For the LORD will vindicate his people and have compassion on his servants" (Ps. 135:14 ESV).

"Thus says the LORD of hosts, the God of Israel: Amend your ways and your deeds, and I will let you dwell in this place" (Jer. 7:3 ESV).

"He will make your innocence radiate like the dawn, and the justice of your cause will shine like the noonday sun" (Ps. 37:6 NLT).

"That being justified by his grace, we should be made heirs according to the hope of eternal life" (Titus 3:7 KJV).

"Of his own will begat he us with the word of truth, that we should be a kind of first fruits of his creatures" (James 1:18 KJV).

"I, even I, *am* the LORD; And besides Me *there is* no savior" (Isaiah 43:11 KJV).

"But you have an anointing from the Holy One [you have been set apart, specially gifted and prepared by the Holy Spirit], and all of you know [the truth because He teaches us, illuminates our minds, and guards us from error]" (1 John 2:20 AMP).

"The Lord directs the steps of the godly. He delights in every detail of their lives" (Ps. 37:23 NLT).

"I am Alpha and Omega, the beginning and the ending, saith the Lord, which is, and which was, and which is to come, the Almighty" (Rev. 1:8 KJV).

"Behold, I come quickly: blessed is he that keepeth the saying of the prophecy of this book" (Rev. 22:7 KJV).

"Blessed is he that readeth and they that hear the words of this prophecy, and keep those things which are written therein: for the time is at hand" (Rev. 1:3 KJV).

"Do not abandon me, O Lord. Do not stand at a distance, my God" (Ps. 38:21 NLT).

"Come quickly to help me, O Lord my savior" (Ps. 38:22 NLT).

"Then the word of the LORD came to me" (Jer. 24:4 ESV).

"He which testifieth these things saith, Surely I come quickly. Amen. Even so, come Lord Jesus" (Rev. 22:20 KJV).

*In Jesus name, amen.*

## Notes

_____
_____
_____

# God's Favor

## (Prayer)

"I will extol thee, O Lord; for thou hast lifted me up, and hast not made my foes to rejoice over me" (Ps. 30:1 KJV).

"I will praise thee; for I am fearfully and wonderfully made: marvelous are thy works; and that my soul knoweth right well" (Ps. 139:14 KJV).

"Surely the righteous shall give thanks unto thy name: the upright shall dwell in thy presence" (Ps. 140:13 KJV).

"Thus says the Lord of hosts: consider your ways" (Hag. 1:7 ESV).

"There shall be no strange god among you; you shall not bow down to a foreign god" (Ps. 81:9 ESV).

"Then man prays to God, and he accepts him; he sees his face with a shout of joy, and he restores to man his righteousness" (Job 33:26 ESV).

"For thou, Lord, wilt bless the righteous; with favour wilt thou compass him as with a shield" (Ps. 5:12 KJV).

"The Lord protects them and keeps them alive. He gives them prosperity in the land and rescues them from their enemies" (Ps. 41:2 NLT).

"He keepeth back his soul from the pit, and his life from perishing by the sword" (Job 33:18 KJV).

"Have mercy upon me, O Lord; for I am weak: O Lord, heal me; for my bones are vexed" (Ps. 6:2 KJV).

"My soul is also sore vexed: but thou, O Lord, how long" (Ps. 6:3 KJV).

"Hear, please, and I will speak; I will ask You, and You instruct [and answer] me" (Job 42:4 AMP).

"Stop being angry! Turn from your rage! Do not lose your temper- it only leads to harm" (Ps. 37:8 NLT).

"A good man obtaineth favour of the Lord: but a man of wicked devices will he condemn" (Prov. 12:2 KJV).

"For length of days, and long life, and peace, shall they add to thee" (Prov. 3:2 KJV).

"For whoso findeth me findeth life, and shall obtain favour of the Lord" (Prov. 8:35 KJV).

"Let not mercy and truth forsake thee: bind them about thy neck; write them upon the table of thine heart" (Prov. 3:3 KJV).

"Let my prayer be set forth before thee as incense; and the lifting up of my hands as the evening sacrifice" (Ps. 141:2 KJV).

"Gracious is the Lord, and righteous; yea, our God is merciful" (Ps. 116:5 KJV).

"He lifted me out of the pit of despair, out of the mud and mire. He set my feet on solid ground and steadied me as I walked along" (Ps. 40:2 NLT).

"Cause me to hear thy lovingkindness in the morning; for in thee do I trust: cause me to know the way wherein I should walk; for I lift up my soul unto thee" (Ps. 143:8 KJV).

"Keep me from the snares which they have laid for me, and the gins of the workers of iniquity" (Ps. 141:9 KJV).

"Keep me as the apple of the eye, hide me under the shadow of thy wings" (Ps. 17:8 KJV).

"God says, 'At the time I have planned, I will bring justice against the wicked'" (Ps. 75:2 NLT).

"My son, forget not my law; but let thine heart keep my commandments" (Prov. 3:1 KJV).

"So shalt thou find favour and good understand in the sight of God and man" (Prov. 3:4 KJV).

"Therefore the Lord waits to be gracious to you, and therefore he exalts himself to show mercy to you. For the Lord is a God of justice; blessed are all those who wait for him" (Isa. 30:18 ESV).

"Make thy face to shine upon thy servant; and teach me thy statues" (Ps. 119:135 KJV).

"I take joy in doing your will, my God, for your instructions are written on my heart" (Ps. 40:8 NLT).

"O Lord my God, you have performed many wonders for us. Your plans for us are too numerous to list. If I tried to recite all your wonderful deeds, I would never come to the end of them" (Ps. 40:5 NLT).

"Look down and have mercy on me. Give your strength to your servant; save me, the son of your servant" (Ps. 86:16 NLT).

"Protect me, for I am devoted to you. Save me, for I serve you and trust you. You are my God" (Ps. 86:2 NLT).

"Let your favor shine on your servant. In your unfailing love, rescue me" (Ps. 31:16 NLT).

"The Lord your God is in your midst, a mighty one who will save; he will rejoice over you with gladness; he will quiet you by his love; he will exult over you with loud singing" (Zeph. 3:17 ESV).

"'Therefore wait for me,' declares the Lord, 'for the day when I rise up to seize the prey. For my decision is to gather nations, to assemble Kingdoms, to pour out upon them my indignation, all my burning anger; for in the fire of my jealousy all the earth shall be consumed'" (Zeph. 3:8 ESV).

*In Jesus name, amen.*

# Notes

_____
_____
_____

# Peace

Let the peace of Christ [The inner calm of one who walks daily with Him] be the controlling factor in your hearts [deciding and settling questions that arise]. To this peace indeed you were called as members in one body [of believers]. And be thankful [to God always] (Col. 3:15 AMP)

# God's Peace

## Surpassing Peace
## (A Word from God in Prayer)

"Hear and give ear; be not proud, for the Lord has spoken" (Jer. 13:15 ESV).

"You will seek me and find me, when you seek me with all your heart" (Jer. 29:13 ESV).

"Strive for peace with everyone, and for the holiness without which no one will see the Lord" (Heb. 12:14 ESV).

"Blessed are the peacemakers, for they will be called children of God" (Matt. 5:9 NIV).

"Blessed be the God and Father of our Lord Jesus Christ, who has blessed us in Christ with every spiritual blessing in the heavenly places" (Eph. 1:3 ESV).

"Even as he chose us in him before the foundation of the world, that we should be holy and blameless before him. In love (Eph. 1:4 ESV).

"He predestined us for adoption to himself as sons through Jesus Christ, according to the purpose of his will" (Eph. 1:5 ESV).

"To the praise of his glorious grace, with which he has blessed us in the Beloved" (Eph. 1:6 ESV).

"I love the Lord, because he has heard my voice and my pleas for mercy" (Ps. 116:1 ESV).

"Gracious is the Lord, and righteous; our God is merciful" (Ps. 116:5 ESV).

"Blessed is the nation whose God is the Lord, the people whom he has chosen as his heritage!" (Ps. 33:12 ESV).

"For from the rising of the sun to its setting my name will be great among the nations, and in every place incense will be offered to my name, and pure offering. For my name will be great among the nations, says the Lord of hosts" (Mal. 1:11 ESV).

"If it be possible, as much as lieth in you, live peaceably with all men" (Rom. 12:18 KJV).

"And the peace of God, which passeth all understanding, shall keep your hearts and minds through Christ Jesus" (Phil. 4:7 KJV).

"The Lord is slow to anger and great in power, and the Lord will by no means clear the guilty. His way is in the whirlwind and storm, and the clouds are the dust of his feet" (Nah. 1:3 ESV).

"For he that will love life, and see good days, let him refrain his tongue from evil, and his lips that they speak no guile" (1 Pet. 3:10 KJV).

"Let him turn away from evil and do good; let him seek peace and pursue it" (1 Pet. 3:11 ESV).

"Peace I leave with you, My peace I give unto you: not as the world giveth, give I unto you. Let not your heart be troubled, neither let it be afraid" (John 14:27 KJV).

"The Lord watches over the innocent day by day and they possess a permanent inheritance" (Ps. 37:18 ESV).

"He did this when he revealed to us the secret of his will, according to his good pleasure that he set forth in Christ" (Eph. 1:9 NET).

"So then, strengthen hands that are weak and knees that tremble" (Heb. 12:12 AMP).

"Cut through and make smooth, straight paths for your feet [that are safe and go in the right direction], so that the leg which is lame may not be put out of joint, but rather may be healed" (Heb. 12:13 AMP).

"See to it that no one falls short of God's grace; that no root of resentment springs up and causes trouble, and by it many be defiled" (Heb. 12:15 AMP).

## PRAY IN GOD'S WORD FOR ENCOURAGEMENT AND CHANGE

"Bearing with one another and, if one has a complaint against another, forgiving each other; as the Lord has forgiven you, so you also must forgive" (Col. 3:13 ESV).

"For the wrong doer will be paid back for the wrong he has done, and there is no partiality" (Col. 3:25 ESV).

"Let your speech always be gracious, seasoned with salt, so that you may know how you ought to answer each person" (Col. 4:6 ESV).

"Peacemakers who sow in peace reap a harvest of righteousness" (James 3:18 NIV).

"I say to the Lord, 'You are my Lord; I have no good apart from you'" (Ps. 16:2 ESV).

"Lead me in your truth and teach me, for you are the God of my salvation; for you I wait all the day long" (Ps. 25:5 ESV).

"In peace I will lie down and sleep, for you alone, Lord, make me dwell in safety" (Ps. 4:8 NIV).

*In Jesus name, amen.*

## Notes

_____
_____
_____

# Reflecting on God's Miracles

## (Prayer)

"When the Lord restored the fortunes of Zion, we were like those who dreamed" (Ps. 126:1 NIV).

"Blessed be the God and Father of our Lord Jesus Christ, who has blessed us in Christ with every spiritual blessing in the heavenly places" (Eph. 1:3 ESV).

"For who is God except the Lord? Who but our God is a solid rock?" (Ps. 18:31 NLT).

"Blessed be the Lord, who daily loadeth us with benefits, even the God of our salvation" (Ps. 68:19 KJV).

"The word of the Lord came to me" (Ezek. 18:1 ESV).

"Behold, all souls are mine, the soul of the father as well as the soul of the son is mine: the soul who sins shall die" (Ezek. 18:4 ESV).

"He therefore that ministereth to you the Spirit, and worketh miracles among you, doeth he

It by the works of the law, or by the hearing of faith?" (Gal. 3:5 KJV).

"Even as Abraham believed God, and it was accounted to him for righteousness" (Gal. 3:6 KJV).

"For as many as are of the works of the law are under the curse: for it is written, Cursed is Every one that continueth not in all things which are written in the book of the law to do Them" (Gal. 3:10 KJV).

"But that no man is justified by the law in the sight of God, it is evident: for, The just shall live By faith" (Gal. 3:11 KJV).

"You will teach me the right way to live. Just being with you will bring complete happiness. Being at Your right side will make me happy" (Ps. 16:11 ERV).

"Lord our Lord, your name is most wonderful in all the earth! It brings you praise everywhere in heaven" (Ps. 8:1 ERV).

"I look at the heavens you made with your hands. I see the moon and the stars you created" (Ps. 8:3 ERV).

"And I wonder, 'Why are people so important to you? Why do you even think about them? Why do you care so much about humans? Why do you even notice them?'" (Ps. 8:4 ERV).

"But you made them almost like gods and crowned them with glory and honor" (Ps. 8:5 ERV).

"The heavens declare the glory of God, and the sky above proclaims his handiwork" (Ps. 19:1 ESV).

"Praise him who alone does wonderful miracles! His faithful love will last forever" (Ps. 136:4 ERV).

"Praise the one who used wisdom to make the skies! His faithful love will last forever" (Ps. 136:5 ERV).

"Who covereth the heaven with clouds, who prepareth rain for the earth, who maketh grass to grow upon the mountains" (Ps. 147:8 KJV).

"He giveth to the beast his food, and to the young ravens which cry" (Ps. 147:9 KJV).

"He telleth the number of the stars; he calleth them all by their names" (Ps. 147:4 KJV).

"How great is our Lord! His power is absolute! His understanding is beyond comprehension!" (Ps. 147:5 NLT).

"I am the Lord: that is my name: and my glory will I not give to another, neither my praise to graven images" (Isa. 42:8 KJV).

"Who hath wrought and done it, calling the generations from the beginning? I the Lord, the first, and with the last; I am he" (Isa. 41:4 KJV).

"Who is like me? Let him step forward and prove to you his power. Let him do as I have done since ancient times when I established a people and explained its future" (Ps. 44:7 NLT).

"For I know that the LORD is great, and that our Lord is above all gods" (Ps. 135:5 KJV).

"To him that by wisdom made the heavens: for his mercy endureth for ever" (Ps. 136:5 KJV).

"To him that stretched out the earth above the waters; for his mercy endureth for ever" (Ps. 136:6 KJV).

"To him that made great lights: for his mercy endureth for ever" (Ps. 136:7 KJV).

"The sun to rule by day: for his mercy endureth for ever" (Ps. 136:8 KJV).

"The moon and star to rule by night: for his mercy endureth for ever" (Ps. 136:9 KJV).

"To him that smote Egypt in their firstborn: for his mercy endureth for ever" (Ps. 136:10 KJV).

"To him which divided the Red sea into parts: for his mercy endureth for ever" (Ps. 136:13 KJV).

"And made Israel to pass through the midst of it: for his mercy endureth for ever" (Ps. 136:14 KJV).

"To him that rideth upon the heavens of heavens, which were of old; lo, he doth send out his voice, and that a mighty voice" (Ps. 68:33 KJV).

"Ascribe ye strength unto God: his excellency is over Israel, and his strength is in the clouds" (Ps. 68:34 KJV).

"O God, thou art terrible out of thy holy places: the God of Israel is he that giveth strength and power unto his people. Blessed be God" (Ps. 68:35 KJV).

*In Jesus name, amen.*

## Notes

_____
_____
_____

# Forgiving

## (Prayer)

"This I recall to my mind, therefore have I hope" (Lam. 3:21 KJV).

"The Lord will not suffer the soul of the righteous to famish: but he casteth away the substance of the wicked" (Prov. 10:3 KJV).

"Who shall ascend the hill of the Lord? And who shall stand in his holy place?" (Ps. 24:3 ESV).

"He who has clean hands and a pure heart, who does not lift up his soul to what is false and does not swear deceitfully" (Ps. 24:4 ESV).

"Behold, the eye of the Lord is upon them that fear him, upon them that hope in his mercy" (Ps. 33:18 KJV).

"If we confess our sins, he is faithful and just to forgive us our sins, and to cleanse us from all unrighteousness" (1 John 1:9 KJV).

"The fool hath said in his heart, There is no God. Corrupt are they, and have done abominable iniquity: there is none that doeth good" (Ps. 53:1 KJV).

"The heart of him that hath understanding seeketh knowledge: but the mouth of fools feedeth on foolishness" (Prov. 15:14 KJV).

"All the paths of the Lord are mercy and truth unto such as keep his covenant and his testimonies" (Ps. 25:10 KJV).

"The earth is the Lord's, and the fullness of it, The world, and those who dwell in it" (Ps. 24:1 AMP).

"God looked down from heaven upon the children of men, to see if there were any that did understand, that did seek God" (Ps. 53:2 KJV).

"To the Lord our God belongs mercies and forgiveness, though we have rebelled against him" (Dan. 9:9 KJV).

"If we are faithless, he remains faithful-for he cannot deny himself" (2 Tim. 2:13 ESV).

"So repent [change your inner self—your old way of thinking, regret past sins] and return [to God—seek His purpose for your life], so that your sins may be wiped away [blotted out, completely erased], so that times of refreshing may come from the presence of the Lord [restoring you like a cool wind on a hot day]" (Acts 3:19 AMP).

"Devote yourselves to prayer with an alert mind and a thankful heart" (Col. 4:2 NLT).

"Let this mind be in you, which was also in Christ Jesus" (Phil. 2:5 KJV).

"And the peace of God, which passeth all understanding, shall keep your hearts and minds through Christ Jesus" (Phil. 4:7 KJV).

"Give your burdens to the Lord, and he will take care of you. He will not permit the godly to slip and fall" (Ps. 55:22 NLT).

"Morning, noon, and night I cry out in my distress, and the Lord hears my voice" (Ps. 55:17 NLT).

"The LORD takes delight in his faithful followers, and in those who wait for his loyal love" (Ps. 147:11 NET).

"'Yet even now,' declares the LORD, 'return to me with all your heart, with fasting, with weeping, and with mourning'" (Joel 2:12 ESV).

"And when ye stand praying, forgive, if ye have ought against any: that your Father also which is in heaven may forgive you your trespasses" (Mark 11:25 KJV).

"Let all bitterness, and wrath, and anger, and clamor, and evil speaking, be put away from you, with all malice" (Eph. 4:31 KJV).

"And be ye kind one to another, tenderhearted, forgiving one another, even as God for Christ's sake hath forgiven you" (Eph. 4:32 KJV).

## PRAY IN GOD'S WORD FOR ENCOURAGEMENT AND CHANGE

"But if ye forgive not men their trespasses, neither will your Father forgive your trespasses" (Matt. 6:15 KJV).

"For if ye love them which love you, what reward have ye? do not even the publicans the same?" (Matt. 5:46 KJV).

"A man shall not be established by wickedness: but the root of the righteous shall not be moved" (Prov. 12:3 KJV).

"Be ye therefore perfect, even as your Father which is in heaven is perfect" (Matt. 5:48 KJV).

"If thine enemy be hungry, give him bread to eat; and if he be thirsty, give him water to drink" (Prov. 25:21 KJV).

"For thou shalt heap coals of fire upon his head, and the Lord shall reward thee" (Prov. 25:22 KJV).

"Never stop praying" (1 Thess. 5:17 NLT).

"A man shall be satisfied with good by the fruit of his mouth: and the recompense of a man's hands shall be rendered unto him" (Prov. 12:14 KJV).

"For thy name's sake, O Lord, pardon mine iniquity, for it is great" (Ps. 25:11 KJV).

"Remember not the sins of my youth, nor my transgressions: according to thy mercy remember thou me for thy goodness' sake, O Lord" (Ps. 25:7 KJV).

""Come now, let's settle this," says the Lord. "Though your sins are like scarlet, I will make them as white as snow. Though they are red like crimson, I will make them as white as wool" (Isa. 1:18 NLT).

"Then he says, 'I will never again remember their sins and lawless deeds'" (Heb. 10:17 NLT).

"Blessed be God, which hath not turned away my prayer, nor his mercy from me" (Ps. 66:20 KJV).

*In Jesus name, amen.*

## Notes

_____

_____

_____

# Trust in the Lord Your God

## (Prayer)

"O God, have mercy on me, for people are hounding me. My foes attack me all day long" (Ps. 56:1 NLT).

"I am constantly hounded by those who slander me, and many are boldly attacking me" (Ps. 56:2 NLT).

"But when I am afraid, I will put my trust in you" (Ps. 56:3 NLT).

"The Lord is good, a stronghold in the day of trouble; and he knoweth them that trust in him" (Nah. 1:7 KJV).

"Mine eyes are ever toward the Lord; for he shall pluck my feet out of the net" (Ps. 25:15 KJV).

"Then the word of the Lord came to me" (Jer. 13:8 ESV).

"Faithful is he that calleth you, who also will do it" (1 Thess. 5:24 KJV).

"I praise God for what he has promised. I trust in God, so why should I be afraid? What can mere mortals do to me?" (Ps. 56:4 NLT).

"My help comes from the Lord, who made heaven and earth" (Ps. 121:3 NLT).

"I will boast only in the Lord; let all who are helpless take heart" (Ps. 34:2 NLT).

"Those who look to him for help will be radiant with joy; no shadow of shame will darken their faces" (Ps. 34:5 NLT).

"Blessed is the man that trusteth in the Lord, and whose hope the Lord is" (Jer. 17:7 KJV).

"And this hope will not lead to disappointed. For we know how dearly God loves us, because he has given us the Holy Spirit to fill our hearts with his love" (Rom. 5:5 NLT).

"For our heart shall rejoice in him, because we have trusted in his holy name" (Ps. 33:21 KJV).

"Many sorrows shall be to the wicked: but he that trusteth in the Lord, mercy shall compass him about" (Ps. 32:10 KJV).

"Once I was young, and now I am old. Yet I have never seen the godly abandoned or their children begging for bread" (Ps. 37:25 NLT).

"Show me the right path, O Lord; point out the road for me to follow" (Ps. 25:4 NLT).

"Lead me by your truth and teach me, for you are the God who saves me. All day long I put my hope in you" (Ps. 25:5 NLT).

"Send out your light and your truth; let them guide me. Let them lead me to your holy mountain, to the place where you live" (Ps. 43:3 NLT).

"Oh, the joys of those who trust the Lord, who have no confidence in the proud or in those who worship idols" (Ps. 40:4 NLT).

"O Lord, you know; remember me and visit me, and take vengeance for me on my persecutors. In your forbearance take me not away; know that for your sake I bear reproach" (Jer. 15:15 ESV).

"I have seen wicked and ruthless people flourishing like a tree in its native soil" (Ps. 37:35 NLT).

"But when I looked again, they were gone! Though I searched for them, I could not find them!" (Ps. 37:36 NLT).

"The Lord rescues the godly; he is their fortress in times of trouble" (Ps. 37:39 NLT).

"The Lord openeth the eyes of the blind: the Lord raiseth them that are bowed down: the Lord loveth the righteous" (Ps. 146:8 KJV).

"Happy is he that hath the God of Jacob for his help, whose hope is in the Lord his God" (Ps. 146:5 KJV).

"You have made a wide path for my feet to keep them from slipping" (Ps. 18:36 NLT).

"See, God has come to save me. I will trust in him and not be afraid. The Lord God is my strength and my song; he has given me victory" (Isa. 12:2 NLT).

"I called on the Lord, who is worthy of praise, and he saved me from my enemies" (Ps. 18:3 NLT).

*In Jesus name, amen.*

## Notes

_____
_____
_____

# The Honor of God's Name Upheld

## (Prayer)

"A good name is better than precious ointment; and the day of death than the day of one's birth" (Eccles. 7:1 KJV).

"A good name is rather to be chosen than great riches, and loving favour rather than silver and gold" (Prov. 22:1 KJV).

"Have mercy upon me, O God, according to thy lovingkindness: according unto the multitude of thy tender mercies blot out my transgressions" (Ps. 51:1 KJV).

"Wash me thoroughly from mine iniquity, and cleanse me from my sin" (Ps. 51:2 KJV).

"I the LORD search the heart, I try the reins, even to give every man according to his ways, and according to the fruit of his doings" (Jeremiah 17:10 KJV).

"Gather to me my faithful ones, who made a covenant with me by sacrifice!" (Ps. 50:5 ESV).

"For my name's sake will I defer mine anger, and for my praise will I refrain for thee, that I cut thee not off" (Isa. 48:9 KJV).

"Behold, I have refined thee, but not with silver; I have chosen thee in the furnace of affliction" (Isa. 48:10 KJV).

"For mine own sake, even for mine own sake, will I do it: for how should my name be polluted? and I will not give my glory unto another" (Isa. 48:11 KJV).

[God loves His people and will release them from their captivity. Not because they/we are worthy of release (for He owes them/ us nothing). But because He does not want His name to be polluted by the triumph of the heathen.]

"And in that day thou shalt say, O Lord, I will praise thee: though thou wast angry with me, thine anger is turned away, and thou comfortedst me" (Isa. 12:1 KJV).

"Thou hast shewed thy people hard things: thou hast made us to drink the wine of astonishment" (Ps. 60:3 KJV).

"I said, Lord, be merciful unto me: heal my soul; for I have sinned against thee" (Ps. 41:4 KJV).

"For innumerable evils have compassed me about: mine iniquities have taken hold upon me, so that I am not able to look up; they are more than the hairs of mine head: therefore my heart faileth` me" (Ps. 40:12 KJV).

"All that hate me whisper together against me: against me do they devise my hurt" (Ps. 41:7 KJV).

"But I will hope continually, and will yet praise thee more and more" (Ps. 71:14 KJV).

"Thou hast given a banner to them that fear thee, that it may be displayed because of the truth" (Ps. 60:4 KJV). *Selah*.

"Unto thee, O my strength, will I sing: for God is my defense, and the God of my mercy" (Ps. 59:17 KJV).

"Turn, O backsliding children, saith the Lord; for I am married unto you: and I will take you one of a city, and two of a family, and I will bring you to Zion" (Jer. 3:14 KJV).

"I the Lord search the heart, I try the reins, even to give every man according to his ways, and according to the fruit of his doings" (Jeremiah 17:10 KJV)

"Make us glad according to the days wherein thou hast afflicted us, and the years wherein we have seen evil" (Ps. 90:15 KJV).

"O satisfy us early with thy mercy; that we may rejoice and be glad all our days" (Ps. 90:14 KJV).

"That thy beloved may be delivered; save with thy right hand, and hear me" (Ps. 60:5 KJV).

"Let thy work appear unto thy servants, and thy glory unto their children" (Ps. 90:16 KJV).

## PRAY IN GOD'S WORD FOR ENCOURAGEMENT AND CHANGE

"For the Lord is righteous; he loves righteous deeds; the upright shall behold his face" (Ps. 11:7 ESV).

"And let the beauty of the Lord our God be upon us: and establish thou the work of our hands upon us; yea, the work of our hands establish thou it" (Ps. 90:17 KJV).

"You have not handed me over to my enemies but have set me in a safe place" (Ps. 31:8 NLT).

"Righteous are You, O Lord, And upright are Your judgments" (Ps. 119:137 NAS).

"For the Lord loves justice, and he will never abandon the godly. He will keep them safe forever, but the children of the wicked will die" (Ps. 37:28 NLT).

"Those who desert him will perish, for you destroy those who abandon you" (Ps. 73:27 KJV).

"Who can comprehend the power of your anger? Your wrath is as awesome as the fear you deserve" (Ps. 90:11 NLT).

"The highest angelic powers stand in awe of God. He is far more awesome than all who surround his throne" (Ps. 89:7 NLT).

"Your name, O Lord, endures forever; your fame, O Lord, is known to every generation" (Ps. 135:13 NLT).

"For the Lord will give justice to his people and have compassion on his servants" (Ps. 135:14 NLT).

"They will receive the Lord's blessing and have a right relationship with God their savior" (Ps. 24:5 NLT).

"The humble will see their God at work and be glad. Let all who seek God's help be encourage" (Ps. 69:32 NLT).

*In Jesus name, amen.*

## Notes

_____
_____
_____

# Patience

"May the Lord direct your hearts into the love of God and into the steadfastness and patience of Christ" (2 Thess. 3:5).

"In your patience possess ye your souls" (Luke 21:19 KJV).

# God's Patience

## Operating in Patience
## (A Word from God in Prayer)

"To every thing is a season, and a time for every matter under heaven" (Eccles. 3:1 KJV).

"I know that, whatsoever God doeth, it shall be for ever: nothing can be put to it: and God doeth it, that men should fear before him" (Eccles. 3:14 KJV).

"Forever, O Lord, your word is firmly fixed in the heavens" (Ps. 119:89 ESV).

"Your faithfulness continues from generation to generation; You have established the earth, and it stands [securely]" (Ps. 119:90 AMP).

"For in the hand of the Lord there is a cup, and the wine is red; It is full of mixture; and he poureth out of the same: But the dregs thereof, All the wicked of the earth shall wring them out, and drink them" (Ps. 75:8 KJV).

"Come, my people, enter thou into thy chambers, and shut thy doors about thee: hide thyself as it were for a little moment, until the indignation be overpast" (Isa. 26:20 KJV).

"Cast not away therefore your confidence, which hath great recompense of reward" (Heb. 10:35 KJV).

"For ye have need of patience, that, after ye have done the will of God, ye might receive the promise" (Heb. 10:36 KJV).

"But let patience have her perfect work, that ye may be perfect and entire, wanting nothing" (James 1:4 KJV).

"Every good and perfect gift is from above, and cometh down from the Father of lights, with whom is no variableness, neither shadow of turning" (James 1:17 KJV).

"You have multiplied, O Lord my God, your wondrous deeds and your thoughts toward us; none can compare with you! I will proclaim and tell of them, yet they are more than can be told" (Ps. 40:5 ESV).

"He appointed the moon for seasons: the sun knoweth his going down" (Ps. 104:19 KJV).

"O Lord, how manifold are thy works! In wisdom hast thou made them all: the earth is full of thy riches" (Ps. 104:24 KJV).

"I will praise thee, O Lord, with my whole heart; I will shew forth all thy marvelous works" (Ps. 9:1 KJV).

"Lead me in thy truth, and teach me: for thou art the God of my salvation; on thee do I wait all the day" (Ps. 25:5 KJV).

"Let integrity and uprightness preserve me; for I wait on thee" (Ps. 25:21 KJV).

"Rest in the Lord, and wait patiently for him: fret not thyself because of him who prospereth in his way, because of the man who bringeth wicked devices to pass" (Ps. 37:7 KJV).

"Wait on the Lord: be of good courage, and he shall strengthen thine heart: wait, I say, on the
Lord" (Ps. 27:14 KJV).

"For yet a little while, and the wicked shall not be: yea, thou shalt diligently consider his place, and it shall not be" (Ps. 37:10 KJV).

"Wait on the Lord, and keep his way, and he shall exalt thee to inherit the land: when the wicked are cut off, thou shalt see it" (Ps. 37:24 KJV).

"You did it: you changed wild lament into whirling dance; You ripped off my black mourning band and decked me with wildflowers. I'm about to burst with song; I can't keep quiet about you God, my God, I can't thank you enough" (Ps. 30:11–12 MSG).

"For in this hope we were saved. But hope that is seen is no hope at all. Who hopes for what they already have?" (Rom. 8:24 NIV).

"But if we hope for what we do not yet have, we wait for it patiently" (Rom. 8:25 NIV).

"In God will I praise his word: in the Lord will I praise his word" (Ps. 56:10 KJV).

"I will fulfill my vows to you, O God, and will offer a sacrifice of thanks for your help" (Ps. 56:12 NLT).

*In Jesus name, amen.*

## Notes

_____
_____
_____

# Reflections

# I Have Been Chosen

## (Prayer)

"Say this to those who worship other gods: 'Your so-called gods, who did not make the heavens and earth, will vanish from the earth and from under the heavens'" (Jer. 10:11 NLT).

"But the LORD made the earth by his power, and he preserves it by his wisdom. With his own understanding he stretched out the heavens" (Jer. 10:12 NLT).

"When he speaks in the thunder, the heavens roar with rain. He causes the clouds to rise over the earth. He sends the lightening with rain and releases the wind from his storehouses" (Jer. 13:13 NLT).

"Thou whom I have taken from the ends of the earth, and called thee from the chief men thereof, and said unto thee, Thou art servant; I have chosen thee, and not cast thee away" (Isa. 41:9 KJV).

"Fear thou not; for I am with thee: be not dismayed; for I am thy God: I will strengthen thee; yea, I will help thee; yea, I will uphold thee with the right hand of my righteousness" (Isa. 41:10 KJV).

"When the poor and needy seek water, and there is none, and their tongue faileth for thirst, I the Lord will hear them, I the God of Israel will not forsake them" (Isa. 41:17 KJV).

"Because of your unfailing love, I can enter your house; I will worship at your temple with deepest awe" (Ps. 5:7 KJV).

"For no one is abandoned by the Lord forever" (Lam. 3:31 NLT).

"Though he brings grief, he also shows compassion because of the greatness of his unfailing love" (Lam. 3:32 NLT).

"For he does not enjoy hurting people or causing them sorrow" (Lam. 3:33 NLT).

"O Lord, hear me as I pray; pay attention to my groaning" (Ps. 5:1 NLT).

"Listen to my cry for help, my King and my God, for I pray to no one but you" (Ps. 5:2 NLT).

"Because for thy sake I have borne reproach; shame hath covered my face" (Ps. 69:7 KJV).

"For the zeal of thine house hath eaten me up; and the reproaches of them that reproached thee are fallen upon me" (Ps. 69:9 KJV).

"Deliver me, O my God, out of the hand of the wicked, out of the hand of the unrighteous and cruel man" (Ps. 71:4 KJV).

"For thou art my hope, O Lord God: thou art my trust from my youth" (Ps. 71:5 KJV).

"By thee have I been holden up from the womb: thou art he that took me out of my mother's bowels: my praise shall be continually of thee" (Ps. 71:6 KJV).

"Do not drag me away with the wicked- with those who do evil- those who speak friendly words to their neighbors while planning evil in their hearts" (Ps. 28:3 NLT).

"Like emery harder than flint have I made your forehead. Fear them not, nor be dismayed at their looks, for they are a rebellious house" (Ezek. 3:9 ESV).

"Moreover, he said to me, "Son of man. All my words that I shall speak to you receive in your heart, and hear with your ears" (Ezek. 3:10 ESV).

"Ye have not chosen me, but I have chosen you, and ordained you, that ye should go and bring forth fruit, and that your fruit should remain: that whatsoever ye shall ask of the Father in my name, he may give it you" (John 15:16 KJV).

"Turn to me and be saved, all the ends of the earth! For I am God, and there is no other" (Isa. 45:22 ESV).

"That day of judgment will come, says the Sovereign Lord. Everything will happen just as I have declared it" (Ezek. 39:8 NLT).

# PRAY IN GOD'S WORD FOR ENCOURAGEMENT AND CHANGE

"If I shut up heaven that there be no rain, or if I command the locusts to devour the land, or if I send pestilence among my people" (2 Chron. 7:13 KJV).

"If my people, which are called by my name, shall humble themselves, and pray, and seek my face, and turn from their wicked ways; then will I hear from heaven, and will forgive their sin, and will heal their land" (2 Chron. 7:14 KJV).

"I have made the earth, and created man upon it: I, even my hands, have stretched out the heavens, and all their host have I commanded" (Isa. 45:12 KJV).

"Therefore also now, saith the Lord, turn ye even to me with all your heart and with fasting, and with weeping, and with mourning" (Joel 2:12 KJV).

"I cried unto the Lord with my voice, and he heard me out of his holy hill" (Ps. 3:4 KJV). *Selah.*

"Salvation belongeth unto the Lord: thy blessing is upon thy people" (Ps. 3:8 KJV). *Selah.*

"Please guarantee a blessing for me. Don't let the arrogant oppress me!" (Ps. 119:122 NLT).

"With all my heart I will want your blessings. Be merciful as you promised" (Ps. 119:58 NLT).

"I ponder the direction of my life, and I turned to follow your laws" (Ps. 119:59 NLT).

"Even when we were dead in sins, hath quickened us together with Christ" (By grace ye are saved;) (Eph. 2:5 KJV).

"For we are his workmanship, created in Christ Jesus unto good works, which God hath before ordained that we should walk in them" (Eph. 2:10 KJV).

"And hath raised us up together, and made us sit together in heavenly places in Christ Jesus" (Eph. 2:6 KJV).

"I know, O Lord, that your regulations are fair; you disciplined me because I needed it" (Ps. 119:75 NLT).

"I am silent before you; I won't say a word, for my punishment is from you" (Ps. 39:9 NLT).

"But please stop striking me! I am exhausted by the blows from your hand" (Ps. 39:10 NLT).

"Morning, noon, and night I cry out in my distress, and the Lord hears my voice" (Ps. 55:17 NLT).

"Now let your unfailing love comfort me, just as you promised me, your servant" (Ps. 119:76 NLT).

"I entrust my spirit into your hand. Rescue me, Lord, for you are a faithful God" (Ps. 31:5 NLT).

"I will exalt you, Lord, for you rescued me. You refused to let my enemies triumph over me" (Ps. 30:1 NLT).

"Great is our Lord, and of great power: his understanding is infinite" (Ps. 147:5 KJV).

"The voice of the Lord is powerful; the voice of the Lord is majestic" (Ps. 29:4 NLT).

"O Lord God, thou hast begun to shew thy servant thy greatness, and thy mighty hand: for what God is there in heaven or in earth, that can do according to thy works, and according to thy might" (Deut. 3:24 KJV).

"And the word of the LORD came unto me the second time, saying" (Jer. 13:3 KJV).

"Do not be afraid or discouraged, for the Lord will personally go ahead of you. He will be with you; he will neither fail you nor abandon you." (Deut. 31:8 NLT).

"Your right hand, O Lord, is glorious in power. Your right hand, O Lord, smashes the enemy" (Exod. 15:6 NLT).

"The Lord is a warrior; Yahweh is his name!" (Exod. 15:3 NLT).

"In the greatness of your majesty, you overthrow those who rise against you. You unleashed your blazing fury; it consumes them like straw" (Exod. 15:7 NLT).

"Who is like unto thee, O Lord, among the gods? who is like thee, glorious in holiness, fearful in praises, doing wonders?" (Exod. 15:11 KJV).

"The Lord shall reign for ever and ever" (Exod. 15:18 KJV).

"For when God made promise to Abraham, because he could swear by no greater, he swear by himself" (Heb. 6:13 KJV).

"Saying, Surely blessing I will bless thee, and multiplying I will multiply thee" (Heb. 6:14 KJV).

"And so, after he had patiently endured, he obtained the promise" (Heb. 6:15 KJV).

"And this is the promise that he hath promised us, even eternal life" (1 John 2:25 KJV).

"I will delight in your decrees and not forgot your word" (Ps. 119:16 NLT).

"Lord, there is no one like you! For you are great, and your name is full of power" (Jer. 10:6 NLT).

"Help me abandon my shameful ways; for your regulations are good" (Ps. 119:39 NLT).

"Remember me, O my God, concerning this, and wipe not out my good deeds that I have done for the house of my God, and for the offices thereof" (Neh. 13:14 KJV).

"Thou, O Lord, remainest for ever; thy throne from generation to generation" (Lam. 5:19 KJV).

*In Jesus name, amen.*

## Notes

_____
_____
_____

# Kindness

So then, while we [as individual believers] have the opportunity, let us do good to all people [not only being helpful, but also doing that which promotes their Spiritual well-being], and especially [be a blessing] to those of the household of faith.[Born-again believers]. (Gal. 6:10 AMP)

# God's Kindness

## God's Kindness to Us
## (A Word from God in Prayer)

"He that believeth on me, as the scripture hath said, out of his belly shall flow rivers of living water" (John 7:3 KJV).

"Hear; for I will speak of excellent things; and the opening of my lips shall be right things" (Prov. 8:6 KJV).

"For my mouth shall speak truth; and wickedness is an abomination to my lips" (Prov. 8:7 KJV).

"ALL the words of my mouth are in righteousness; there is nothing froward or perverse in them" (Prov. 8:8 KJV).

"Put on therefore, as the elect of God, holy and beloved, bowels of mercies, kindness, humbleness of mind, meekness, longsuffering" (Col. 3:12 KJV).

"I will declare the decree: the LORD hath said unto me, Thou art my son; this day have I begotten thee" (Ps. 2:7 KJV).

"My flesh and my heart faileth: but God is the strength of my heart, and my portion forever" (Ps. 73:26 KJV).

"Blessed be the God and Father of our Lord Jesus Christ! According to his great mercy, he has caused us to be born again to a living hope through the resurrection of Jesus Christ from the dead" (1 Pet. 1:3 ESV).

"To an inheritance that is imperishable, undefiled, and unfading, kept in heaven for you" (1 Pet. 1:4 ESV).

"He hath made the earth by his power, he hath established the world by his wisdom, and hath stretched out the heavens by his discretion" (Jer. 10:12 KJV).

"Who then will condemn us? No one- for Christ Jesus died for us and was raised to life for us, and he is sitting in the place of honor at God's right hand, pleading for us" (Rom. 8:34 NLT).

"Can anything ever separate us from Christ's love? Does it mean he no longer loves us if we have trouble or calamity, or are persecuted, or hungry, or destitute, or in danger, or threatened with death?" (Rom. 8:35 NLT).

"No, despite all these things, overwhelming victory is ours through Christ, who loved us" (Rom. 8:37 NLT).

"Hold up my goings in thy paths, that my footsteps slip not" (Ps. 17:5 KJV).

"Thou shalt guide me with thy counsel, and afterward receive me to glory" (Ps. 73:24 KJV).

*In Jesus name, amen.*

## Notes

_____

_____

_____

# God's Blessings and Promises

## (Prayer)

"Oh, taste and see that the Lord is good! Blessed is the man who takes refuge in him!" (Ps. 34:8 ESV).

"If I say, "I will not mention him, or speak any more in his name," there is in my heart as it were a burning fire shut up in my bones, and I am weary with holding it in, and I cannot" (Jer. 20:9 ESV).

"For I hear many whispering. Terror is on ever side! 'Denounce him! Let us denounce him!' say all my close friends, watching for my fall. 'Perhaps he will be deceived; then we can overcome him and take our revenge on him'" (Jer. 20:10 ESV).

"But the Lord is with me as a dread warrior; therefore my persecutors will stumble; they will not overcome me. They will be greatly shamed, for they will not succeed. There eternal dishonor will never be forgotten" (Jer. 20:11 ESV).

"Based on the hope and divine guarantee of eternal life, [the life] which God, who is ever truthful and without deceit, promised before the ages of time began" (Titus 1:2 AMP).

"Oh, continue your steadfast love to those who know you, and your righteousness to the upright of hearts!" (Ps. 36:10 ESV).

"And may these words that I have prayed in the presence of the Lord be before him constantly, day and night, so that the Lord our God may give justice to me and to his people Israel, according to each day's needs" (1 Kings 8:59 NLT).

"Then people all over the earth will know that the Lord alone is God and there is no other" (1 Kings 8:60 NLT).

"Be gracious to me, O Lord, for to you do I cry all the day" (Ps. 86:3 ESV).

"In the day of my trouble I called upon you, for you answer me" (Ps. 86:7 ESV).

"I am the God of Abraham, and the God of Isaac, and the God of Jacob? God is not the God of the dead, but of the living" (Matt. 22:32 KJV).

""They shall be mine, says the Lord of hosts, in the day when I make up my treasured possession, and I will spare them as a man spares his son who serves him" (Mal. 3:17 ESV).

"I will instruct you and teach you in the way you should go, I will counsel you [who are willing to learn] with My eye upon you" (Ps. 32:8 AMP).

"When you go through deep waters, I will be with you. When you go through rivers of difficulty, you will not drown. When you walk through the fire of oppression, you will not be burned up; the flames will not consume you" (Isa. 43:2 NLT).

"Then once more you shall see the distinction between the righteous and the wicked, between one who serves God and one who does not serve him" (Mal. 3:18 ESV).

"The fear of the Lord is clean, enduring for ever: the judgments of the Lord are true and righteous altogether" (Ps. 19:9 KJV).

"On the day when I act, you will tread upon the wicked as if they were dust under your feet," says the Lord of Heaven's Armies" (Mal. 4:3 NLT).

"Now know I that the Lord saveth his anointed; he will hear him from his holy heaven with the saving strength of his right hand" (Ps. 20:6 KJV).

"Do thy diligence to come shortly unto me" (2 Tim. 4:9 KJV).

"Teach me your way, O Lord, that I may walk in your truth; unite my heart to fear your name" (Ps. 86:11 ESV).

"Bring all the tithes into the storehouse so there will be enough food in my Temple. If you do," says the Lord of Heaven's Armies, "I will open the windows of heaven for you. I will pour out a blessing so great you won't have enough room to take it in! Try it! Put me to the test!" (Mal. 3:10 NLT).

"And I will rebuke the devourer for your sakes, and he shall not destroy the fruits of your ground; neither shall your vine cast her fruit before the time in the field, saith the Lord of hosts" (Mal. 3:11 KJV).

"'All nations shall call you happy and blessed, for you shall be a land of delight,' says the Lord of hosts" (Mal. 3:12 AMP).

"You have done many good things for me, Lord, just as you promised" (Ps. 119:65 NLT).

My victory and honor come from God alone. He is my refuge, a rock where no enemy can reach me" (Ps. 62:7 NLT).

"For God is the King over all the earth. Praise him with a psalm" (Ps. 47:7 NLT).

"God reigns above the nations, sitting on his holy throne" (Ps. 47:8 NLT).

"Therefore I will look unto the Lord; I will wait for the God of my salvation: my God will hear me" (Mic. 7:7 KJV).

"And the Lord shall deliver me from every evil work, and will preserve me unto his heavenly Kingdom: to whom be glory for ever and ever. Amen" (2 Tim. 4:18 KJV).

*In Jesus name, amen.*

## Notes

_____
_____
_____

# Receiving God's Spiritual Gifts

## (Prayer)

"Search for the Lord and his strength; continually seek him" (1 Chron. 16:11 NLT).

"Seek him that maketh the seven stars and Orion, and turneth the shadow of death into the morning, and maketh the day dark with night: that calleth for the waters of the sea, and poureth them out upon the face of the earth: The Lord is his name" (Amos 5:8 KJV).

"Behold, to the LORD your God belong heaven and the heaven of heavens, the earth with all that is in it" (Deut. 10:14 ESV).

"My gifts are better than gold, even the purest gold, my wages better than sterling silver!" (Prov. 8:19 NLT).

"Wherewithal shall a young man cleanse his way? by taking heed thereto according to thy word" (Psalm 119:9 KJV)

"With my whole heart have I sought thee: O let me not wander from thy commandments" (Psalm 119:10 KJV)

"Thy word have I hid in mine heart, that I might not sin against thee" (Psalm 119:11 KJV)

"You shall remember the LORD your God, for it is he who gives you power to get wealth, that he may confirm his covenant that he swore to your fathers, as it is this day" (Deut. 8:18 ESV).

"Seek the Lord, all who are humble, and follow his commands. Seek to do what is right and to live humbly. Perhaps even yet the Lord will protect you—protect you from his anger on that day of destruction" (Zeph. 2:3 NLT).

"The stupid man cannot understand this" (Ps. 92:6 ESV).

"The Lord by wisdom founded the earth; by understanding he established the heavens" (Prov. 3:19 ESV).

"I will praise you with an upright heart, when I learn your righteous rules" (Ps. 119:7 ESV).

"Blessed is the one who finds wisdom, and the one who gets understanding" (Prov. 3:13 ESV).

"I entreated thy favour with my whole heart: be merciful unto me according to thy word" (Ps. 119:58 KJV).

"Surround me with your tender mercies so I may live, for your instructions are my delight" (Ps. 119:77 NLT).

"Thy faithfulness is unto all generations: thou hast established the earth, and it abideth" (Ps. 119:90 KJV).

"For the vision is yet for an appointed time, but at the end it shall speak, and not lie: though it tarry, wait for it; because it will surely come, it will not tarry" (Hab. 2:3 KJV).

"Christ is the visible image of the invisible God. He existed before anything was created and is supreme over all creation" (Col. 1:15 NLT).

"For in him dwelleth all the fulness of the Godhead bodily" (Col. 2:9 KJV).

"For through him God created everything in the heavenly realms and on earth. He made the things we can see and the things we can't see- such as thrones, kingdoms, rulers, and authorities in the unseen world. Everything was created through him and for him" (Col. 1:16 NLT).

"He existed before anything else, and he holds all creation together" (Col. 1:17 NLT).

"Saying with a loud voice, Worthy is the lamb that was slain to receive power, and riches, and wisdom, and strength, and honour, and glory, and blessing" (Rev. 5:12 KJV).

"For He satisfies the parched throat, And fills the hungry appetite with what is good" (Ps. 107:9 AMP).

"How good you are- how kind! Teach me your commands" (Ps. 119:68 GNT).

"For, behold, the Lord cometh forth out of his place, and will come down, and tread upon the high places of the earth" (Mic. 1:3 KJV).

"But to the saints that are in the earth, And to the excellent, in whom is all my delight" (Ps. 16:3 KJV).

"For with the heart one believes and is justified, and with the mouth one confesses and is saved" (Rom. 10:10 ESV).

"For the Son of man is come to seek and to save that which was lost" (Luke 19:10 KJV).

"And he gave some, apostles; and some prophets; and some, evangelists; and some, pastors and teachers" (Eph. 4:11 KJV).

"For to one is given by the Spirit the word of wisdom; to another the word of knowledge by the same Spirit" (1 Cor. 12:8 KJV).

"To another faith by the same Spirit; to another the gifts of healing by the same Spirit" (1 Cor. 12:9 KJV).

"To another the working of miracles; to another prophecy; to another discerning of spirits; to another divers kinds of tongues; to another the interpretation of tongues" (1 Cor. 12:10 KJV).

"It is the one and only Spirit who distributes all these gifts. He alone decides which gift each person should have" (1 Cor. 12:11 NLT).

"But the manifestation of the Spirit is given to every man to profit withal" (1 Cor. 12:7 KJV).

"For the body is not one member, but many" (1 Cor. 12:14 KJV).

"All of you together are Christ's body, and each of you is a part of it" (1 Cor. 12:27 KJV).

"And these signs shall follow them that believe; In my name shall they cast out devils; they shall speak with new tongues" (Mark 16:17 KJV).

"They shall take up serpents; and if they drink any deadly thing, it shall not hurt them; they shall lay hands on the sick, and they shall recover" (Mark 16:18 KJV).

"Behold, I give unto you power to tread on serpents and scorpions, and over all the power of the enemy: and nothing shall by any means hurt you" (Luke 10:19 KJV).

"For I will give you a mouth and wisdom, which all your adversaries shall not be able to gainsay nor resist" (Luke 21:15 KJV).

"But covet earnestly the best gifts: and yet shew I unto you a more excellent way" (1 Cor. 12:31 KJV).

"Let love be your highest goal! But you should also desire the special abilities the Spirit gives- especially the ability to prophesy" (1 Cor. 14:1 NLT).

"Therefore, believers, desire earnestly to prophesy [to foretell the future, to speak a new message from God to the people], and do not forbid speaking in unknown tongues" (1 Cor. 14:39 AMP).

"For he that speaketh in an unknown tongue speaketh not unto men, but unto God: for no man understandeth him; howbeit in the spirit he speaketh mysteries" (1 Cor. 14:2 KJV).

"Wherefore tongues are for a sign, not to them that believe, but to them that believe not: but prophesying serveth not for them that believe not, but for them which believe" (1 Cor. 14:22 KJV).

"Let all things be done decently and in order" (1 Cor. 14:40 KJV).

"The one who speaks in a tongue builds up himself, but the one who prophesies builds up the church" (1 Cor. 14:4 ESV).

"I will behave myself wisely in a perfect way. O when wilt thou come unto me? I will walk within my house with a perfect heart" (Ps. 101:2 KJV).

"Let the redeemed of the Lord say so, Whom he has redeemed from the hand of the adversary" (Ps. 107:2 AMP).

"Sing unto the Lord with the harp; with the harp, and the voice of a psalm" (Ps. 98:5 KJV).

"Every word of God is pure: he is a shield unto them that put their trust in him" (Prov. 30:5 KJV).

"Your promises have been thoroughly tested; that is why I love them so much" (Ps. 119:140 NLT).

"Therefore my heart is glad, and my glory rejoiceth: my flesh also shall rest in hope" (Ps. 16:9 KJV).

"For he satisfies the thirsty and fills the hungry with good things" (Ps. 107:9 NLT).

"Thou hast dealt well with thy servant, O Lord, according unto thy word" (Ps. 119:65 KJV).

*In Jesus name, amen.*

## Notes

_____
_____
_____

# Goodness

"He has told you, O man, what is good; And what does the Lord require of you Except to be just, and to love [and to diligently practice] kindness (compassion)" (Mic. 6:8 ESV).

"Do not devise evil in your hearts against one another, and love no false oath, for all these things I hate, declares the Lord" (Zech. 8:17 ESV).

# God's Goodness

## God's Goodness Eternal
## (A Word from God in Prayer)

"O give thanks unto the Lord, for he is good: for His mercy endureth for ever" (Ps. 107:1 KJV).

"Ascribe to the Lord, O heavenly beings, ascribe to the Lord glory and strength" (Ps. 29:1 ESV).

"Ascribe to the Lord the glory due his name; worship the Lord in the splendor of holiness" (Ps. 29:2 ESV).

"Let us search and try our ways, and turn again to the Lord" (Lam. 3:40 KJV).

"For you bless the godly, O Lord; you surround them with your shield of love" (Ps. 5:12 NLT).

"And all things are of God, who hath reconciled us to himself by Jesus Christ, and hath given to us the ministry of reconciliation" (2 Cor. 5:18 KJV).

"Oh that men would praise the Lord for his goodness, and for his wonderful works to the children of men!" (Ps. 107:68 KJV).

"The Lord is good to all: and his tender mercies are over all his works" (Ps. 145:9 KJV).

"Thou art good, and doest good; teach me thy statues" (Ps. 119:68 KJV).

"My soul makes its boast in the Lord; The humble and downtrodden will hear it and rejoice" (Ps. 34:2 AMP).

# PRAY IN GOD'S WORD FOR ENCOURAGEMENT AND CHANGE

"Everything good comes from God. Every perfect gift is from him. These good gifts come down from the Father who made all the lights in the sky. But God never changes like the shadows from those lights. He is always the same" (James 1:17 ERV).

"Oh how great is thy goodness, which thou hast laid up for them that fear thee, which thou hast wrought for them that trust in thee before the sons of man" (Ps. 31:19 KJV).

"For the Lord God is a sun and shield: the Lord will give grace and glory: no good thing will he withhold from them that walk uprightly" (Ps. 84:11 KJV).

"For the eyes of the Lord are over the righteous, and his ears are open unto their prayers: but the face of the Lord is against them that do evil" (1 Pet. 3:12 KJV).

"And who is he that will harm you if ye be followers of that which is good?" (1 Pet. 3:13KJV).

"For as in Adam all die, even so in Christ shall all be made alive" (1 Cor. 15:22 KJV).

"For he hath put all things under his feet. But when he saith all things are put under him, it is manifest that he is excepted which did put all things under him" (1 Cor. 15:27 KJV).

"Blessed be the God and Father of our Lord Jesus Christ, which according to his abundant mercy hath begotten us again unto a lively hope by the resurrection of Jesus Christ from the dead" (1 Pet. 1:3 KJV).

"Who is gone into heaven, and is on the right hand of God; angels and authorities and powers being made subject unto him" (1 Pet. 3:22 KJV).

"The Lord gave the word: great was the company of those that published it" (Ps. 68:11 KJV).

"Blessed be the Lord, who daily loath us with benefits, even the God of our salvation" (Ps. 68:19 KJV).

*In Jesus name, amen.*

## Notes

# A Promise

## (Prayer)

"Behold, God is my helper and ally; The Lord is the sustainer of my soul [my upholder]" (Ps. 54:4 AMP).

"Hear my prayer, O God; give ear to the words of my mouth" (Ps. 54:2 KJV).

"For from days of old no one has heard, nor has ear perceived, Nor has the eye seen a God besides You, Who works and acts in behalf of the one who [gladly] waits for Him" (Isa. 64:4 AMP).

"O God, my heart is steadfast [with confident faith]; I will sing, I will sing praises, even with my soul" (Ps. 108:1 AMP).

"Be exalted [in majesty], O God, above the heavens, And Your glory above all the earth" (Ps. 108:5 AMP).

"That Your beloved [ones] may be rescued, Save with Your hand, and answer me!" (Ps. 108:6 AMP).

"This is what the Lord says- your Redeemer, the Holy One of Israel: "I am the Lord your God, who teaches you what is good for you and leads you along the paths you should follow" (Isa. 48:17 NLT).

"Call unto me, and I will answer thee, and shew thee great and mighty things, which thou knowest not" (Jer. 33:3 KJV).

"Be gracious to me, O God, for man has trampled on me; All day long the adversary oppresses and torments me" (Ps. 56:1 AMP).

"Listen to me and answer me; I am restless and distraught in my complaint and distracted" (Ps. 55:2 AMP).

""The LORD who rules over all said, 'Exercise true judgment and show brotherhood and compassion to each other'" (Zech. 7:9 NET).

"Listen, O my people, to my teaching; Incline your ears to the words of my mouth [and be willing to learn]" (Ps. 78:1 AMP).

"For as a snare shall it come on all them that dwell on the face of the earth" (Luke 21:35 KJV).

"But stay awake at all times, praying that you may have strength to escape all these things that are going to take place, and to stand before the Son of Man." (Luke 21:36 ESV).

"Oh, that my people would listen to me, that Israel would walk in my ways!" (Ps. 81:13 ESV).

"Then I would quickly subdue and humble their enemies And turn My hand against their adversaries" (Ps. 81:14 AMP).

"And I will make an everlasting covenant with them, that I will not turn away from them, to do them good; but I will put my fear in their hearts, that they shall not depart from me" (Jer. 32:40 KJV).

"And they shall be my people, and I will be their God" (Jer. 32:38 KJV).

"Remember ye not the former things, neither consider the things of old" (Isa. 43:18 KJV).

"Behold, I will do a new thing; now it shall spring forth; shall ye not know it? I will even make a way in the wilderness, and rivers in the desert" (Isa. 43:19 KJV).

"I, even I, am he that blotteth out thy transgressions for mine own sake, and will not remember thy sins" (Isa. 43:25 KJV).

"I have been with you wherever you have gone, and have cut off all your enemies from before you; and I will make you a great name, like that of the great men of the earth" (2 Sam. 7:9 AMP).

"Yea, I will rejoice over them to do them good, and I will plant them in this land assuredly with my whole heart and with my whole soul" (Jer. 32:41 KJV).

"For thus saith the Lord; like as I have brought all this evil upon this people, so will I bring upon them all the good that I have promised them" (Jer. 32:42 KJV).

"You are the [awesome] God who works [powerful] wonders; You have demonstrated Your power among the people" (Ps. 77:14 AMP).

"You, Lord, will keep the needy safe and will protect us forever from the wicked" (Ps. 12:7 NIV).

"For this is God, Our God forever and ever; He will be our guide even until death" (Ps. 48:14 AMP).

"For the Lord will not cast off for ever" (Lam. 3:31 KJV).

"But though he cause grief, yet will he have compassion according to the multitude of his mercies" (Lam. 3:32 KJV).

"For he doth not afflict willingly nor grieve the children of men" (Lam. 3:33 KJV).

"For God alone my soul waits in silence and quietly submits to Him, For my hope is from Him" (Ps. 62:5 AMP).

"Therefore now let it please thee to bless the house of thy servant, that it may continue for ever before thee: for thou, O Lord God, hast spoken it: and with thy blessing let the house of thy servant be blessed for ever" (2 Sam. 7:29 KJV).

*In Jesus name, amen.*

## Notes

_____

_____

_____

# Blessings

## (Prayer)

"Shout for joy in the LORD, O you righteous! Praise befits the upright" (Ps. 33:1 ESV).

"Lift up your hands to the holy place and bless the Lord!" (Ps. 134:2 ESV).

"Give thanks to him who alone does mighty miracles. His faithful love endures forever" (Ps. 136:4 NLT).

"Give thanks to him who made the heavens so skillfully. His faithful love endures forever" (Ps. 136:5 NLT).

"Give thanks to him who placed the earth among the waters. His faithful love endures forever" (Ps. 136:6 NLT).

"Give thanks to him who made the heavenly lights- His faithful love endures forever" (Ps. 136:7 NLT).

"Blessed is every one that feareth the Lord; that walketh in his ways" (Ps. 128:1 KJV).

"O Lord God of heaven's Armies, hear my prayer. Listen, O God of Jacob" (Ps. 84:8 NLT).

## (Interlude)

"Hear the right, O Lord, attend unto my cry, give ear unto my prayer, that goeth not out of feigned lips" (Ps. 17:1 KJV).

"I am praying to you because I know you will answer, O God. Bend down and listen as I pray" (Ps. 17:6 NLT).

## PRAY IN GOD'S WORD FOR ENCOURAGEMENT AND CHANGE

"I cry out to God Most High, to God who fulfills his purpose for me" (Ps. 57:2 ESV).

"For there is one God, and one mediator between God and men, the man Christ Jesus" (1 Tim. 2:5 KJV).

"May all who seek you rejoice and be glad in you! May those who love your salvation say evermore, 'God is great!'" (Ps. 70:4 ESV).

"But I am poor and needy; hasten to me, O God! You are my help and my deliverer; O Lord, do not delay!" (Ps. 70:5 ESV).

"This is what the Lord of Heaven's Armies says: Look at what's happening to you!" (Hag. 1:5 NLT).

"Commit your actions to the Lord, and your plans will succeed" (Prov. 16:3 NLT).

"The lot is cast into the lap; but the whole disposing thereof is of the Lord" (Prov. 16:33 KJV).

"The godly people in the land are my true heroes! I take pleasure in them!" (Ps. 16:3 NLT).

"For your shame ye shall have double; and for confusion they shall rejoice in their portion: therefore in their land they shall possess the double: everlasting joy shall be unto them" (Isa. 61:7 KJV).

"Then shall thy light break forth as the morning, and thine health shall spring forth speedily: and thy righteousness shall go before thee; the glory of the Lord shall be thy rearward" (Isa. 58:8 KJV).

"You will be blessed in the city, and you will be blessed in the field" (Deut. 28:3 AMP).

"Wherever you go and whatever you do, you will be blessed" (Deut. 28:6 NLT).

"The Lord will conquer your enemies when they attack you. They will attack you from one direction, but they will scatter from you in seven!" (Deut. 28:7 NLT).

"All these blessings will come upon you and overtake you if you pay attention to the voice of the Lord your God" (Deut. 28:2 AMP).

"Your steadfast love, O Lord, extends to the heavens, your faithfulness to the clouds" (Ps. 36:5 ESV).

"Gracious is the Lord, and righteous; our God is merciful" (Ps. 116:5 ESV).

"The Lord preserves the simple; when I was brought low, he saved me" (Ps. 116:6 ESV).

"I will lift up the cup of salvation and call on the name of the Lord" (Ps. 116:13 ESV).

"I will keep my promise to the Lord in the presence of all his people" (Ps. 116:14 NLT).

"Let the words of my mouth, and the meditation of my heart, be acceptable in thy sight, O Lord, my strength, and my redeemer" (Ps. 19:14 KJV).

"Let my soul be at rest again, for the Lord has been good to me" (Ps. 116:7 NLT).

*In Jesus name, amen.*

## Notes

_____
_____
_____

# Faithfulness

For with the heart a person believes [in Christ as Savior] resulting in his justification [that is, being made righteous-being freed of guilt of sin and made acceptable to God]; and with the mouth he acknowledges and confess [his *faith openly*], resulting in and confirming [his] salvation. (Rom. 10:10 AMP)

If we are faithless, He remains faithful [true to His word and His Righteous character], for He cannot deny Himself. (2 Tim. 2:13 AMP)

# God's Faithfulness

## The Reason for Our Faith
## (A Word from God in Prayer)

"Looking unto Jesus the author and finisher of our faith; who for the joy that was set before him endured the cross, despising the shame, and is set down at the right hand of the throne of God" (Heb. 12:2 KJV).

"This is a faithful and trustworthy saying: If we died with Him, we will also live with Him" (2 Tim. 2:11 AMP).

"If we endure, we will also reign with Him; If we deny Him, He will also deny us" (2 Tim. 2:12 AMP).

"Let all that I am wait quietly before God, for my hope is in him" (Ps. 62:5 NLT).

"He alone is my rock and my salvation, my fortes where I will not be shaken" (Ps. 62:6 NLT).

"Now faith is the substance of things hoped for, the evidence of things not seen" (Heb. 11:1 KJV).

"I cling to you; your strong right hand holds me securely" (Ps. 63:8 NLT).

"I lie awake thinking of you, meditating on you through the night" (Ps. 63:6 NLT).

"Now the Lord All-Powerful says, 'Think about what is happening'" (Hag. 1:5 ERV).

"For by grace are ye saved through faith; and that not of yourselves: it is the gift of God" (Eph. 2:8 KJV).

"One Lord, one faith, one baptism" (Eph. 4:5KJV).

"One God and Father of all, who is above all, and through all, and in you all" (Eph. 4:5 KJV).

"Even as Abraham believed God, and it was accounted to him for righteousness" (Gal. 3:6 KJV).

"So then they which be of faith are blessed with faithful Abraham" (Gal. 3:9 KJV).

"That the blessing of Abraham might come on the gentiles through Jesus Christ; that we might receive the promise of the Spirit through faith" (Gal. 3:14 KJV).

"That your faith should not stand in the wisdom of men, but in the power of God" (1 Cor. 2:5 KJV).

"Blessed and reverently praised are You, O Lord; Teach me Yours statutes" (Ps. 119:12 AMP).

"O send out thy light and thy truth: let them lead me; let them bring me unto thy holy hill, and to thy tabernacles" (Ps. 43:3 KJV).

"Faithful is he that calleth you, who also will do it" (1 Thess. 5:24 KJV).

*In Jesus name, amen.*

## Notes

_____

_____

_____

# Boasting in the Lord

## (Prayer)

"I lift my eyes to you, O God, enthroned in heaven" (Ps. 123:1 NLT).

"Give ear to my prayer, O God; and hide not thyself from my supplication" (Ps. 55:1 KJV).

"With my soul have I desired thee in the night; yea, with my spirit within me will I seek thee early: for when thy judgments are in the earth, the inhabitants of the world will learn righteousness" (Isa. 26:9 KJV).

"For in that day every man shall cast away his idols of silver, and his idols of gold, which your own hands have made unto you for sin" (Isa. 31:7 KJV).

"In his wisdom, the Lord will send great disaster; he will not change his mind. He will rise against the wicked and against their helpers" (Isa. 31:2 NLT).

"They have greatly oppressed me from my youth, but they have not gained the victory over me" (Ps. 129:2 NIV).

"Surely the righteous will never be shaken; they will be remembered forever" (Ps. 112:6 NIV).

"Blessed be the Lord, who hath not given us as a prey to their teeth" (Ps. 124:6 KJV).

"Our help is in the name of the Lord, who made heaven and earth" (Ps. 124:8 KJV).

## PRAY IN GOD'S WORD FOR ENCOURAGEMENT AND CHANGE

"For whatsoever is born of God overcometh the world: and this is the victory that overcometh the world, even our faith" (1 John 5:4 KJV).

"Who is he that overcometh the world, but he that believeth that Jesus is the Son of God?" (1 John 5:5 KJV).

"O Lord, thou art my God; I will exalt thee, I will praise thy name; for thou hast done wonderful things; thy counsels of old are faithfulness and truth" (Isa. 25:1 KJV).

"For thou hast been a strength to the poor, a strength to the needy in his distress, a refuge from the storm, a shadow from the heat, when the blast of the terrible ones is as a storm against the wall" (Isa. 25:4 KJV).

"Thou shalt bring down the noise of strangers, as the heat in a dry place; even the heat with the shadow of a cloud: the branch of the terrible ones shall be brought low" (Isa. 25:5 KJV).

"Thou shalt make them as a fiery oven in the time of thine anger: the Lord shall swallow them up in his wrath, and the fire shall devour them" (Ps. 21:9 KJV).

"Thou didst march through the land in indignation, thou didst thresh the heathen in anger" (Hab. 3:12 KJV).

"Sing to the Lord, for he has done glorious things; let this be known to all the world" (Isa. 12:5 NIV).

"As for me, I will call upon God; and the Lord shall save me" (Ps. 55:16 KJV).

"The Lord is my rock, and my fortress, and my deliverer; my God, my strength, in whom I will trust; my buckler, and the horn of my salvation, and my high tower" (Ps. 18:2 KJV).

"For in the time of trouble he shall hide me in his pavilion: in the secret of his tabernacle shall he hide me; he shall set me up upon a rock" (Ps. 27:5 KJV).

"For thy lovingkindness is before mine eyes: and I have walked in thy truth" (Ps. 26:3 KJV).

"Gather not my soul with sinners, nor my life with bloody men" (Ps. 26:9 KJV).

"In whose hands is mischief, And their right hand is full of bribes" (Ps. 26:10 KJV).

"Hold up my goings in thy paths, that my footsteps slip not" (Ps. 17:5 KJV).

*In Jesus name, amen.*

## Notes

_____
_____
_____

# My God Is Faithful

## (Prayer)

"Come and hear, all ye that fear God, and I will declare what he hath done for my soul" (Ps. 66:16 KJV).

"For I cried out to him for help, praising him as I spoke" (Ps. 66:17 NLT).

"Shew thy marvellous lovingkindness, O thou that saveth by thy right hand them which put their trust in thee from those that rise up against them" (Ps. 17:7 KJV).

"'Behold, the days are coming,' declares the LORD, 'when the plowman overtake the reaper and the treader of grapes him who sows the seed; the mountains shall drip sweet wine, and all the hills shall flow with it'" (Amos 9:13 ESV).

"My child, listen and be wise: Keep your heart on the right course" (Prov. 23:19 NLT).

"Be careful for nothing; but in every thing by prayer and supplication with thanksgiving let your requests be made known unto God" (Phil. 4:6 KJV).

"To him who is able to keep you from stumbling and to present you before his glorious presence without fault and with great joy" (Jude 1:24 NIV).

"Being confident of this very thing, that he which hath begun a good work in you will perform it until the day of Jesus Christ" (Phil. 1:6 KJV).

"As your name deserves, O God, you will be praised to the ends of the earth. Your strong right hand is filled with victory" (Ps. 48:10 NLT).

"For me to live is Christ, and to die is gain" (Phil. 1:21 KJV).

"The godly are showered with blessings; the words of the wicked conceal violent intentions" (Prov. 10:6 NLT).

"This is what the Lord says: "Cursed are those who put their trust in mere humans, who rely on human strength and turn their hearts away from the Lord" (Jer. 17:5 NLT).

"But the Lord is faithful. He will establish you and guard you against the evil one" (2 Thess. 3:3 EVS).

"For it is God which worketh in you both to will and to do of his good pleasure" (Phil. 2:13 KJV).

"O that my ways were directed to keep thy statutes!" (Ps. 119:5 KJV).

"The stone which the builders refused is become the head stone of the corner" (Ps. 118:22 KJV).

"Who hath delivered us from the power of darkness, and hath translated us into the kingdom of his Son" (Col. 1:13 KJV).

"Who purchased our freedom and forgave our sins" (Col. 1:14 NLT).

"For surely there is an end; and thine expectation shall not be cut off" (Prov. 23:18 KJV).

"Therefore the Lord, the God of hosts, the Lord, saith thus; Wailing shall be in all streets; and they shall say in all the highways, Alas! Alas! And they shall call the husbandman to mourning, and such as are skillful of lamentation to wailing" (Amos 5:16 KJV).

"And the times of this ignorance God winked at; but now all men every where to repent" (Acts 17:30 KJV).

"Because he hath appointed a day in the which he will judge the world in righteousness by that man whom he hath ordained; where of he hath given assurance unto all men, in that he hath raised him from the dead" (Acts 17:31 KJV).

"Woe unto you that desire the day of the Lord! to what end is it for you? the day of the Lord is darkness, and not light" (Amos 5:18 KJV).

# PRAY IN GOD'S WORD FOR ENCOURAGEMENT AND CHANGE

"I spoke to the prophets; it was I who multiplied visions, and through the prophets gave parables" (Hosea 12:10 ESV).

"The law and the prophets were until John; since then the good news of the Kingdom of God is preached, and everyone forces his way into it" (Luke 16:16 ESV).

"And I heard a loud voice in heaven, saying, "Now the salvation and the power and the kingdom of our God and the authority of his Christ have come, for the accuser of our brothers has been thrown down, who accuses them day and night before our God" (Rev. 12:10 ESV).

"The Lord is righteous: he hath cut asunder the cords of the wicked" (Ps. 129:4 KJV).

"Blessed be the God and Father of our Lord Jesus Christ, which according to his abundant mercy hath begotten us again unto a lively hope by resurrection of Jesus Christ from the dead" (1 Pet. 1:3 KJV).

"Who his own self bare our sins in his own body on the tree, that we, being dead to sins, should live unto righteousness: by whose stripes ye were healed" (1 Pet. 2:24 KJV).

"The LORD is good, a stronghold in the day of trouble; he knows those who take refuge in him" (Nah. 1:7 ESV).

"For in him we live and move and exist. As some of your own poets have said, 'We are his offspring'" (Acts 17:28 NLT).

"At that time I will bring you in, at the time when I gather you together; for I will make you renowned and praised among all the peoples of the earth, when I restore your fortunes before your eyes," says the LORD" (Zeph. 3:20 ESV).

"For at that time I will change the speech of the peoples to a pure speech, that all of them may call upon the name of the LORD and serve him with one accord" (Zeph. 3:9 ESV).

"Whoever has the Son has life; whoever does not have God's Son does not have life" (1 John 5:12 NLT).

"Behold, at that time I will deal with all your oppressors. And I will save the lame and gather the outcast, and I will change their shame into praise and renown in all the earth" (Zeph. 3:19 ESV).

"For the Lord your God is he who goes with you to fight for you against your enemies, to give you the victory" (Deut. 20:4 ESV).

"Therefore all they that devour thee shall be devoured; and all thine Look! The Lord's anger bursts out like a storm, a driving wind that swirls down on the heads of the wicked" (Jer. 30:23 NLT).

"Behold, the whirlwind of the Lord goeth forth with fury, a continuing whirlwind: it shall fall with pain upon the head of the wicked" (Jer. 30:23 KJV).

"Adversaries, every one of them, shall go into captivity; and they that spoil thee shall be a spoil, and all that prey upon thee will I give for a prey" (Jer. 30:16 KJV).

"I will love thee, O Lord, my strength" (Ps. 18:1 KJV).

"I can do all things through Christ which strengtheneth me" (Phil. 4:13 KJV).

"You are my hiding place; you will protect me from trouble and surround me with songs of deliverance" (Ps. 32:7 NIV).

"The Lord will be terrible unto them: for he will famish all the gods of the earth; and men shall worship him, every one from his place, even all the isles of the heathen" (Zeph. 2:11 KJV).

"Evil shall slay the wicked: and they that hate the righteous shall be desolate" (Ps. 34:21 KJV).

"My enemies turn back; they stumble and perish before you" (Ps. 9:3 NIV).

"For you have upheld my right and my cause, sitting enthroned as the righteous judge" (Ps. 9:4 NIV).

"What do you plot against the LORD? He will make a complete end; trouble will not rise up a second time" (Nah. 1:9 ESV).

"To the only wise God our Saviour, be glory and majesty, dominion and power, both now and ever. Amen" (Jude 1:25 KJV).

*In Jesus name, amen.*

# Notes

_____
_____
_____

# God's Promise of Protection

## (Prayer)

"The Lord is a jealous and avenging God; the Lord is avenging and wrathful; the Lord takes vengeance on his adversaries and keeps wrath for his enemies" (Nah. 1:2 ESV).

"In the Lord I take refuge. How then can you say to me: "Flee like a bird to your mountain" (Ps. 11:1 NIV).

"For look, the wicked bend their bows; they set their arrows against the strings to shoot from the shadows at the upright in heart" (Ps. 11:2 NIV).

"The Lord is in his holy temple; the Lord is on his heavenly throne. He observes everyone on earth; his eyes examine them" (Ps. 11:4 NIV).

"Who can stand before his indignation? Who can endure the heat of his anger? His wrath is poured out like fire, and the rocks are broken into pieces by him" (Nah. 1:6 ESV).

"Thou, even thou, art Lord alone; thou hast made heaven, the heaven of heavens, with all their host, the earth, and all things that are therein, the seas, and all that is therein, and thou preservest them all; and the host of heaven worshippeth thee" (Neh. 9:6 KJV).

"Bless the Lord, ye his angels, that excel in strength, that do his commandments, hearkening unto the voice of his word" (Ps. 103:20 KJV).

"Bless ye the Lord, all ye his hosts; ye ministers of his, that do his pleasure" (Ps. 103:21 KJV).

"Bless the Lord, all his works in all places of his dominion: bless the Lord, O my soul" (Ps. 103:22 KJV).

"My health may fail, and my spirit may grow weak, but God remains the strength of my heart; he is mine forever" (Ps. 73:26 NLT).

"For the Lord is our judge, the Lord is our lawgiver, the Lord is our King; he will save us" (Isa. 33:22 KJV).

"Even when I am old and gray, do not forsake me, my God, till I declare your power to the next generation, your mighty acts to all who are to come" (Ps. 71:18 NIV).

"Be merciful unto me, O Lord: for I cry unto thee daily" (Ps. 86:3 KJV).

"The Lord replies, 'I have seen violence done to the helpless, and I have heard the groans of the poor. Now I will rise up to rescue them, as they longed for me to do'" (Ps. 12:5 NLT).

"Do not fret because of those who are evil or be envious of those who do wrong" (Ps. 37:1 NIV).

"For they are like entangled thorns, like drunkards as they drink; they are consumed like stubble fully dried" (Nah. 1:10 ESV).

"All the horns of the wicked also will I cut off; but the horns of the righteous shall be exalted" (Ps. 75:10 KJV).

"Trust in the Lord and do good; dwell in the land and enjoy safe pasture" (Ps. 37:3 NIV).

"Take delight in the Lord, and he will give you the desires of your heart" (Ps. 37:4 NIV).

"'Come now, and let us reason together,' Says the Lord. Though your sins are like scarlet, They shall be as white as snow; Though they are red like crimson, They shall be like wool" (Isa. 1:18 ESV).

"Therefore the Lord waits to be gracious to you, and therefore he exalts himself to show mercy to you. For the Lord is a God of justice; blessed are all those who wait for him" (Isa. 30:18 ESV).

"It is good that a man should both hope and quietly wait for the salvation of the Lord" (Lam. 3:26 KJV).

"'And I will compensate you for the years That the swarming locust has eaten, The creeping locust, the stripping locust, and the gnawing locust - My great army which I sent among you" (Joel 2:25 AMP).

"Moreover the light of the moon shall be as the light of the sun, and the light of the sun shall be sevenfold, as the light of seven days, in the day that the Lord bindeth up the breach of his people, and healeth the stroke of their wound" (Isa. 30:26 KJV).

"For, behold, the darkness shall cover the earth, and gross darkness the people: but the Lord shall arise upon thee, and his glory shall be seen upon thee" (Isa. 60:2 KJV).

"Whereas thou hast been forsaken and hated, so that no man went through thee, I will make thee an eternal excellency, a joy of many generations" (Isa. 60:15 KJV).

"For ye shall go out with joy, and be led forth with peace: the mountains and the hills shall break forth before you into singing, and all the trees of the field shall clap their hands" (Isa. 55:12 KJV).

"Blessed is the man that walketh not in the counsel of the ungodly, nor standeth in the way of sinners, nor sitteth in the seat of the scornful" (Ps. 1:1 KJV).

"And he will be like a tree firmly planted [and fed] by streams of water, Which yields fruit in its season; Its leaf does not wither; And in whatever he does, he prospers [and But his delight is in the law of the Lord; and in his law doth he meditate day and night" (Ps. 1:2 KJV).

"Wealth and riches shall be in his house: and his righteousness endureth for ever" (Ps. 112:3 KJV).

"And he will be like a tree firmly planted [and fed] by streams of water, Which yields its fruit in its season; Its leaf does not wither; And in whatever he does, he prospers [and comes to maturity]" (Ps. 1:3 AMP).

"Blessed is the man that trusteth in the Lord, and whose hope the Lord is" (Jer. 17:7 KJV).

"For he shall be as a tree planted by the waters, and that spreadeth out her roots by the river, and shall not see when heat cometh, but her leaf shall be green; and shall not be careful in the year of drought, neither shall cease from yielding fruit" (Jer. 17:8 KJV).

"His heart is upheld, he will not fear While he looks [with satisfaction] on his adversaries" (Ps. 112:8 AMP).

"Lord, all my desire is before You; And my sighing is not hidden from You" (Ps. 38:9 AMP).

"My heart throbs violently, my strength fails me; And as for the light of my eyes, even that has also gone from me" (Ps. 38:10 AMP).

"For mine enemies speak against me; and they that lay wait for my soul take counsel together" (Ps. 71:10 KJV).

"Saying, God hath forsaken him: persecute and take him; for there is none to deliver him" (Ps. 71:11 KJV).

"'He trusts in the Lord,' they say, 'let the Lord rescue him. Let him deliver him, since he delights in him'" (Ps. 22:8 NIV).

"Hear, O Lord, when I cry with my voice: have mercy also upon me, and answer me" (Ps. 27:7 KJV).

"Hear my prayer, O Lord, give ear to my supplications: in thy faithfulness answer me, and in thy righteousness" (Ps. 143:1 KJV).

"Let them be ashamed and confounded together that seek after my soul to destroy it; let them be driven backward and put to shame that wish me evil" (Ps. 40:14 KJV).

"Keep me from the snares which they have laid for me, and the gins of the workers of iniquity" (Ps. 141:9 KJV).

"Give them sorrow of heart, thy curse unto them" (Lam. 3:65 KJV).

"Persecute and destroy them in anger from under the heavens of the Lord" (Lam. 3:66 KJV).

"In my distress I cried unto the Lord, and he heard me" (Ps. 120:1 KJV).

"The Lord's message came to me" (Jer. 1:4 ERV).

"Behold, all they that were incensed against thee shall be ashamed and confounded: they shall be as nothing; and they that strive with thee shall perish" (Isa. 41:11 KJV).

"Thou shalt seek them, and shalt not find them, even them that contended with thee: they that war against thee shall be as nothing, and as a thing of nought" (Isa. 41:12 KJV).

"For I the Lord thy God will hold thy right hand, saying unto thee, Fear not; I will help thee" (Isa. 41:13 KJV).

"In peace I will lie down and sleep, for you alone, O Lord, will keep me safe" (Ps. 4:8 NLT).

PRAY IN GOD'S WORD FOR ENCOURAGEMENT AND CHANGE

"By this I know that thou favourest me, because mine enemy doth not triumph over me" (Ps. 41:11 KJV).

*In Jesus name, amen.*

## Notes

_____
_____
_____

# God Is Able

## (Prayer)

"Now unto him that is able to do exceeding abundantly above all that we ask or think, according to the power that worketh in us" (Eph. 3:20 KJV).

"And what is the exceeding greatness of his power to us-ward who believe, according to the working of his mighty power" (Eph. 1:19 KJV).

"Which he wrought in Christ, when he raised him from the dead, and set him at his own right hand in the heavenly places" (Eph. 1:20 KJV).

"Far above all principality, and power and might, and dominion, and every name that is named, not only in this world, but also in that which is to come" (Eph. 1:21 KJV).

"Great is the Lord, and greatly to be praised; and his greatness is unsearchable" (Ps. 145:3 KJV).

"One generation shall praise thy works to another, and shall declare thy mighty acts" (Ps. 145:4 KJV).

"They shall abundantly utter the memory of thy great goodness, and shall sing of thy righteousness" (Ps. 145:7 KJV).

"Thy right hand, O Lord, is become glorious in power: thy right hand, O Lord, hath dashed in in pieces the enemy" (Exod. 15:6 KJV).

"The Lord's message came to me" (Jer. 2:1 ERV).

"Great is our Lord and mighty in power; his understanding has no limit" (Ps. 147:5 NIV).

"He alone is your God, the only one who is worthy of your praise, the one who has done these mighty miracles that you have seen with your own eyes" (Deut. 10:21 NLT).

"And God is able to make all grace abound toward you; that ye, always having all sufficiency in all things, may abound to every good work" (2 Cor. 9:8 KJV).

The Lord God is Able: "And Moses stretched out his hand over the sea; and the Lord caused the sea to go back by a strong east wind all night, and made the sea dry land, and the waters were divided" (Exod. 14:21 KJV).

The Lord God is Able: "And he cried unto the Lord; and the Lord shewed him a tree, which when he had cast into the waters, the waters were made sweet: there he made for them a statue and an ordinance, and there he proved them" (Exod. 15:25 KJV).

The Lord God is Able: "And Moses lifted up his hand, and with his rod he smote the rock twice: and the water came out abundantly, and the congregation drank, and their beasts also" (Num. 20:11 KJV).

The Lord God is Able: "And Moses made a serpent of brass, and put it upon a pole, and it came to pass, that if a serpent had bitten any man, when he beheld the serpent of brass, he lived" (Num. 21:9 KJV).

The Lord God is Able: "And the Lord opened the mouth of the ass, and she said unto Balaam, What have I done unto thee, that thou hast smitten me these three times?" (Num. 22:28 KJV).

The Lord God is Able: "And the priests that bare the ark of the covenant of the Lord stood firm on dry ground in the midst of Jordan, and all the Israelites passed over on dry ground, until all the people were passed clean over Jordan" (Josh. 3:17 KJV).

The Lord God is Able: "So the people shouted when the priests blew with the trumpets: and it came to pass, when the people heard the sound of the trumpet, and the people shouted with a great shout, that the wall fell down flat, so that the people went up into the city, every man straight before him, and they took the city" (Josh. 6:20 KJV).

The LORD GOD is Able: "And the sun stood still, and the moon stayed, until the people had avenged themselves upon their enemies. Is not this written in the book of Jasher? So the sun stood still in the midst of heaven, and hasted not to go down about a whole day" (Josh. 10:13 KJV).

The LORD GOD is Able: "And the King answered and said unto the man of God, entreat now the face of the Lord thy God, and pray for me, that my hand may be restored me again. And the man of God besought the Lord, and the King's hand was restored him again, and became as it was before" (1 Kings 13:6 KJV).

The LORD GOD is Able: "And Elijah the Tishbite, who was of the inhabitants of Gilead, said unto Ahab, As the Lord God of Israel liveth, before whom I stand, there shall not be dew nor rain these years, but according to my word" (1 Kings 17:1 KJV).

"And it came to pass after many days, that the word of the Lord came to Elijah in the third year, saying, Go, shew thyself unto Ahab; and I will send rain upon the earth" (1 Kings 18:1 KJV).

The LORD GOD is Able: [speaking of Elijah] "And the ravens brought him bread and meat in the morning, and bread and meat in evening; and he would drink from the brook" (1 Kings 17:6 AMP).

The LORD GOD is Able: "And she went and did according to the saying of Elijah: and she, and he, and her house, did eat many days" (1 Kings 17:15 KJV).

"And the barrel of meal wasted not, neither did the cruse of oil fail, according to the word of the LORD, which he spake by Elijah" (1 Kings 17:16 KJV).

The LORD GOD is Able: "And the Lord heard the voice of Elijah; and the soul of the child came into him again, and he revived" (1 Kings 17:22 KJV).

"And Elijah took the child, and brought him down out of the chamber into the house, and delivered him unto his mother: and Elijah said, see, thy son liveth" (1 Kings 17:23 KJV).

The LORD GOD is Able: "Then the fire of the Lord fell, and consumed the burnt sacrifice, and the wood, and the stones, and the dust, and licked up the water that was in the trench" (1 Kings 18:39 KJV).

"And when all the people saw it, they fell on their faces: and they said, The Lord, he is God; the Lord, he is the God" (1 Kings 18:39 KJV).

The LORD GOD is Able: "And Elijah said unto Ahab, Get thee up, eat and drink; for there is a sound of abundance of rain" (1 Kings 18:41 KJV).

The LORD GOD is Able: "And the hand of the Lord was on Elijah; and he girded up his loins, and ran before Ahab to the entrance of Jezreel" (1 Kings 18:46 KJV).

The LORD GOD is Able: "And Elijah answered and said to the captain of fifty, If I be a man of God, then let fire come down from heaven, and consume thee and thy fifty. And there came down fire from heaven, and consumed him and his fifty" (2 Kings 1:10 KJV).

The LORD GOD is Able: "And Elijah took his mantle, and wrapped it together, and smote the waters, and they were divided hither and thither, so that they two went over on dry ground" (2 Kings 2:8 KJV).

The LORD GOD is Able: "And it came to pass, as they still went on, and talked, that, behold, there appeared a chariot of fire, and horses of fire, and parted them both asunder; and Elijah went up by a whirlwind into heaven" (2 Kings 2:11 KJV).

The LORD GOD is Able: "And he took the mantle of Elijah that fell from him, and smote the waters, and said, where is the Lord God of Elijah? and when he also had smitten the waters, they parted hither and thither: and Elisha went over" (2 Kings 2:14 KJV).

The LORD GOD is Able: "And he went forth unto the spring of the waters, and cast the salt in there, and said, Thus saith the Lord, I have healed these waters; there shall not be from thence any more death or barren land" (2 Kings 2:21 KJV).

"So the waters were healed unto this day, according to the saying of Elisha" (2 Kings 2:22 KJV).

The LORD GOD is Able: "And he went up from thence unto Beth-el: and as he was going up by the way, there came forth little children out of the city, and mocked him, and said unto him, Go up, thou bald head; go up thou bald head" (2 Kings 2:23 KJV).

"And he turned back, and looked on them, and cursed them in the name of the Lord. And there came forth two she bears out of the wood, and tare forty and two children of them" (2 Kings 2:24 KJV).

The LORD GOD is Able: "For thus saith the Lord, ye shall not see wind, neither shall ye see rain; yet that valley shall be filled with water, that ye may drink, both ye, and your cattle, and your beasts" (2 Kings 3:17 KJV).

"And this is but a light thing in the sight of the Lord: he will deliver the Moabites also into your hand" (2 Kings 3:18 KJV).

"And it came to pass in the morning, when the meat offering was offered, that, behold, there came water by the way of Edom, and the country was filled with water" (2 Kings 3:20 KJV).

The LORD GOD is Able: "Then he said, Go, borrow thee vessels abroad of all thy neighbours, even empty vessels; borrow not a few" (2 Kings 4:3 KJV).

"And it came to pass, when the vessels were full, that she said unto her son, Bring me yet a vessel more. And the oil stayed" (2 Kings 4:6 KJV).

"Then she came and told the man of God. And he said, Go sell the oil, and pay thy debt, and live thou and thy children of the rest" (2 Kings 4:7 KJV).

The LORD GOD is Able: "And he said, About this season, according to the time of life, thou shalt embrace a son. And she said, Nay, my lord, thou man of God, do not lie unto thine handmaid" (2 Kings 4:16 KJV).

"And the woman conceived, and bare a son at that season that Elisha had said unto her, according to the time of life" (2 Kings 4:17 KJV).

The LORD GOD is Able: "And when Elisha was come into the house, behold, the child was dead, and laid upon his bed" (2 Kings 4:32 KJV).

"He went in therefore, and shut the door upon them twain, and prayed unto the Lord" (2 Kings 4:33 KJV).

# PRAY IN GOD'S WORD FOR ENCOURAGEMENT AND CHANGE

"And he went up, and lay upon the child, and put his mouth upon his mouth, and his eyes upon his eyes, and his hands upon his hands: and he stretched himself upon the child; and the flesh of the child waxed warm" (2 Kings 4:34 KJV).

"Then he returned, and walked in the house to and fro; and went up, and stretched himself upon him: and the child sneezed seven times, and the child opened his eye (2 Kings 4:35 KJV).

The LORD GOD is Able: "So they poured out for the men to eat. And it came to pass, as they were eating of the pottage, that they cried out, and said, O thou man of God, there is death in the pot. And they could not eat thereof" (2 Kings 4:40 KJV).

"But he said, Then bring meal. And he cast it into the pot; and he said, Pour out for the people, that they may eat. And there was no harm in the pot" (2 Kings 4:41 KJV).

The LORD GOD is Able: "And there came a man from Baal-shalishah, and brought the man of God bread of the firstfruits; twenty loaves of barley, and full ears of corn in the husk thereof. And he said, Give unto the people, that they may eat" (2 Kings 4:42 KJV).

"And his servitor said, What, should I set this before an hundred man? He said again, Give the people, that they may eat: for thus saith the Lord, They shall eat, and shall leave thereof" (2 Kings 4:43 KJV).

"So he set it before them, and they did eat, and left thereof, according to the word of the LORD" (2 Kings 4:44 KJV).

The LORD GOD is Able: "And Elisha sent a messenger unto him, saying, Go and wash in Jordan seven times, and thy flesh shall come again to thee, and thou shalt be clean" (2 Kings 5:10 KJV).

"Then went he down, and dipped himself seven times in Jordan, according to the saying of the man of God: and his flesh came again like unto the flesh of a little child, and he was clean" (2 Kings 5:14 KJV).

The LORD GOD is Able: "As one of them was cutting down a tree, the iron ahead fell into the water. 'O no, my lord!' he cried out. 'It was borrowed!'" (2 Kings 6:5 NIV).

"And the man of God said, Where fell it? And he shewed him the place. And he cut down a stick, and cast it in thither; and the iron did swim" (2 Kings 6:6 KJV).

The Lord God is Able: "And it came to pass, as they were burying a man, that, behold, they spied a band of men; and they cast the man into the sepulcher of Elisha: and when the man was let down, and touched the bones of Elisha, he revived, and stood up on his feet" (2 Kings 13:21 KJV).

The Lord God is Able: "Jesus saith unto them, Fill the waterpots with water. And they filled them up to the brim" (John 2:7 KJV).

"And he saith unto them, Draw out now, and bear unto the governor of the feast. And they bare it" (John 2:8 KJV).

"When the ruler of the feast had tasted the water that was made wine, and knew not whence it was: (but the servants which drew the water knew;) the governor of the feast called the bridegroom" (John 2:9 KJV).

"And saith unto him, Every man at the beginning doth set forth good wine; and when men have well drunk, then that which is worse: but thou hast kept the good wine until now" (John 2:10 KJV).

The Lord God is Able: "When he had thus spoken, he spat on the ground, and made clay of the spittle, and he anointed the eyes of the blind man with the clay" (John 9:6 KJV).

"And said unto him, Go, wash in the pool of Siloam" (which is by interpretation, sent.).

"He went his way therefore, and washed, and came seeing" (John 9:7 KJV).

The Lord God is Able: "And Jesus said unto the centurion, Go thy way: and as thou hast believed, so be it done unto thee. And his servant was healed in the selfsame hour" (Matt. 8:13 KJV).

The Lord God is Able: "Now when he had left speaking, he said unto Simon, Launch out into the deep, and let down your nets for a draught" (Luke 5:4 KJV).

"And when they had this done, they inclosed a great multitude of fishes: and their net brake" (Luke 5:6 KJV).

The Lord God is Able: "And there was in their synagogue a man with an unclean spirit; and he cried out" (Mark 1:23 KJV).

"And Jesus rebuked him, saying, Hold thy peace, and come out of him" (Mark 1:25 KJV).

"And when the unclean spirit had torn him, and cried a loud voice, he came out of him" (Mark 1:26 KJV).

The LORD GOD is Able: "And when Jesus was come into Peter's house, he saw his wife's mother laid, and sick of fever" (Matt. 8:14 KJV).

"And he touched her hand, and the fever left her: she arose, and ministered unto them" (Matt. 8:15 KJV).

The LORD GOD is Able: "And, behold, there came a leper and worshipped him, saying, Lord, if thou wilt, thou canst make me clean" (Matt. 8:2 KJV).

"And Jesus put forth his hand, and touched him, saying, I will; be thou clean. And immediately his leprosy was cleansed" (Matt. 8:3 KJV).

The LORD GOD is Able: "When Jesus saw their faith, he said unto the sick of the palsy, Son, thy sins be forgiven thee" (Mark 2:5 KJV).

The LORD GOD is Able: "And when Jesus saw her, he called her to him, and said unto her, Woman, thou art loosed from thine infirmity" (Luke 13:12 KJV).

"And he laid his hands on her: and immediately she was made straight, and glorified God" (Luke 13:13 KJV).

The LORD GOD is Able: "And he commanded the multitude to sit down on the grass, and took the five loaves, and the two fishes, and looking up to heaven, he blessed, and brake, and gave the loaves to his disciples, and the disciples to the multitude" (Matt. 14:19 KJV).

"And they did all eat, and were filled: and they took up of the fragments that remained twelve baskets full" (Matt. 14:20 KJV).

"And they that had eaten were about five thousand men, beside women and children" (Matt. 14:21 KJV).

The LORD GOD is Able: "And he took the seven loaves and the fishes, and gave thanks, and brake them, and gave to his disciples, and the disciples to the multitude" (Matt. 15:36 KJV).

"And they did all eat, and were filled: and they took up of the broken meat that was left even baskets full" (Matt. 15:37 KJV).

"And they that did eat were four thousand men, beside women and children" (Matt. 15:38 KJV).

The Lord God is Able: "And when he thus had spoken, he cried with a loud voice, Lazarus, come forth" (John 11:43 KJV).

"And he that was dead came forth, bound hand and foot with graveclothes: and his face was bound about with a napkin. Jesus saith unto them, Loose him, and let him go" (John 11:44 KJV).

The Lord God is Able: "He is not here, but is risen: remember how he spake unto you when he was yet in Galilee" (Luke 24:6 KJV).

"No man taketh it from me, but I lay it down of myself. I have power to lay it down, and I have power to take it again. This commandment have I received of my Father" (John 10:18 KJV).

The Lord God is Able: "And in the fourth watch of the night Jesus went unto them, walking on the sea" (Matt. 14:25 KJV).

The Lord God is Able: "And Jesus answered and said, Suffer ye thus far. And he touched his ear, and healed him" (Luke 22:51 KJV).

The Lord God is Able: "And they found the stone rolled away from the sepulchre" (Luke 24:2 KJV).

"Hearken unto me, ye that know righteousness, the people in whose heart is my law; fear ye not the reproached of men, neither be ye afraid of their revilings" (Isa. 51:7 KJV).

"But the Lord your God ye shall fear; and he shall deliver you out of the hand of all your enemies" (2 Kings 17:39 KJV).

"For the moth shall eat them up like a garment, and the worm shall eat them like wool: but my righteousness shall be for ever, and my salvation from generation to generation" (Isa. 51:8 KJV).

"All those people will fight against you, but they will not defeat you, because I am with you, and will save you" This message is from the Lord" (Jer. 1:19 ERV).

"The Lord upholdeth all that fall, and raiseth up all those that be bowed down" (Ps. 145:14 KJV).

"Keep me as the apple of the eye, hide me under the shadow of thy wings" (Ps. 17:8 KJV).

"Thou openest thine hand, and satisfiest the desire of every living thing" (Ps. 145:16 KJV).

"Your awe-inspiring deeds will be on every tongue; I will proclaim your greatness" (Ps. 145:6 NLT).

"For your kingdom is an everlasting kingdom. You rule throughout all generations. The Lord always keeps his promises; he is gracious in all he does" (Ps. 145:13 NLT).

"Now unto God and our Father be glory for ever and ever. Amen" (Phil. 4:20 KJV).

*In Jesus name, amen.*

## Notes

_____
_____
_____

# I Believe

## (Prayer)

"Don't be afraid of anyone. I am with you, and I will protect you." This message is from the Lord" (Jer. 1:8 ERV).

"Ponder the path of thy feet, and let all thy ways be established" (Prov. 4:26 KJV).

"The instructions of the Lord are perfect, reviving the soul. The decrees of the Lord are trustworthy, making wise the simple" (Ps. 19:7 NLT).

"Blessed be the Lord God, the God of Israel, who only doeth wonderous things" (Ps. 72:18 KJV).

"By faith we understand that the entire universe was formed at God's command, that what we now see did not come from anything that can be seen" (Heb. 11:3 NLT).

"Faith shows the reality of what we hope for; it is the evidence of things we cannot see" (Heb. 11:1 NLT).

"But without faith it is impossible to [walk with God and] please Him, for whoever comes [near] to God must [necessarily] believe that God exist and that He rewards those who [earnestly and diligently] seek Him" (Heb. 11:6 AMP).

"Lord, there is no one like you. You are great! Your name is great and powerful!" (Jer. 10:6 ERV).

"The Lord is my portion, saith my soul; therefore will I hope in him" (Lam. 3:24 KJV).

"For with God nothing shall be impossible" (Luke 1:37 KJV).

"The Lord is the portion of mine inheritance and of my cup: thou maintainest my lot" (Ps. 16:5 KJV).

"The Lord is my rock, and my fortress, and my deliverer, my God, my strength, in whom I will trust; my buckler, and the horn of my salvation, and high tower" (Ps. 18:2 KJV).

"I have chosen to be faithful; I have determined to live by your regulations" (Ps. 119:30 NLT).

"Fulfill your promise to your servant, so that you may be feared" (Ps. 119:38 NIV).

I believe: "For who is God save the Lord? who is a rock save our God?" (Ps. 18:31 KJV).

"The law of the Lord is perfect, converting the soul: the testimony of the Lord is sure, making wise the simple" (Ps. 19:7 KJV).

I believe: "He maketh my feet like hind's feet, and setteth me upon my high places" (Ps. 18:33 KJV).

I believe: "O Lord, thou hast brought up my soul from the grave: thou hast kept me alive, that I should not go down to the pit" (Ps. 30:3 KJV).

I believe: "The blessing of the Lord, it maketh rich, and he addeth no sorrow with it" (Prov. 10:22 KJV).

I believe: "The Lord will give strength unto his people; the Lord will bless his people with peace" (Ps. 29:11 KJV).

I Believe: "I will be glad and rejoice in thy mercy: for thou hast considered my trouble; thou hast known my soul in adversities" (Ps. 31:7 KJV).

I believe: "Blessed is he whose transgression is forgiven, whose sin is covered" (Ps. 32:1 KJV).

I believe: "Blessed is the man unto whom the Lord imputeth not iniquity, and in whose spirit there is no guile" (Ps. 32:2 KJV).

I believe: "Thou art my hiding place: thou shalt preserve me from trouble; thou shalt compass me about with songs of deliverance" (Ps. 32:7 KJV). *Selah.*

I believe: "It is of the Lord's mercies that we are not consumed, because his compassions fail not" (Lam. 3:22 KJV).

I believe: The Lord is good unto them that wait for him, to the soul that seeketh him" (Lam. 3:25 KJV).

I believe: "It is good that a man should both hope and quietly wait for the salvation of the Lord" (Lam. 3:26 KJV).

I believe: "O Lord, thou hast pleaded the causes of my soul; thou hast redeemed my life" (Lam. 3:58 KJV).

I believe: "The angel of the Lord encampeth round about them that fear him, and delivereth them" (Ps. 34:7 KJV).

I believe: "The eyes of the Lord are upon the righteous, and his ears are open unto their cry" (Ps. 34:15 KJV).

I believe: "The righteous cry, and the Lord heareth, and delivereth them out of all their troubles" (Ps. 34:17 KJV).

I believe: "The steps of a good man are ordered by the Lord: and he delighteth in his way" (Ps. 37:23 KJV).

"Though he fall, he shall not be utterly cast down: for the Lord upholdeth him with his hand" (Ps. 37:24 KJV).

I believe: "In peace I will lie down and sleep, for you alone, O Lord, will keep me safe" (Ps. 4:8 NLT).

I believe: "God is our refuge and strength, a very present help in trouble" (Ps. 46:1 KJV).

I believe: "In God is my salvation and my glory: the rock of my strength, and my refuge, is in God" (Ps. 62:7 KJV).

I believe: "The Lord is good, a strong hold in the day of trouble; and he knoweth them that trust in him" (Nah. 1:7 KJV).

"Because of his strength will I wait upon thee: for God is my defence" (Ps. 59:9 KJV).

I believe: "God hath spoken once; twice have I heard this; that power belongeth unto God" (Ps. 62:11 KJV).

"Also unto thee, O Lord, belongeth mercy: for thou renderest to every man according to his work" (Ps. 62:12 KJV).

I believe: "He shall spare the poor and needy, and shall save the souls of the needy" (Ps. 72:13 KJV).

"He shall redeem their soul from deceit and violence: and precious shall their blood be in his sight" (Ps. 72:14 KJV).

"I believed when the Lord said: Verily, verily, I say unto you, if a man keep my saying, he shall never see death" (John 8:51 KJV).

I believe: "There is none holy as the Lord: for there is none beside thee: neither is there any rock like our God" (1 Sam. 2:2 KJV).

## PRAY IN GOD'S WORD FOR ENCOURAGEMENT AND CHANGE

I believe: "You have a mighty arm; strong is your hand, high your right hand" (Ps. 89:13 ESV).

"Justice and judgment are the habitation of thy throne: mercy and truth shall go before thy face" (Ps. 89:14 KJV).

I believe: "For thou, Lord, wilt bless the righteous; with favour wilt thou compass him as with a shield" (Ps. 5:12 KJV).

I believe: "For thou, Lord, hast made me glad through thy work: I will triumph in the works of thy hands" (Ps. 92:4 KJV).

I believe: "The Lord hath heard my supplication; the Lord will receive my prayer" (Ps. 6:9 KJV).

"For thou wilt light my candle: the Lord my God will enlighten my darkness" (Ps. 18:31 KJV).

"Let thine hand help me; for I have chosen thy precepts" (Ps. 119:173 KJV).

"Let, I pray thee, thy merciful kindness be for my comfort, according to thy word unto thy servant" (Ps. 119:76 KJV).

"Let thy mercies come also unto me, O Lord, even thy salvation, according to thy word" (Ps. 119:41 KJV).

"Thy testimonies are wonderful: therefore doth my soul keep them" (Ps. 119:129 KJV)S

*In Jesus name, amen.*

## Notes

_____

_____

_____

# Speak a Word

## (Prayer)

"O Lord, hear me as I pray; pay attention to my groaning" (Ps. 5:1 NLT).

"Hear my cry for help, my King and my God, for to you I pray" (Ps. 5:2 NIV).

"Make haste, O God, to deliver me; make haste to help me, O Lord" (Ps. 70:1 KJV).

"In thee, O Lord, do I put my trust: let me never be put to confusion" (Ps. 71:1 KJV).

"Deliver me in thy righteousness, and cause me to escape: incline thine ear unto me, and save me" (Ps. 71:2 KJV).

"That thy beloved may be delivered; save with thy right hand, and hear me" (Ps. 60:5 KJV).

"The word of the LORD came to me, saying" (Jer. 1:4 NIV).

"We have different gifts, according to the grace given to each of us. If your gift is prophesying, then prophesy in accordance with your faith" (Rom. 12:6 NIV).

"Follow the way of love and eagerly desire gifts of the Spirit, especially prophecy" (1 Cor. 14:1 NIV).

*I declare and decree, God's Power to overcome any problem, sickness or bondage for me (us) in Jesus name.*

"And Jesus looking upon them saith, With men it is impossible, but not with God: for with God all things are possible" (Mark 10:27 KJV).

*I declare and decree, God's Peace in the face of any conflict, large or small for me (us) in Jesus name.*

"And the peace of God, which passeth all understanding, shall keep your hearts and minds through Christ Jesus" (Phil. 4:7 KJV).

*I declare and decree, God's Favor over my (our) finances in Jesus name.*

"The blessing of the Lord brings wealth, without painful toil for it" (Prov. 10:22 NIV).

"You open your hand and satisfy the desires of every living thing" (145:16 NIV).

*I declare and decree, God will cause favorable increase in my (our) life (lives) in Jesus name.*

"And God is able to make all grace abound toward you; that ye, always having all sufficiency in all things, may abound to every good work" (2 Cor. 9:8 KJV).

*I declare and decree, God will give a special years blessing to me (us) in Jesus name.*

"He that spared not his own Son, but delivered him up for us all, how shall he not with him also freely give us all things?" (Rom. 8:32 KJV).

*I declare and decree, that God equip me (us) with multiple windows of income in Jesus name.*

"Bring ye all the tithes into the storehouse, that there may be meat in mine house, and prove me now herewith, saith the Lord of hosts, if I will not open you the windows of heaven, and pour you out a blessing, that there shall not be room enough to receive it" (Malachi 3:10 KJV).

*I declare and decree, the LORD God will perform miracles for me (us), in Jesus name.*

"I will make rivers flow on barren heights, and springs within the valleys. I will turn the desert into pools of water, and the parched ground into springs" (Isa. 41:18 NIV).

*I declare and decree, God will instantly turn my (our) bad circumstances to good, in Jesus name.*

"Instead of the thorn shall come up the fir tree, and instead of the brier shall come up the myrtle tree: and it shall be to the Lord for a name, for an everlasting sign that shall not be cut off" (Isa. 55:13 KJV).

*I declare and decree, that the enemy will not prevail over me, in Jesus name.*

"No evil will conquer you; no plague will come near your home" (Ps. 91:10 NLT).

"So do not fear, for I am with you; do not be dismayed, for I am your God. I will uphold you with my righteous right hand" (Isa. 41:10 NIV).

"The Lord is my light and my salvation; whom shall I fear? the Lord is the strength of my life; whom shall I be afraid?" (Ps. 27:1 KJV).

"In God will I praise his word: in the Lord will I praise his word" (Ps. 56:10 KJV).

"For the Lord will not abandon His people, Nor will He abandon His inheritance" (Ps. 94:14 AMP).

"That they may see, and know, and consider, and understand together, that the hand of the Lord hath done this, and the Holy One of Israel hath created it" (Isa. 41:20 KJV).

"May the glory of the Lord endure forever; May the Lord rejoice and be glad in His works—" (Ps. 104:31 AMP).

"May my tongue sing of your word, for all your commands are righteous" (Ps. 162:172 NIV).

"It is written: 'I believed; therefore I have spoken.' Since we have that same spirit of faith, we also believe and therefore speak" (2 Cor. 4:13 NIV).

*In Jesus name, amen.*

## Notes

_____
_____

# Reflections

# Gentleness

"Let your gentle spirit [your graciousness, unselfishness, mercy, tolerance, and patience] *be known to all people. The Lord is near*" (Phil. 4:5 AMP).

# God's Gentleness

## I AM Is Gentle
## (A Word from God in Prayer)

"I will bless the Lord at all times: his praise shall continually be in my mouth" (Ps. 34:1 KJV).

"I sought the Lord, and he heard me, and delivered me from all my fears" (Ps. 34:4 KJV).

"The eyes of the Lord are upon the righteous, and his ears are open unto their cry" (Ps. 34:15 KJV).

"As for God, his way is perfect: the Lord is tried: he is a buckler to all those that trust in him" (Ps. 18:30 KJV).

"For thou hast possessed my reins: thou hast covered me in my mother's womb" (Ps. 139:13 KJV).

"How precious also are thy thoughts unto me, O God! how great is the sum of them!" (Ps. 139:17 KJV).

"Thou hast also given me the shield of thy salvation: and thy right hand hath holden me up, and thy gentleness hath made me great" (Ps. 18:35 KJV).

"The Lord hath broken the staff of the wicked, and the scepter of the rulers" (Isa. 14:5 KJV).

"Yes, the Sovereign Lord is coming in power. He will rule with a powerful arm. See, he brings his reward with him as he comes" (Isa. 40:10 NLT).

"He will feed his flock like a shepherd. He will carry the lambs in his arms, holding them close to his heart. He will gently lead the mother sheep with their young" (Isa. 40:11 NLT).

"Have you never heard? Have you never understood? The Lord is the everlasting God, the creator of all the earth. He never grows weak or weary. No one can measure the depths of his understanding" (Isa. 40:28 NLT).

"He hath made the earth by his power, he hath established the world by his wisdom, and hath stretched out the heavens by his discretion" (Jer. 10:12 KJV).

"I will teach all your children, and they will enjoy great peace" (Isa. 54:13 NLT).

"You will be secure under a government that is just and fair. Your enemies will stay far away. You will live in peace, and terror will not come near" (Isa. 54:14 NLT).

"If any nation comes to fight you, it is not because I sent them. Whoever attacks you will go down in defeat" (Isa. 54:15 NLT).

"But in that coming day no weapon turned against you will succeed. You will silence every voice raised up to accuse you. These benefits are enjoyed by the servants of the Lord; their vindication will come from me. I, the Lord, have spoken!" (Isa. 54:17 NLT).

"I will praise you forever, O God, for what you have done. I will trust in your good name in the presence of your faithful people" (Ps. 52:9 NLT).

*In Jesus name, amen.*

## Notes

_____
_____
_____

# Giving Thanks to God Almighty

## (Prayer)

"O give thanks unto the Lord, for he is good: for his mercy endureth for ever" (Ps. 107:1 KJV).

"O give thanks unto the God of gods: for his mercy endureth for ever" (Ps. 136:2 KJV).

"O give thanks to the Lord of lords: for his mercy endureth for ever" (Ps. 136:3 KJV).

"To him who alone doeth great wonders: for his mercy endureth for ever" (Ps. 136:4 KJV).

"Who is a God like unto thee, that pardoneth iniquity, and passeth by the transgression of the remnant of his heritage? he retaineth not his anger for ever, because he delighteth in mercy" (Mic. 7:18 KJV).

"This is the message from the Lord" (Jer. 11:1 ERV).

"All this is for your benefit, so that the grace that is reaching more and more people may cause thanksgiving to overflow to the glory of God" (2 Cor. 4:15 NIV).

"And let the peace of God rule in your hearts, to the which also ye are called in one body; and be ye thankful" (Col. 3:15 KJV).

"Be thankful in all circumstances, for this is God's will for you who belong to Christ Jesus" (1 Thess. 5:18 NLT).

"Neither is there salvation in any other: for there is none other name under heaven given among men, whereby we must be saved" (Acts 4:12 KJV).

I thank you: "O Lord of Heaven's Armies, what joy for those who trust in you" (Ps. 84:12 NLT).

I thank you, LORD: "Thy testimonies are very sure: holiness becometh thine house, O Lord, for ever" (Ps. 93:5 KJV).

I thank you, LORD: "For thou, Lord, art high above all the earth: thou art exalted far above all gods" (Ps. 97:9 KJV).

I thank you, LORD: "For the Lord is good. His unfailing love continues forever, and his faithfulness continues to each generation" (Ps. 100:5 NLT).

I thank you, LORD, for: "Light is sown for the righteous, and gladness for the upright in heart" (Ps. 97:11 KJV).

I thank you, LORD: "For he satisfieth the longing soul, and filleth the hungry soul with goodness" (Ps. 107:9 KJV).

I thank you, LORD, for: "The Lord openeth the eyes of the blind: the Lord raiseth them that are bowed down: the Lord loveth the righteous" (Ps. 146:8 KJV).

I thank the LORD, for: "He healeth the broken in heart, and bindeth up their wounds" (Ps. 147:3 KJV).

I thank you, LORD, for: "Blessed is he that considereth the poor: the Lord will deliver him in time of trouble" (Ps. 41:1 KJV).

I thank you, LORD, for: "The meek also shall increase their joy in the Lord, and the poor among men shall rejoice in the Holy One of Israel" (Isa. 29:19 KJV).

I thank you, LORD, for your word that says: "He that believeth on me, as the scripture hath said, out of his belly shall flow rivers of living water" (John 7:38 KJV).

I thank you LORD, for you: "God is our refuge and strength, a very present help in trouble" (Ps. 46:1 KJV).

I thank you LORD, for: "The Lord is good, a strong hold in the day of trouble; and he knoweth them that trust in him" (Nah. 1:7 KJV).

I thank you, LORD, for: "Unto thee, O my strength, will I sing: for God is my defence, and the God of my mercy" (Ps. 59:17 KJV).

I thank you, LORD, for you: "Give us help from trouble: for vain is the help of man" (Ps. 60:11 KJV).

I thank you, Lord, for: "Through God we shall do valiantly: for he it is that shall tread down our enemies" (Ps. 60:12 KJV).

I thank you, Lord: "For thou hast been a shelter for me, and a strong tower from the enemy" (Ps. 61:3 KJV).

I thank you, Lord, for: "God hath spoken once; twice have I heard this; that power belongeth unto God" (Ps. 62:11 KJV).

I thank you, Lord: "For every one that asketh recieveth; and he that seeketh findeth; and to him that knocketh it shall be opened" (Matt. 7:8 KJV).

I thank you, Lord, for: "Thou shalt increase my greatness, and comfort me on every side" (Ps. 71:21 KJV).

I thank you, Lord, for: "You have given me the shield of your salvation, and your gentleness made me great" (2 Sam. 22:36 ESV).

I thank you Lord for your word that says: "He will rescue the poor when they cry to him; he will help the oppressed, who have no one to defend them" (Ps. 72:15 NLT).

"He feels pity for the weak and the needy, and he will rescue them" (Ps. 72:13 NLT).

I thank the Lord: "For the Lord God is our sun and our shield. He gives us grace and glory. The Lord will withhold no good thing from those who do what is right" (Ps. 84:11 NLT).

I thank you, Lord, for: "There is none holy as the Lord: for there is none beside thee: neither is there any rock like our God" (1 Sam. 2:2 KJV).

I thank you, Lord, for: "In the day of my trouble I will call upon thee: for thou wilt answer me" (Ps. 86:7 KJV).

I thank you, Lord: "For thou, Lord, art good, and ready to forgive; and plenteous in mercy unto all them that call upon thee" (Ps. 86:5 KJV).

I thank you, Lord: "For great is thy mercy toward me: and thou hast delivered my soul from the lowest hell" (Ps. 86:13 KJV).

I thank you, Lord, for: "Thou hast a mighty arm: strong is thy hand, and high is thy right hand" (Ps. 89:13 KJV).

I thank you, Lord, for your word that says: "My covenant will I not break, nor alter the thing that is gone out of my lips" (Ps. 89:34 KJV).

I thank you, Lord, for your word that says: "He giveth power to the faint; and to them that have no might he increaseth strength" (Isa. 40:29 KJV).

I thank you, Lord: "For thou, Lord, hast made me glad through thy work: I will triumph in the works of thy hands" (Ps. 92:4 KJV).

I thank you, Lord, for: "Mine eye also shall see my desire on mine enemies, and mine ears shall hear my desire of the wicked that rise up against me" (Ps. 92:11 KJV).

I thank you, Lord, for: "Those that be planted in the house of the Lord shall flourish in the courts of our God" (Ps. 92:13 KJV).

I thank you, Lord, for: "In the way of righteousness is life; and in the pathway thereof there is no death" (Prov. 12:28 KJV).

I thank you, Lord, for your word that says: "But those who trust in the Lord will find new strength. They will soar high on wings like eagles. They will run and not grow weary. They will walk and not faint" (Isa. 40:31 NLT).

I thank you, Lord, for: "The fear of the Lord is a fountain of life, to depart from the snares of death" (Prov. 14:27 KJV).

I thank you, Lord, for: "The name of the Lord is a strong tower: the righteous runneth into it, and is safe" (Prov. 18:10 KJV).

I thank you, Lord, for: "He that hath pity upon the poor lendeth unto the Lord; and that which he hath given will he pay him again" (Prov. 19:17 KJV).

I thank you, Lord, for: "He that followeth after righteousness and mercy findeth life, righteousness, and honour" (Prov. 21:21 KJV).

I thank you, Lord, for: "There is no wisdom nor understanding nor counsel against the Lord" (Prov. 21:30 KJV).

I thank you, Lord, for your word that says: "He sent his word, and healed them, and delivered them from their destructions" (Ps. 107:20 KJV).

I thank you, Lord, for: "Every word of God is pure: he is a shield unto them that put their trust in him" (Prov. 30:5 KJV).

I thank the Lord, for: "He restoreth my soul: he leadeth me in the paths of righteousness for his name's sake" (Ps. 23:3 KJV).

I thank you, Lord, for your word that says: "Ye are blessed of the Lord which made heaven and earth" (Ps. 115:15 KJV).

## PRAY IN GOD'S WORD FOR ENCOURAGEMENT AND CHANGE

I thank you, Lord: "For thou hast delivered my soul from death, mine eyes from tears, and my feet from falling" (Ps. 116:8 KJV).

I thank you, Lord, for: "Thou hast dealt well with thy servant, O Lord, according unto thy word" (Ps. 119:65 KJV).

I thank you, Lord, for being: "The God of my rock; in him will I trust: he is my shield, and the horn of my salvation, my high tower, and my refuge, my saviour, thou savest me from violence" (2 Sam. 22:3 KJV).

I thank you, Lord, for: "Thy testimonies that thou hast commanded are righteous and very faithful" (Ps. 119:138 KJV).

I thank you Lord, for: Thy righteousness is an everlasting righteousness, and thy law is the truth" (Ps. 119:142 KJV).

I thank you Lord, for: He maketh me to lie down in green pastures: he leadeth me beside the still waters" (Ps. 23:2 KJV).

I thank you Lord, for: Great are thy tender mercies, O Lord: quicken me according to thy judgments" (Ps. 119:156 KJV).

I thank you Lord, for your word that says: As for God, his way is perfect; the word of the Lord is tried: he is a buckler to all them that trust in him" (2 Sam. 22:31 KJV).

I thank you, Lord: For the Lord is our judge, the Lord is our lawgiver, the Lord is our king; he will save us" (Isa. 33:22 KJV).

I thank you, Lord: "For thou art my lamp, O Lord: and the Lord will lighten my darkness" (2 Sam. 22:29 KJV).

I thank you, Lord, for: "He maketh my feet like hind's feet, and setteth me upon my high places" (Ps. 18:33 KJV).

I thank the Lord for: "God is my strength and power: and he maketh my way perfect" (2 Sam. 22:33 KJV).

I thank you, Lord, for your word that says: "The Lord shall preserve thee from all evil: he shall preserve thy soul" (Ps. 121:7 KJV).

I thank you, Lord, for your word that says: "As the mountains are round about Jerusalem, so the Lord is round about his people from henceforth even for ever" (Ps. 125:2 KJV).

I thank you, Lord, for your word that says: "They that sow in tears shall reap in joy" (Ps. 126:5 KJV).

I thank you, Lord: "For I know that the Lord is great, and that our Lord is above all gods" (Ps. 135:5 KJV).

I thank the Lord for: "He teaches my hands to war; so that a bow of steel is broken by mine arms" (2 Sam. 22:35 KJV).

I thank you, Lord, for: "Thou hast also given me the shield of thy salvation: and thy gentleness hath made me great" (2 Sam. 22:36 KJV).

I thank you, Lord, for: "Thou hast enlarge my steps under me, that my feet did not slip" (Ps. 18:36 KJV).

I thank you, Lord, for: "Thou preparest a table before me in the presence of mine enemies: thou anoints my head with oil; my cup runneth over" (Ps. 23:5 KJV).

I thank you, Lord: "For thou hast girded me with strength to battle: them that rose up against me hast thou subdued under me" (2 Sam. 22:40 KJV).

"Thou hast also given me the necks of mine enemies; that I might destroy them that hate me" (Ps. 18:40 KJV).

"Now I stand on solid ground, and I will publicly praise the Lord" (Ps. 26:12 NLT).

"He gives strength to the weary and increases the power of the weak" (Isa. 40:29 NIV).

"All the nations you have made will come and worship before you, Lord" (Ps. 86:9 NIV).

"For you are great and do marvelous deeds; you alone are God" (Ps. 86:10 NIV).

"I will praise you, Lord my God, with all my heart; I will glorify your name forever" (Ps. 86:12 NIV).

"Be exalted, O God, above the heavens; let your glory be over all the earth" (Ps. 57:11 NIV).

*In Jesus name, amen.*

## Notes

_____

_____

_____

# Communing with God

## (Prayer)

"Have mercy on me, Lord, for I am in distress. Tears blur my eyes. My body and soul are withering away" (Ps. 31:9 NLT).

"For you are God, my only safe haven. Why have you tossed me aside? Why must I wander around in grief, oppressed by my enemies?" (Ps. 43:2 NLT).

"But I am trusting you, O Lord, saying, 'You are my God!'" (Ps. 31:14 NLT).

"You saw me before I was born. Every day of my life was recorded in your book. Every moment was laid out before a single day had passed" (Ps. 139:16 NLT).

"O Lord, what is man that you regard him; or the son of man that you think of him?" (Ps. 144:3 ESV).

"I have heard all about you, Lord. I am filled with awe by your amazing works. In this time of our deep need, help us again as you did in years gone by. And in your anger, remember your mercy" (Hab. 3:2 NLT).

"This is what the LORD says: "Don't live like people from other nations. Don't be afraid of special signs in the sky. The other nations are afraid of what they see in the sky. But you must not be afraid of them" (Jer. 10:2 ERV).

"Open the heavens, Lord, and come down. Touch the mountains so they billow smoke" (Ps. 144:5 NLT).

"Then the earth quaked and trembled. The foundations of the mountains shook; they quaked because of his anger" (Ps. 18:7 NLT).

"He opened the heavens and came down; dark storm clouds were beneath his feet" (Ps. 18:9 NLT).

"Therefore, the Lord, the LORD of Heaven's Armies, the Mighty One of Israel, says, "I will take revenge on my enemies and pay back my foes!" (Isa. 1:24 NLT).

"He shot his arrows and scattered his enemies; great bolts of lightning flashed, and they were confused" (Ps. 18:14 NLT).

"He reached down from heaven and rescued me; he drew me out of deep waters" (Ps. 18:16 NLT).

"He rescued me from my powerful enemies, from those who hated me and were too strong for me" (Ps. 18:17 NLT).

"They attacked me at a moment when I was in distress, but the Lord supported me" (Ps. 18:18 NLT).

"So shall they fear the name of the Lord from the west, and his glory from the rising of the sun. When the enemy shall come in like a flood, the Spirit of the Lord shall lift up a standard against him" (Isa. 59:19 KJV).

"The LORD's message came to me" (Jer. 1:4 ERV).

"Behold, I give unto you power to tread on serpents and scorpions, and over all the power of the enemy: and nothing shall by any means hurt you" (Luke 10:19 KJV).

"Therefore saith the LORD, the LORD of hosts, the mighty One of Israel, Ah, I will ease me of mine adversaries, and avenge me of mine enemies" (Isa. 1:24 KJV).

"The LORD said to my Lord, 'Sit in the place of honor at my right hand until I humble your enemies, making them a footstool under your feet'" (Ps. 110:1 NLT).

"The Lord is on my side; I will not fear: what can man do to me?" (Ps. 118:6 KJV).

"He frustrates the plans of schemers so the work of their hands will not succeed" (Job 5:12 NLT).

"Do good to your servant according to your word, Lord" (Ps. 119:65 NIV).

## PRAY IN GOD'S WORD FOR ENCOURAGEMENT AND CHANGE

"He traps the wise in their own cleverness so their cunning schemes are thwarted" (Job 5:12 NLT).

"But the Lord watches over those who fear him, those who rely on his unfailing love" (Ps. 33:18 NLT).

"He rescues them from death and keeps them alive in times of famine" (Ps. 33:19 NLT).

"He gives prosperity to the poor and protects those who suffer" (Job 5:11 NLT).

"In the cover of your presence you hide them from the plots of men; you store them in your shelter from the strife of tongues" (Ps. 31:20 ESV).

"Therefore, let all the godly pray while there is still time, that they may not drown in the floodwaters of judgment" (Ps. 32:6 NLT).

"With my lips have I declared all the judgments of thy mouth" (Ps. 119:13 KJV).

"Thou hast dealt well with thy servant, O Lord, according unto thy word" (Ps. 119:65 KJV).

""The days are coming," declares the Lord, "when the reaper will be overtaken by the plowman and the planter by the one treading grapes. New wine will drip from the mountains and flow from all the hills" (Amos 9:13 NIV).

"May those who fear you rejoice when they see me, for I have put my hope in your word" (Ps. 119:24 NIV).

"May your unfailing love be my comfort, according to your promised to your servant" (Ps. 119:76 NIV).

"I will pray to the LORD, and he will answer me from his holy mountain" (Ps. 3:4 ERV). *Selah.*

*In Jesus name, amen.*

## Notes

_____
_____
_____

# Self-Control

"Set a guard, O Lord, over my mouth; keep watch over the door of my lips [to keep me from speaking thoughtlessly]" (Ps. 141:3 AMP).

"He who guards his mouth and his tongue Guards himself from troubles" (Prov. 21:23 AMP).

# God's Temperance

## Self-Control in the Lord
## (A Word from God in Prayer)

"Thus saith the Lord, Learn not the way of the heathen, and be not dismayed at the signs of heaven; for the heathen are dismayed at them" (Jer. 10:20KJV).

"Forasmuch as there is none like unto thee, O Lord; thou art great, and thy name is great in might" (Jer. 10:6 KJV).

"He rules the world with righteousness; he judges the nations with justice" (Ps. 9:8 GNT).

"I study your teachings very carefully so that I will not sin against you" (Ps. 119:11 ERV).

"Lord, you are worthy of praise! Teach me your laws" (Ps. 119:12 ERV).

"Judge not, and ye shall not be judged: condemn not, and ye shall not be condemned: forgive, and ye shall be forgiven" (Luke 6:37KJV).

"Be not hasty in the spirit to be angry: for anger resteth in the bosom of fools" (Eccles. 7:9 KJV).

"I will instruct thee and teach thee in the way which thou shalt go: I will guide thee with mine eye" (Ps. 32:8 KJV).

"Humble yourselves therefore under the mighty hand of God, that he may exalt you in due time (1 Pet. 5:6 KJV).

"Let all bitterness, and wrath, and anger, and clamor, and evil speaking, be put away from you, with all malice" (Eph. 4:31 KJV).

"That ye would walk worthy of God, who hath called you unto his kingdom and glory" (1 Thess. 2:12 KJV).

"Put on the whole armor of God, that ye may be able to stand against the wiles of the devil" (Eph. 6:11 KJV).

"The LORD's laws are right. They make people happy. The LORD's commands are good. They show people the right way to live" (Ps. 19:8 ERV).

"For we wrestle not against flesh and blood, but against principalities, against powers, against the rulers of the darkness of this world, against spiritual wickedness in high places" (Eph. 6:12 KJV).

"The LORD's message came to me" (Jer. 1:4 ERV).

"Death and life are in the power of the tongue, and those who love it shall eat the fruit thereof" (Prov. 18:21 KJV).

"But ye, beloved, building up yourselves on your most holy faith, praying in the Holy Ghost" (Jude 1:20 KJV).

"I have no greater joy than to hear that my children walk in truth" (3 John 1:4).

"I will instruct you and teach you in the way you should go; I will counsel you with my eye upon you" (Ps. 32:8 ESV).

"Be exalted, O God, above the highest heavens. May your glory shine over all the earth" (Ps. 57:11 NLT).

"For your unfailing love is as high as the heavens. Your faithfulness reaches to the clouds" (Ps. 57:10 NLT).

"Let me live forever in your sanctuary, safe beneath the shelter of your wings!" (Ps. 61:4 NLT).

*In Jesus name, amen.*

## Notes

_____
_____
_____

# Confession and Repentance

## (Prayer)

"If we say that we have no sin, we deceive ourselves, and the truth is not in us" (1 John 1:8 KJV).

"If we confess our sins, he is faithful and just to forgive us our sins, and to cleans us from all unrighteousness" (1 John 1:9 KJV).

"Order my steps in thy word: and let not any iniquity have dominion over me" (Ps. 119:133 KJV).

"Be surety for thy servant for good: let not the proud oppress me" (Ps. 119:122 KJV).

"Your word is a lamp to guide my feet and a light for my path" (Ps. 119:105 NLT).

"For ever, O Lord, thy word is settled in heaven" (Ps. 119:89 KJV).

"O keep my soul, and deliver me: let me not be ashamed; for I put my trust in thee" (Ps. 25:20 KJV).

"Then the message from the Lord came to me" (Jer. 13:8 ERV).

"I will teach you wisdom's ways and lead you in straight paths" (Prov. 4:11 NLT).

"When you walk, you won't be held back; when you run, you won't stumble" (Prov. 4:12 NLT).

"And call upon me in the day of trouble: I will deliver thee, and thou shalt glorify me" (Ps. 50:15 KJV).

*"Confess with your mouth, your sin unto God."*

"Come with great power, O God, and rescue me!" (Ps. 54:1 NLT).

"Listen to my prayer, O God. Pay attention to my plea" (Ps. 54:2 NLT).

"Have mercy upon me, O God, according to thy lovingkindness: according unto the multitude of thy tender mercies blot out my transgressions" (Ps. 51:1 KJV).

"Listen and pay attention. The LORD has spoken to you. Do not be proud" (Jer. 13:15 ERV).

"I, I am he who blots out your transgressions for my own sake, and I will not remember your sins" (Isa. 43:25 ESV).

"The Lord executeth righteousness and judgment for all that are oppressed" (Ps. 103:6 KJV).

"For as the heaven is high above the earth, so great is his mercy toward them that fear him" (Ps. 103:11 KJV).

"As far as the east is from the west, so far hath he removed our transgressions from us" (Ps. 103:12 KJV).

"He hath not dealt with us after our sins; nor rewarded us according to our iniquities" (Ps. 103:10 KJV).

"The Lord is merciful and gracious, slow to anger, and plenteous in mercy" (Ps. 103:8 KJV).

"Now repent of your sins and turn to God, so that your sins may be wiped away" (Acts 3:19 NLT).

"LORD, I repent for…"

"Behold, thou desirest truth in the inward parts: and in the hidden part thou shalt make me to know wisdom" (Ps. 51:6 KJV).

"I reflect at night on who you are, O Lord; therefore, I obey your instructions" (Ps. 119:55 NLT).

"For I acknowledge my transgressions: and my sin is ever before me" (Ps. 51:3 KJV).

"Against thee, thee only, have I sinned, and done this evil in thy sight: that thou mightest be justified when thou speakest, and be clear when thou judgest" (Ps. 51:4 KJV).

"Behold, I was shapen in iniquity; and in sin did my mother conceive me" (Ps. 51:5 KJV).

"Purge me with hyssop, and I shall be clean: wash me, and I shall be whiter than snow" (Ps. 51:7 KJV).

"Make me to hear joy and gladness; that the bones which thou hast broken may rejoice" (Ps. 51:8 KJV).

"Hide thy face from my sins, and blot out all mine iniquities" (Ps. 51:9 KJV).

"Remember not the sins of my youth, nor my transgressions: according to thy mercy remember thou me for thy goodness' sake, O Lord" (Ps. 25:7 KJV).

"Look upon mine affliction and my pain; and forgive all my sins" (Ps. 25:18 KJV).

"Create in me a clean heart, O God; and renew a right spirit within me" (Ps. 51:10 KJV).

"Cast me not away from thy presence; and take not thy holy spirit from me" (Ps. 51:11 KJV).

"Restore unto me the joy of thy salvation; and uphold me with thy free spirit" (Ps. 51:12 KJV).

"The like figure whereunto even baptism doth also now save us (not the putting away of the filth of the flesh, but the answer of good conscience toward God,) by the resurrection of Jesus Christ" (1 Pet. 3:21 KJV).

"Therefore I take pleasure in infirmities, in reproaches, in necessities, in persecution, in distress for Christ's sake: for when I am weak, then am I strong" (2 Cor. 12:10 KJV).

"The sacrifices of God are a broken spirit: a broken and contrite heart, O God, thou wilt not despise" (Ps. 51:17 KJV).

"Come and show me mercy, as you do for all who love your name" (Ps. 119:132 NLT).

"Like as a father pitieth his children, so the Lord pitieth them that fear him" (Ps. 103:13 KJV).

"My meditation of him shall be sweet: I will be glad in the Lord" (Ps. 104:34 KJV).

"Your faithful love is higher than the highest clouds in the sky!" (Ps. 108:4 ERV).

"Rise above the heavens, God. Let all the world see your glory" (Ps. 108:5 ERV).

CRAIG WILLIAMS

*In Jesus name, amen.*

## Notes

# Reflections

# The Two Shall Be One

## (Prayer)

"Praise the LORD! I thank the LORD with all my heart in the assembly of his good people" (Ps. 111:1 ERV).

"The LORD does wonderful things, more than anyone could ask for" (Ps. 111:2 ERV).

"The earth is the Lord's, and everything in it, the world, and all who live in it" (Ps. 24:1 NIV).

"Everything he does is good and fair. All his commandments can be trusted" (Ps. 111:7 ERV).

"The Lord of host is with us; the God of Jacob is our refuge" (Ps. 46:11 KJV). *Selah.*

"Blessed art thou, O Lord: teach me thy statues" (Ps. 119:12 KJV).

"Open thou mine eyes, that I may behold wondrous things out of thy law" (Ps. 119:18 KJV).

"The day is thine, the night also is thine: thou hast prepared the light and the sun" (Ps. 74:16 KJV).

"Thou hast set all the borders of the earth: thou hast made summer and winter" (Ps. 74:17 KJV).

"Who is like You among the gods, O LORD? Who is like You, majestic in holiness, Awesome in splendor, working wonders" (Exod. 15:11 AMP).

"I will follow your teachings forever and ever" (Ps. 119:44 ERV).

"So I will live in freedom, because I do my best to know your instructions" (Ps. 119:45 ERV).

"The LORD God said, 'It is not good for the man to be alone. I will make a helper suitable for him'" (Gen. 2:18 NIV).

So the LORD God caused the man to fall into a deep sleep; and while he was sleeping, he took one of the man's ribs and then closed up the place with flesh" (Gen. 2:21 NIV).

"Then the LORD God made a woman from the rib he had taken out of the man, and he brought her to the man" (Gen. 2:22 NIV).

"The man said, 'This is now bone of my bones and flesh of my flesh; she shall be called "woman," for she was taken out of man'" (Gen. 2:23 NIV).

"Therefore shall a man leave his father and his mother, and shall cleave unto his wife: and they shall be one flesh" (Gen. 2:24 KJV).

"It shall be health to thy navel, and marrow to thy bones" (Prov. 3:8 KJV).

"Is not my word like as a fire? saith the Lord; and like a hammer that breaketh the rock in pieces?" (Jeremiah 23:29 KJV).

"Be ye therefore followers of God, as dear children" (Eph. 5:1 KJV).

"And walk in love, as Christ also hath loved us, and hath given himself for us an offering and a sacrifice to God for a sweet-smelling savour" (Eph. 5:2 KJV).

"Proving what is acceptable unto the Lord" (Eph. 5:10 KJV).

"Speaking to yourselves in psalms and hymns and spiritual songs, singing and making melody in your heart to the Lord" (Eph. 5:19 KJV).

"Giving thanks always for all things unto God and the Father in the name of our Lord Jesus Christ" (Eph. 5:20 KJV).

"The LORD made the earth, and he keeps it safe. The LORD is his name. He says" (Jer. 33:2 ERV).

"Wives, submit yourselves unto your own husbands, as unto the Lord" (Eph. 5:22 KJV).

"Even as Sara obeyed Abraham, calling him lord: whose daughters ye are, as long as ye do well, and are not afraid with any amazement" (1 Pet. 3:6 KJV).

"Husbands, love your wives, even as Christ also loved the church, and gave himself for it" (Eph. 5:25 KJV).

"Likewise, ye husbands, dwell with them according to knowledge, giving honour unto the wife, as unto the weaker vessel, and as being heirs together of the grace of life; that your prayers be not hindered" (1 Pet. 3:7 KJV).

"Live happily with the woman you love through all the meaningless days of life that God has given you under the sun. The wife God gives you is your reward for all your earthly toil" (Eccles. 9:9 NLT).

"That ye might walk worthy of the Lord unto all pleasing, being fruitful in every good work, and increasing in the knowledge of God" (Col. 1:10 KJV).

"Strengthen with all might, according to his power, unto all patience and longsuffering with joyfulness" (Col. 1:11 KJV).

"Lie not one to another, seeing that ye have put off the old man with his deeds" (Col. 3:9 KJV).

"Let thy fountain be blessed: and rejoice with the wife of thy youth" (Prov. 5:18 KJV).

"Submitting yourselves one to another in the fear of God" (Eph. 5:21 KJV).

"Put on therefore, as the elect of God, holy and beloved, bowels of mercies, kindness, humbleness of mind, meekness, longsuffering" (Col. 3:12 KJV).

"Forbearing one another, and forgiving one another, if any man have a quarrel against any: even as Christ forgave you, so also do ye" (Col. 3:13 KJV).

"Continue steadfastly in prayer, being watchful in it with thanksgiving" (Col. 4:2 ESV).

"And you must love the LORD your God with all your heart, all your soul, all your mind, and all your strength" (Mark 12:30 NLT).

"That the communication of thy faith may become effectual by the acknowledging of every good thing which is in you in Christ Jesus" (Philem. 1:6 KJV).

"I have no greater joy than to hear that my children walk in truth" (3 John 1:3 KJV).

"For a man indeed ought not to cover his head, forasmuch as he is the image and glory of God: but the woman is the glory of the man" (1 Cor. 11:7 KJV).

"For the man is not of the woman; but the woman of the man" (1 Cor. 11:8 KJV).

"Neither was the man created for the woman; but the woman for the man" (1 Cor. 11:9 KJV).

"Nevertheless neither is the man without the woman, neither the woman without the man, in the Lord" (1 Cor. 11:11 KJV).

"Then the message from the LORD came to me" (Jer. 13:8 ERV).

"For we are God's masterpiece. He has created us anew in Christ Jesus, so we can do the good things he planned for us long ago" (Eph. 2:10 NLT).

"Open my eyes to see the wonderful truths in your instructions" (Ps. 119:18 NLT).

"How good and pleasant it is when God's people live together in unity!" (Ps. 133:1 NIV).

"I will study your commandments and reflect on your ways" (Ps. 119:15 NLT).

*In Jesus name, amen.*

## Notes

_____

_____

_____

# Walking in God's Plan

## (Prayer)

"From the depths of despair, O Lord, I call for your help" (Ps. 133:1 NLT).

"Hear my cry, O Lord. Pay attention to my prayer" (Ps. 130:2 NLT).

"Let my cry come near before thee, O Lord: give me understanding according to thy word" (Ps. 119:169 KJV).

"Declare me innocent, O Lord, for I have acted with integrity; I have trusted in the Lord without wavering" (Ps. 26:1 NLT).

"Because it is written, be ye holy; for I am holy" (1 Pet. 1:16 KJV).

"Lord, who shall abide in thy tabernacle? who shall dwell in thy holy hill?" (Ps. 15:1 KJV).

"And the word of Jehovah came to me saying" (Jer. 2:1 ASV).

"Those who lead blameless lives and do what is right, speaking the truth from sincere hearts" (Ps. 15:2 NLT).

"He that hath clean hands, and a pure heart; Who hath not lifted up his soul unto falsehood, And hath not sworn deceitfully" (Ps. 24:4 ASV).

"Those who refuse to gossip or harm their neighbors or speak evil of their friends" (Ps. 15:3 NLT).

"Those who despise flagrant sinners, and honor the faithful followers of the Lord, and keep their promises even when it hurts" (Ps. 15:4 NLT).

"Those who lend money without charging interest, and who cannot be bribed to lie about the innocent. Such people will stand firm forever" (Ps. 15:5 NLT).

"For by grace are ye saved through faith; and that not of yourselves: it is the gift of God" (Eph. 2:8 KJV).

"Not of works, lest any man should boast" (Eph. 2:9 KJV).

"And thou shalt love the Lord thy God with all thy heart, and with all thy soul, and with all thy mind, and with all thy strength: this is the first commandment" (Mark 12:30 KJV).

"And the second is like, namely this, Thou shalt love thy neighbor as thyself. There is none other commandment greater than these" (Mark 12:31 KJV).

"That it may be well with thee, and thou mayest live long on the earth" (Eph. 6:3 KJV).

"I have longed for thy salvation, O Lord; and thy law is my delight" (Ps. 119:174 KJV).

"Let my soul live, and it shall praise thee; and let thy judgments help me" (Ps. 119:175 KJV).

"My tongue shall speak of thy word: for all thy commandments are righteousness" (Ps. 119:172 KJV).

"O Lord, I love the habitation of your house and the place where your glory dwells" (Ps. 26:8 ESV).

"Do good, O Lord, unto those that be good, and to them that are upright in their hearts" (Ps. 125:4 KJV).

*In Jesus name, amen.*

## Notes

_____
_____
_____

# It Is Written

## (Wisdom Prayer)

"The fear of the LORD is the beginning of wisdom: and the knowledge of the holy is understanding" (Prov. 9:10 KJV).

"Thou hast commanded us to keep thy precepts diligently" (Ps. 119:4 KJV).

"Open thou mine eyes, that I may behold wondrous things out of thy law" (Ps. 119:18 KJV).

"My tongue shall speak of thy word: for all thy commandments are righteousness" (Ps. 119:172 KJV).

"Make me to go in the path of thy commandments; for therein do I delight" (Ps. 119:35 KJV).

"Let thy mercies come also unto me, O LORD, even thy salvation, according to thy word" (Ps. 119:41 KJV).

"Establish Your word to Your servant, As that which produces reverence for You" (Ps. 119:38 NASB).

"For therein is the righteousness of God revealed from faith to faith: as it is written, The just shall live by faith" (Rom. 1:17 KJV).

*For it is written*: "The LORD possessed me in the beginning of his way, before his works of old" (Prov. 8:22 KJV).

*For it is written*: "In the fear of the LORD is strong confidence: and his children shall have a place of refuge" (Prov. 14:26 KJV).

*For it is written:* "The fear of the LORD is a fountain of life, to depart from the snares of death" (Prov. 14:27 KJV).

## PRAY IN GOD'S WORD FOR ENCOURAGEMENT AND CHANGE

*For it is written*: "Counsel is mine, and sound wisdom: I am understanding; I have strength" (Prov. 8:14 KJV).

*For it is written*: "Through wisdom is an house builded; And by understanding it is established" (Prov. 24:3 KJV).

*For it is written*: "For wisdom is better than rubies; and all the things that may be desired are not to be compared to it" (Prov. 8:11 KJV).

*For it is written*: "For the LORD giveth wisdom: out of his mouth cometh knowledge and understanding" (Prov. 2:6 KJV).

*For it is written*: "He layeth up sound wisdom for the righteous: he is a buckler to them that walk uprightly" (Prov. 2:7 KJV).

*For it is written*: "He keepeth the paths of judgment, and preserveth the way of his saints" (Prov. 2:8 KJV).

*For it is written*: "For the upright shall dwell in the land, and the perfect shall remain in it" (Prov. 2:21 KJV).

*For it is written*: "In all thy ways acknowledge him, and he shall direct thy paths" (Prov. 3:6 KJV).

*For it is written*: "For I give you good doctrine, forsake ye not my law" (Prov. 4:2 KJV).

*For it is written*: "Get wisdom, get understanding: forget it not; neither decline from the words of my mouth" (Prov. 4:5 KJV).

*For it is written*: "Hear, O my son, and receive my sayings; and the years of thy life shall be many" (Prov. 4:10 KJV).

*For it is written*: "When you walk, your step will not be hampered, and if you run, you will not stumble" (Prov. 4:12 ESV).

*For it is written*: "The road the righteous travel is like the sunrise, getting brighter and brighter until daylight has come" (Prov. 4:18 GNT).

*For it is written*: "Blessed is the man that heareth me, watching daily at my gates, waiting at the posts of my doors" (Prov. 8:34 KJV).

*For it is written:* "For whoso findeth me findeth life, and shall obtain favour of the LORD" (Prov. 8:35 KJV).

*For it is written*: "The blessing of the LORD, it maketh rich, and he addeth no sorrow with it" (Prov. 10:22 KJV).

*For it is written*: "The LORD is far from the wicked: but he heareth the prayer of the righteous" (Prov. 15:29 KJV).

*For it is written*: "When a man's ways please the Lord, he maketh even his enemies to be at peace with him" (Prov. 16:7 KJV).

*For it is written*: "The name of the Lord is a strong tower: the righteous runneth into it, and is safe" (Prov. 18:10 KJV).

*For it is written*: "He that hath pity upon the poor lendeth unto the Lord; and that which he hath given will he pay him again" (Prov. 19:17 KJV).

*For it is written*: "The fear of the Lord tendeth to life: and he that hath it shall abide satisfied; he shall not be visited with evil" (Prov. 19:23 KJV).

*For it is written*: "He that followeth after righteousness and mercy findeth life, righteousness, and honour" (Prov. 21:21 KJV).

*For it is written*: "There is no wisdom nor understanding nor counsel against the Lord" (Prov. 21:30 KJV).

*For it is written*: "By humility and the fear of the Lord are riches, and honour, and life" (Prov. 22:4 KJV).

*For it is written*: "The eyes of the Lord preserve knowledge, and he overthroweth the words of the transgressor" (Prov. 22:12 KJV).

*For it is written*: "Seest thou a man diligently in his business? he shall stand before king's; he shall not stand before mean men" (Prov. 22:29 KJV).

*For it is written*: "Envy thou not the oppressor, and choose none of his ways" (Prov. 3:31).

For a just man falleth seven times, and riseth up again: but the wicked shall fall into

mischief" (Prov. 24:16 KJV).

*For it is written*: "Whoso causeth the righteous to go astray in an evil way, he shall fall himself into his own pit: but the upright shall have good things in possession" (Prov. 28:10 KJV).

*For it is written*: "The fruit of the righteous is a tree of life; and he that winneth souls is wise" (Prov. 11:30 KJV).

*For it is written*: "For nothing will be impossible with God." (Luke 1:37 ESV).

"Now the word of the Lord came to me, saying" (Jer. 1:4 ESV).

"Concerning his Son, who was descended from David according to the flesh" (Rom. 1:3 ESV).

"And was declared to be the Son of God in power according to the Spirit of holiness by his resurrection from the dead, Jesus Christ our Lord" (Rom. 1:4 ESV).

"And you are included among those Gentiles who have been called to belong to Jesus Christ" (Rom. 1:6 NLT).

"Because that which may be known of God is manifest in them; for God hath shewed it unto them" (Rom. 1:19 KJV).

"Have not I written to thee excellent things in counsels and knowledge" (Prov. 22:20 KJV).

"That your faith should not stand in the wisdom of men, but in the power of God" (1 Cor. 2:5 KJV).

"This is my comfort in my affliction: for thy word hath quicken me" (Ps. 119:50 KJV).

"I have obeyed your laws, for I love them very much" (Ps. 119:167 NLT).

"Yes, I obey your commandment and laws because you know everything I do" (Ps. 119:168 NLT).

"As it is written, He hath dispersed abroad; he hath given to the poor: his righteousness remaineth for ever" (2 Cor. 9:9 KJV).

"Thou art my portion, O Lord: I have said that I would keep thy words" (Ps. 119:57 KJV).

"I have rejoiced in the way of thy testimonies, as much as in all riches" (Ps. 119:14 KJV).

"You have seen, O Lord; be not silent! O Lord, be not far from me!" (Ps. 35:22 ESV).

"Let your hand be ready to help me, for I have chosen your precepts" (Ps. 119:173 ESV).

*In Jesus name, amen.*

## Notes

_____
_____
_____

# Lord, Give Me Your Desires

## (Prayer)

"Hope deferred maketh the heart sick: but when the desire cometh, it is a tree of life" (Prov. 13:12 KJV).

"The Lord is my chosen portion and my cup; you hold my lot" (Ps. 16:5 ESV).

"For I will proclaim the name of the Lord; ascribe greatness to our God!" (Deut. 32:3 KJV).

"Thus says the Lord who made the earth, the Lord who formed it to establish it—the Lord is his name" (Jer. 33:2).

"All the ways of a man are pure in his own eyes, but the Lord weighs the spirit" (Prov. 16:2 ESV).

"The plans of the heart belong to man, but the answer of the tongue is from the Lord" (Prov. 16:1 ESV).

"I will praise thee with uprightness of heart, when I shall have learned thy righteous judgments" (Ps. 119:7 KJV).

"He is the Rock; his deeds are perfect. Everything he does is just and fair. He is a faithful God who does no wrong; how just and upright he is!" (Deut. 32:4 NLT).

"And the word of Jehovah came unto me the second time, saying" (Jer. 13:3 ASV).

"The heart of man plans his way, but the Lord establishes his steps" (Prov. 16:9 ESV).

"Commit your work to the Lord, and your plans will be established" (Prov. 16:3 ESV).

"Commit your way to the LORD; trust in him, and he will act" (Ps. 37:5 ESV).

"Delight yourself in the LORD, and he will give you the desires of your heart" (Ps. 37:4 ESV).

"For where your treasure is, there will your heart be also" (Matt. 6:21 KJV).

"The human heart is most deceitful of all things, and desperately wicked. Who really knows how bad it is?" (Jer. 17:9 NLT).

"But for those who are righteous, the way is not steep and rough. You are a God who does what is right, and you smooth out the path ahead of them" (Isa. 26:7 NLT).

"As the hart panteth after the water brooks, so panteth my soul after thee, O God" (Ps. 42:1 KJV).

"My soul yearns for you in the night; my spirit within me earnestly seeks you. For when your judgments are in the earth, the inhabitants of the world learn righteousness" (Isa. 26:9 ESV).

"My thought will be clear; I will speak words of wisdom" (Ps. 49:3 GNT).

"I will love thee, O LORD, my strength" (Ps. 18:1 KJV).

"I will declare thy name unto my brethren: in the midst of the congregation will I praise thee" (Ps. 22:22 KJV).

"I will bless the LORD, who hath given me counsel: my reins also instruct me in the night seasons" (Ps. 16:7 KJV).

"I will praise the LORD according to his righteousness: and will sing praise to the name of the LORD most high" (Ps. 7:17 KJV).

"Praise ye the LORD. Blessed is the man that feareth the LORD, that delighteth greatly in his commandments" (Ps. 112:1 KJV).

"You are the God who works miracles; you showed your might among the nations" (Ps. 77:14 GNT).

"Blessed are those whose strength is in you, in whose heart are the highways to Zion" (Ps. 84:5 ESV).

"The word of the LORD came to me saying" (Jer. 2:1 ESV).

"Are there any among the false gods of the nations that can bring rain? Or can the heavens give showers? Are you not he, O LORD our God? We set our hope on you, for you do all these things" (Jer. 14:22 ESV).

"Every good gift and every perfect gift is from above, and cometh down from the Father of lights, with whom is no variableness, neither shadow of turning" (James 1:17 KJV).

"Be careful for nothing; but in every thing by prayer and supplication with thanksgiving let your request be made known unto God" (Phil. 4:6 KJV).

"But when ye pray, use not vain repetitions, as the heathen do: for they think that they shall be heard for their much speaking" (Matt. 6:7 KJV).

*Now Make your request be known unto God.*

Your righteousness, O God, reaches to the highest heavens. You have done such wonderful things. Who can compare with you, O God?" (Ps. 71:19 NLT).

"I run in the path of your commands, for you have broadened my understanding" (Ps. 119:32 NIV).

"How sweet your words taste to me; they are sweeter than honey" (Ps. 119:103 NLT).

"I rejoice in your word like one who discovers a great treasure" (Ps. 119:162 NLT).

"You will show me the way of life, granting me joy of your presence and the pleasures of living with you forever" (Ps. 16:11 NLT).

*In Jesus name, amen.*

## Notes

_____
_____
_____

# Ungodly Desires You Want God to Change

# Reflections

# Honoring the Sabbath

## (Prayer)

"Give ear, O ye heavens, and I will speak; and hear, O earth, the words of my mouth" (Deut. 32:1 KJV).

"My doctrine shall drop as the rain, my speech shall distil as the dew, as the small rain upon the tender herb, and as the showers upon the grass" (Deut. 32:2 KJV).

"Because I will publish the name of the Lord: ascribe ye greatness unto our God" (Deut. 32:3 KJV).

"My soul longeth, yea, even fainteth for the courts of the Lord: my heart and my flesh crieth out for the living God" (Ps. 84:2 KJV).

"Blessed is the man whose strength is in thee; in whose heart are the ways of them" (Ps. 84:5 KJV).

"Blessed are they that dwell in thy house: they will be still praising thee" (Ps. 84:4 KJV). *Selah.*

"Then the word of the Lord came unto me, saying" (Jer. 1:4 KJV).

"Remember the sabbath day, to keep it holy" (Exod. 20:8 KJV).

"Six days shalt thou labour, and do all thy work" (Exod. 20:9 KJV).

"But the seventh day is the sabbath of the Lord thy God: in it thou shalt not do any work, thou, nor thy son, nor thy daughter, thy manservant, nor thy maidservant, nor thy cattle, nor thy stranger that is within thy gates" (Exod. 20:10 KJV).

"For in six days the LORD made heaven and earth, the sea, and all that in them is, and rested the seventh day: wherefore the LORD blessed the sabbath day, and hallowed it" (Exod. 20:11 KJV).

"So the Son of man is LORD, even over the Sabbath!" (Mark 2:28 NLT).

"Keep the Sabbath day holy. Don't pursue your own interest on that day, but enjoy the Sabbath and speak of it with delight as the LORD holy day. Honor the Sabbath in everything you do on that day, and don't follow your own desires or talk idly" (Isa. 58:13 NLT).

"Blessed is the man that doeth this, and the son of man that layeth hold on it; that keepeth the sabbath from polluting it, and keepeth his hand from doing any evil" (Isa. 56:2 KJV).

"Then the LORD will be your delight. I will give you great honor and satisfy you with the inheritance I promised to your ancestor Jacob. I, the LORD, have spoken!" (Isa. 58:14 NLT).

"O LORD, how great are thy works! and thy thoughts are very deep" (Ps. 92:5 KJV).

"The righteous shall flourish like the palm tree: he shall grow like a cedar in Lebanon" (Ps. 92:12 KJV).

"Those that be planted in the house of the LORD shall flourish in the courts of our God" (Ps. 92:13 KJV).

"Moreover the word of the LORD came to me, saying" (Jer. 2:1 KJV).

"The heart is hopelessly dark and deceitful, a puzzle that no one can figure out. But I, God, search the heart and examine the mind. I get to the heart of the human. I get to the root of things. I treat them as they really are, not as they pretend to be" (Jer. 17:9–10 MSG).

"You have six days each week for your ordinary work, but the seventh day must be a Sabbath day of complete rest, a holy day dedicated to the LORD. Anyone who works on the Sabbath must be put to death" (Exod. 31:15 NLT).

"Shew me thy ways, O LORD; teach me thy paths" (Ps. 25:4 KJV).

"Moreover also I gave them my sabbaths, to be a sign between me and them, that they might know that I am the LORD that sanctify them" (Ezek. 20:12 KJV).

## PRAY IN GOD'S WORD FOR ENCOURAGEMENT AND CHANGE

"Remember that I, the Lord, have given you a day of rest, and that is why on the sixth day I will always give you enough food for two days. Everyone is to stay where he is on the seventh day and not leave his home" (Exod. 16:29 GNT).

"Neither carry forth a burden out of your houses on the sabbath day, neither do ye any work, but hallow ye the sabbath day, as I commanded your fathers" (Jer. 17:22 KJV).

"And it shall come to pass, if ye diligently hearken unto me, saith the Lord, to bring in no burden through the gates of this city on the sabbath day, but hallow the sabbath day, to do no work therein" (Jer. 17:24 KJV).

"And if you will indeed obey my commandments that I command you today, to love the Lord your God, and to serve him with all your heart and with all your soul" (Deut. 11:13 ESV).

"If you do, he will send rain on your land when it is needed, in the autumn and in the spring, so that there will be grain, wine, and olive oil for you" (Deut. 11:14 GNT).

"And God is able to give you more than you need, so that you will always have all you need for yourselves and more than enough for every good cause" (2 Cor. 9:8 GNT).

"I am the Lord your God; walk in my statues, and keep my judgments, and do them" (Ezek. 20:19 KJV).

"And hallow my sabbaths; and they shall be a sign between me and you, that ye may know that I am the Lord your God" (Ezek. 20:20 KJV).

"And it shall come to pass, that from one new moon to another, and from one sabbath to another, shall all flesh come to worship before me, saith the Lord" (Isa. 66:23 KJV).

"I rejoice at thy word, as one that findeth great spoil" (Ps. 119:162 KJV).

"As the scripture says, 'He gives generously to the needy; his kindness lasts forever'" (2 Cor. 9:9 GNT).

"I rejoice in following your statutes as one rejoices in great riches" (Ps. 119:14 NIV).

"I meditate on your precepts and consider your ways" (Ps. 119:15 NIV).

"I delight in your decrees; I will not neglect your word" (Ps. 119:16 NIV).

"For thou, Lord, hast made me glad through thy work: I will triumph in the works of thy hands" (Ps. 92:4 KJV).

"Be good to your servant while I live, that I may obey your word" (Ps. 119:17 NIV).

"I have chosen the way of faithfulness; I have set my heart on your laws" (Ps. 119:30 NIV).

"I will hasten and not delay to obey your commands" (Ps. 119:60 NIV).

"I will always obey your law, for ever and ever" (Ps. 119:44 NIV).

"This is the day which the Lord hath made; we will rejoice and be glad in it" (Ps. 118:24 KJV).

*In Jesus name, amen.*

## Notes

_____
_____
_____

# Be Ye Holy

## (Prayer)

"My child, listen to what I say, and treasure my commands" (Prov. 2:11 NLT).

"Be still and know that I am God: I will be exalted among the heathen, I will be exalted in the earth" (Ps. 46:10 KJV).

"Wise choices will watch over you. Understanding will keep you safe" (Prov. 2:11 NLT).

"Remember the former things of old: for I am God, and there is none else; I am God, and there is none like me" (Isa. 46:9 KJV).

"I have sworn by my own name; I have spoken the truth, and I will never go back on my word: Every knee will bend to me, and every tongue will declare allegiance to me" (Isa. 45:23 NLT).

"God, all that you do is holy. No god is as great as you are" (Ps. 77:13 ERV).

"Thou art the God that doest wonders: thou hast declared thy strength among the people" (Ps. 77:14 KJV).

"I will fulfill my vows to you, O God, and will offer a sacrifice of thanks for your help" (Ps. 56:12 NLT).

"Thou art more glorious and excellent than the mountains of prey" (Ps. 76:4 KJV).

"The mighty God, even the LORD, hath spoken, and called the earth from the rising of the sun unto the going down thereof" (Ps. 50:1 KJV).

"He shall call to the heavens from above, and to the earth, that he may judge his people" (Ps. 50:4 KJV).

"And the heavens shall declare his righteousness: for God is judge himself" (Ps. 50:6 KJV). *Selah.*

'The human spirit can endure a sick body, but who can bear a crush spirit?" (Prov. 18:14 NLT).

"I have considered my ways and have turned my steps to your statutes" (Ps. 119:59 NIV).

"Only fools say in their hearts, 'There is no God.' They are corrupt, and their actions are evil; not one of them does good!" (Ps. 14:1 NLT).

"The LORD looks down from heaven on the entire human race; he looks to see if anyone is truly wise, if anyone seeks God" (Ps. 14:2 NLT).

"I said to the LORD, 'You are my Master! Every good thing I have comes from you'" (Ps. 16:2 NLT).

"Keep me safe, O God, for I have come to you for refuge" (Ps. 16:1 NLT).

"Open my eyes so that I can see all the wonderful things in your teachings" (Ps. 119:18 ERV).

"I am the LORD, your savior; I am the one who created you. I am the LORD, the creator of all things. I alone stretched out the heavens; when I made the earth, no one helped me" (Isa. 44:24 GNT).

"I, even I, am the LORD; and besides me there is no savior" (Isa. 43:11 KJV).

"Yea, before the day was I am he; and there is none that can deliver out of my hand: I will work, and who shall let it?" (Isa. 43:13 KJV).

"I have declared, and have saved, and I have shewed, when there was no strange god among you: therefore ye are my witnesses, saith the LORD, that I am God" (Isa. 43:12 KJV).

"Declaring the end from the beginning, and from ancient times the things that are not yet done, saying, My counsel shall stand, and I will do all my pleasure" (Isa. 46:9 KJV).

"What sorrow awaits those who argue with their Creator. Does a clay dispute with the one who shapes it, saying, 'Stop, you're doing it wrong!' Does the pot exclaim, 'How clumsy can you be?'" (Isa. 45:9 NLT).

"How terrible it would be if a newborn baby said to its father, 'Why was I born?' or if it said to its mother, 'Why did you make me this way?'"(Isa. 45:10 NLT).

"Look unto me, and be ye saved, all the ends of the earth: for I am God, and there is none else" (Isa. 45:22 KJV).

"Hearken unto me, ye stouthearted, that are far from righteousness" (Isa. 46:12 KJV).

"All of us have become like one who is unclean, and all our righteous acts are like filthy rags; we all shrivel up like a leaf, and like the wind our sins sweep us away" (Isa. 64:6 NIV).

"Behold, I am vile; what shall I answer thee? I will lay mine hand upon my mouth" (Job 40:4 KJV).

"For thou wilt save the afflicted people; but wilt bring down high looks" (Ps. 18:27 KJV).

"For ever since the world was created, people have seen the earth and sky. Through everything God made, they can clearly see his invisible qualities - his eternal power and divine nature. So they have no excuse for not knowing God" (Rom. 1:20 NLT).

"There is no peace, saith the Lord, unto the wicked" (Isa. 48:22 KJV).

"To whom will you compare me? Who is my equal?" (Isa. 46:5).

"I expose the false prophets as liars and make fools of fortune-tellers. I cause the wise to give bad advice, thus proving them to be fools" (Isa. 44:25 NLT).

"Behold, they shall be as stubble; the fire shall burn them; they shall not deliver themselves from the power of the flame: there shall not be a coal to warm at, nor fire to sit before it" (Isa. 47:14 KJV).

"Thy nakedness shall be uncovered, yea, thy shame shall be seen: I will take vengeance, and I will not meet thee as a man" (Isa. 47:3 KJV).

"But you, God's people, will be happy and sing as you do on the night of a sacred festival. You will be as happy as those who walk to the music of flutes on their way to the Temple of the Lord, the defender of Israel" (Isa. 30:29 GNT).

"You whom I took from the ends of the earth, and called from its farthest corners, saying to you, 'You are my servant, I have chosen you and not cast you off'" (Isa. 41:9 ESV).

"Fear not, for I am with you; be not dismayed, for I am your God; I will strengthen you, I will help you, I will uphold you with my righteous right hand" (Isa. 41:10 ESV).

"Once again you will have all the food you want, and you will praise the LORD your God, who does these miracles for you. Never again will my people be disgraced" (Joel 2:26 NLT).

"Oh, the joys of those who trust the LORD, who have no confidence in the proud or in those who worship idols" (Ps. 40:4 NLT).

"For the scripture saith, Whosoever believeth on him shall not be ashamed" (Rom. 10:11 KJV).

"Thy righteousness also, O God, is very high, who hast done great things: O God, who is like unto thee!" (Ps. 71:19 KJV).

"Now I know that the LORD saves his anointed; he will answer him from his holy heaven with the saving might of his right hand" (Ps. 20:6 ESV).

"But not the wicked! They are like worthless chaff, scattered by the wind" (Ps. 1:4 NLT).

"They will be condemned at the time of judgment. Sinners will have no place among the godly" (Ps. 1:5 NLT).

"For the LORD watches over the paths of the godly, but the path of the wicked leads to destruction" (Ps. 1:6 NLT).

"The voice of the LORD is powerful; the voice of the LORD is majestic" (Ps. 29:4 NLT).

"The voice of the LORD splits the mighty cedars; the LORD shatters the cedars of Lebanon" (Ps. 29:5 NLT).

"Come, behold the works of the LORD, what desolations he hath made in the earth" (Ps. 46:8 KJV).

"He sends disease before him and commands death to follow him" (Hab. 3:5 GNT).

"You got ready to use your bow, ready to shoot your arrows. Your lighting split open the earth" (Hab. 3:9 GNT).

"You marched across the earth in anger; in fury you trampled the nations" (Hab. 3:12 GNT).

"But unto the wicked God saith, What hast thou to do declare my statutes, or that thou shouldest take my covenant in thy mouth?" (Ps. 50:16 KJV).

"Seeing thou hatest instruction, And castest my words behind thee" (Ps. 50:17 KJV).

"Thus saith the Lord; Cursed be the man that trusteth in man, and maketh flesh his arm, and whose heart departeth from the Lord" (Jer. 17:5 KJV).

"And I will destroy those who used to worship me but now no longer do. They no longer ask for the Lord's guidance or seek my blessings" (Zeph. 1:6 NLT).

"And in those days shall men seek death, and shall not find it; and shall desire to die, and death shall flee from them" (Rev. 9:6 KJV).

"Then the devil, who had deceived them, was thrown into the fiery lake of burning sulfur, joining the beast and the false prophet. There they will be tormented day and night forever and ever" (Rev. 20:10 NLT).

"And anyone whose name was not found recorded in the Book of Life was thrown into the lake of fire" (Rev. 20:15 NLT).

"These people are the ones who are creating divisions among you. They follow their natural instincts because they do not have God's Spirit in them" (Jude 1:19 NLT).

"Repent, all of you who forget me, or I will tear you apart, and no one will help you" (Ps. 50:22 NLT).

"But giving thanks is a sacrifice that truly honors me. If you keep to my path, I will reveal to you the salvation of God" (Ps. 50:23 NLT).

"Behold, the Lord maketh the earth empty, and maketh it waste, and turneth it upside down, and scattereth abroad the inhabitants thereof" (Isa. 24:1 KJV).

"The grass withers and the flowers fade beneath the breath of the Lord. And so it is with people" (Isa. 40:7 NLT).

"The grass withers and the flowers fade, but the word of our God stands forever." (Isa. 40:8 NLT).

"Bring my faithful people to me—those who made a covenant with me by giving sacrifices." (Ps. 50:5 NLT).

"God will judge us for everything we do, including every secret thing, whether good or bad" (Eccles. 12:14 NLT).

"Have mercy on me, my God, have mercy on me, for in you I take refuge. I will take refuge in the shadow of your wings until the disaster has passed" (Ps. 57:1 NIV).

"Thy mercy, O Lord, is in the heavens; and thy faithfulness reacheth unto the clouds" (Ps. 36:5 KJV).

"Let all the earth fear the Lord: let all the inhabitants of the world stand in awe of him" (Ps. 33:8 KJV).

"Our God shall come, and shall not keep silence: a fire shall devour before him, and it shall be very tempestuous round about him" (Ps. 50:3 KJV).

"He calls on the heavens above and earth below to witness the judgment of his people" (Ps. 50:4 NLT).

"I praise God for what he has promised; yes, I praise the Lord for what he has promised" (Ps. 56:10 NLT).

"I will praise you forever, O God, for what you have done. I will trust in your good name in the presence of your faithful people" (Ps. 52:9 NLT).

"For you have delivered my soul from death, yes, my feet from falling, that I may walk before God in the light of life" (Ps. 56:13 ESV).

*In Jesus name, amen.*

## Notes

_____

_____

_____

# Part 2

## Winning the Battle through the Word of God

"Arise, O LORD, confront him, cast him down; Save my soul from the wicked with your sword" (Ps. 17:13 AMP).

*In Jesus name, amen.*

# Petition for God's Help

## (Prayer)

"I called upon thy name, O Lord, out of the low dungeon" (Lam. 3:55 KJV).

"Thou hast heard my voice: hide not thine ear at my breathing, at my cry" (Lam. 3:56 KJV).

"Thou drewest near in the day that I called upon thee: thou saidst, fear not" (Lam. 3:57 KJV).

"When I called to you for help, you answered me and gave me strength" (Ps. 138:3 ERV).

"Behold, I give unto you power to tread on serpents and scorpions, and over all the power of the enemy: and nothing shall by any means hurt you" (Luke 10:19 KJV).

"If ye abide in me, and my words abide in you, ye shall ask what ye will, and it shall be done unto you" (John 15:7 KJV).

"Call unto me, and I will answer thee, and shew thee great and mighty things, which thou knowest not" (Jer. 33:3 KJV).

"Therefore I say unto you, what things soever ye desire, when ye pray, believe that ye receive them, and ye shall have them" (Mark 11:24 KJV).

"If ye shall ask any thing in my name, I will do it" (John 14:14 KJV).

"Ask, and it shall be given you; seek, and ye shall find; Knock, and it shall be opened unto you" (Matt. 7:7 KJV).

"And whatsoever ye shall ask in my name, that will I do, that the Father may be glorified in the Son" (John 14:13 KJV).

"And all things, whatsoever ye shall ask in prayer, believing, ye shall receive" (Matt. 21:22 KJV).

"For verily I say unto you, that whosoever shall say unto this mountain, be thou removed, and be thou cast into the sea; and shall not doubt in his heart, but shall believe that those things which he saith shall come to pass; he shall have whatsoever he saith" (Mark 11:23 KJV).

"Ask of me, and I shall give thee the heathen for thine inheritance, and the uttermost parts of the earth for thy possession" (Ps. 2:8 KJV).

"O God, have mercy on me, for people are hounding me. My foes attack me all day long" (Ps. 56:1 NLT).

"I am constantly hounded by those who slander me, and many are boldly attacking me" (Ps. 56:2 NLT).

"But when I am afraid, I will put my trust in you" (Ps. 56:3 NLT).

"LORD, you have seen the wrong done to me. Uphold my cause!" (Lam. 3:59 NIV).

"Thou hast seen all their vengeance and all their imaginations against me" (Lam. 3:60 KJV).

"Thou hast heard their reproach, O LORD, and all their imaginations against me" (Lam. 3:61 KJV).

"The lips of those that rose up against me, and their device against me all the day" (Lam. 3:62 KJV).

"They are always twisting what I say; they spend their days plotting to harm me" (Ps. 56:5 NLT).

"Behold their sitting down, and their rising up; I am their musick" (Lam. 3:63 KJV).

"Render unto them a recompense, O LORD, according to the work of their hands" (Lam. 3:64 KJV).

"Give them sorrow of heart, thy curse unto them" (Lam. 3:65 KJV).

"Let their table become a snare before them: and that which should have been for their welfare, let it become a trap" (Ps. 69:22 KJV).

"Persecute and destroy them in anger from under the heavens of the Lord" (Lam. 3:66 KJV).

"Surely thou didst set them in slippery places: thou castedst them down into destruction" (Ps. 73:18 KJV).

"How are they brought into desolation, as in a moment! they are utterly consumed with terrors" (Ps. 73:19 KJV).

"As a dream when one awaketh; so, O Lord, when thou awakes, thou shalt despise their image" (Ps. 73:20 KJV).

"For God is my King of old, working salvation in the midst of the earth" (Ps. 73:12 KJV).

"For I know that my Redeemer liveth, and that he shall stand at the latter day upon the earth" (Job 19:25 KJV).

"I will declare the decree: the Lord hath said unto me, thou art my Son; this day have I begotten thee" (Ps. 2:7 KJV).

"O Lord, thou hast pleaded the causes of my soul; thou hast redeemed my life" (Lam. 3:58 KJV).

"For the righteous Lord loveth righteousness; his countenance doth behold the upright" (Ps. 11:7 KJV).

"For thou art not a God that hath pleasure in wickedness: neither shall evil dwell with thee" (Ps. 5:4 KJV).

"A brutish man knoweth not, neither doth a fool understand this" (Ps. 92:6 KJV).

"When the wicked spring as the grass, and when all the workers of iniquity do flourish; it is that they shall be destroyed for ever" (Ps. 92:7 KJV).

"For, lo, thine enemies, O Lord, for, lo, thine enemies shall perish; all the workers of iniquity shall be scattered" (Ps. 92:9 KJV).

"But my horn shalt thou exalt like the horn of an unicorn: I shall be anointed with fresh oil" (Ps. 92:10 KJV).

"Mine eye also shall see my desire on mine enemies, and mine ears shall hear my desire of the wicked that rise up against me" (Ps. 92:11 KJV).

"Those that be planted in the house of the Lord shall flourish in the courts of our God" (Ps. 92:13 KJV).

"They shall still bring forth fruit in old age; they shall be fat and flourishing" (Ps. 92:14 KJV).

"To shew that the LORD is upright: he is my rock, and there is no unrighteousness in him" (Ps. 92:15 KJV).

*In Jesus name, amen.*

# Notes

_____
_____
_____

# Prayer of Victory

## (Prayer)

Say: I am Victorious!

"For thou LORD, hast made me glad through thy work: I will triumph in the works of thy hands" (Ps. 92:4 KJV).

"The LORD will perfect that which concerneth me, thy mercy, O LORD, endureth for ever: forsake not the works of thine own hands" (Ps. 138:8 KJV).

"Though I walk in the midst of trouble, thou wilt revive me: thou shalt stretch forth thine hand against the wrath of mine enemies, and thy right hand shall save me" (Ps. 138:7 KJV).

"When the wicked, even mine enemies and foes, came upon me to eat up my flesh, they stumbled and fell" (Ps. 27:2 KJV).

"My help cometh from the LORD, which made heaven and earth" (Ps. 121:2 KJV).

"Remember your promise to me; it is my only hope" (Ps. 119:49 NLT).

"They shall not hunger nor thirst; neither shall the heat nor sun smite them: for he that hath mercy on them shall lead them, even by the springs of water shall he guide them" (Isa. 49:10 KJV).

"Your promise revives me; it comforts me in all my troubles" (Ps. 119:50 NLT).

"Who can command things to happen without the LORD's permission?" (Lam. 3:37 NLT).

"This is what the LORD says- your Redeemer and creator: "I am the LORD, who made all things. I alone stretched out the heavens. Who was with me when I made the earth?" (Isa. 44:24 NLT).

"I have swept away your sins like a cloud. I have scattered your offenses like the morning mist. Oh, return to me, for I have paid the price to set you free" (Isa. 44:22 NLT).

"I, even I, am he that comforteth you: who art thou, that thou should be afraid of a man that shall die, and of the son of man which shall be made as grass" (Isa. 51:12 KJV).

"For the moth shall eat them up like a garment, and the worm shall eat them like wool: but my righteousness shall be for ever, and my salvation from generation to generation" (Isa. 51:8 KJV).

"One generation shall praise thy works to another, and shall declare thy mighty acts" (Ps. 145:4 KJV).

"You know what I long for, Lord; you hear my every sigh" (Ps. 38:9 NLT).

"I prayed, 'Don't let my enemies gloat over me or rejoice at my downfall'" (Ps. 38:16 NLT).

"Rid me, and deliver me from the hand of strange children, whose mouth speaketh vanity, and their right hand is a right hand of false hood" (Ps. 144:11 KJV).

"As for the head of those that compass me about, let the mischief of their own lips cover them" (Ps. 140:9 KJV).

"Take hold of shield and buckler, and stand up for mine help" (Ps. 35:2 KJV).

"Bring disgrace and destruction on my accusers. Humiliate and shame those who want to harm me" (Ps. 71:13 NLT).

"Lift up your spear and javelin against those who pursue me. Let me hear you say, "I will give you victory!" (Ps. 35:3 NLT).

"Let them be confounded and put to shame that seek after my soul: let them be turned back and brought to confusion that devise my hurt" (Ps. 35:4 KJV).

"Let them be as chaff before the wind: and let the angel of the LORD chase them" (Ps. 35:5 KJV).

"Let their way be dark and slippery: and let the angel of the LORD persecute them" (Ps. 35:6 KJV).

"Let them be confounded and consumed that are adversaries to my soul; let them be covered with reproach and dishonor that seek my hurt" (Ps. 71:13 KJV).

"Let them be confounded and troubled for ever; yea, let them be put to shame and perish" (Ps. 83:17 KJV).

"Let burning coals fall upon them: let them be cast into the fire; into deep pits, that they rise not up again" (Ps. 140:10 KJV).

"So persecute them with thy tempest, and make them afraid with thy storm" (Ps. 83:15 KJV).

"Keep me, O Lord, from the hands of the wicked; preserve me from the violent man; who have purposed to overthrow my goings" (Ps. 140:4 KJV).

"When he shall be judged, let him be condemned: and let his prayer become sin" (Ps. 109:7 KJV).

"Let his days be few; and let another take his office" (Ps. 109:8 KJV).

"Let the extortioner catch all that he hath; and let the strangers spoil his labour" (Ps. 109:11 KJV).

"As he loved cursing, so let it come unto him; as he delighted not in blessing, so let it be far from him" (Ps. 109:17 KJV).

"As he clothed himself with cursing like as with his garment, so let it come into his bowels like water, and like oil into his bones" (Ps. 109:18 KJV).

"Let it be unto him as the garment which covereth him, and for a girdle wherewith he is girded continually" (Ps. 109:19 KJV).

"May those curses become the Lord's punishment for my accusers who speak evil of me" (Ps. 109:20 NLT).

"But mine eyes are unto thee, O God the Lord; in thee is my trust; leave not my soul destitute" (Ps. 141:8 KJV).

"My life is an example to many, because you have been my strength and protection" (Ps. 71:7 KJV).

"What shall we then say to these things? if God be for us, who can be against us?" (Rom. 8:31 KJV).

"Please, Lord, rescue me! Come quickly, Lord, and help me" (Ps. 40:13 NLT).

"Let them be horrified by their shame, for they said, 'Aha! We've got him now!'" (Ps. 40:15 NLT).

"Moreover the word of the LORD came to me, saying" (Jer. 2:1 KJV).

"He that spared not his own son, but delivered him up for us all, how shall he not with him also freely give us all things?" (Rom. 8:32 KJV).

"Trust in the LORD with all thine heart; and lean not unto thine own understanding" (Prov. 3:5 KJV).

"Then shall thy light break forth as the morning, and thine health shall spring forth speedily: and thy righteousness shall go before thee; the glory of the LORD shall be thy rearward" (Isa. 58:8 KJV).

"I will go before thee, and make the crooked places straight: I will break in pieces the gates of brass, and cut in sunder the bars of iron" (Isa. 45:2 KJV).

"And I will give thee the treasures of darkness, and hidden riches of secret places, that thou mayest know that I, the LORD, which call thee by thy name, am the God of Israel" (Isa. 45:3 KJV).

"And even to your old age I am he; and even to hoar hairs will I carry you: I have made, and I will bear; even I will carry, and will deliver you" (Isa. 46:4 KJV).

"For the LORD God will help me; therefore shall I not be confounded: therefore have I set my face like a flint, and I know that I shall not be ashamed" (Isa. 50:7 KJV).

"Behold, the LORD God will help me; who is he that shall condemn me? Lo, they all shall wax old as a garment; the moth shall eat them up" (Isa. 50:9 KJV).

"Then this message came to me from the LORD" (Ezek. 7:1 NLT).

"Behold, all they that were incensed against thee shall be ashamed and confounded: they shall be as nothing; and they that strive with thee shall perish" (Isa. 41:11 KJV).

"Thou shalt seek them, and shalt not find them, even them that contended with thee: they that war against thee shall be as nothing, and as a thing of nought" (Isa. 41:2 KJV).

"And I will feed them that oppress thee with their own flesh; and they shall be drunken with their own blood, as with sweet wine: and all flesh shall know that I the LORD am thy saviour and thy Redeemer, the mighty One of Jacob" (Isa. 49:26 KJV).

"For the LORD shall be thy confidence, and shall keep thy foot from being taken" (Prov. 3:26 KJV).

"Look! Those who do evil have fallen! They are thrown down, never to rise again" (Ps. 36:12 NLT).

"For there shall be no reward to the evil man; the candle of the wicked shall be put out" (Prov. 24:20 KJV).

"The counsel of the LORD standeth for ever, the thoughts of his heart to all generations" (Ps. 33:11 KJV).

"Let the wicked fall into their own nets, whilst that I withal escape" (Ps. 141:10 KJV).

*In Jesus name, amen.*

# Notes

_____
_____
_____

# The Lord's Vengeance on My Enemies

## (Prayer)

"Now unto him that is able to do exceeding abundantly above all that we ask or think, according to the power that worketh in us" (Eph. 3:20 KJV).

"I will declare the decree: the Lord hath said unto me, Thou art my son; this day have I begotten thee" (Ps. 2:7 KJV).

"The Lord gave me this message" (Jer. 1:4 NLT).

"Dearly beloved, avenge not yourselves, but rather give place unto wrath: for it is written, Vengeance is mine; I will repay, saith the Lord" (Rom. 12:19 KJV).

"Say to them that are of a fearful heart, Be strong, fear not: behold, your God will come with vengeance, even God with a recompense; he will come and save you" (Isa. 35:4 KJV).

"He gives justice to the oppressed and food to the hungry. The Lord frees the prisoners" (Ps. 146:7 NLT).

"Yet, Lord, thou knowest all their counsel against me to slay me: forgive not their iniquity, neither blot out their sin from thy sight, but let them be overthrown before thee; deal thus with them in the time of thine anger" (Jer. 18:23 KJV).

"For the Lord knoweth the way of the righteous: but the way of the ungodly shall perish" (Ps. 1:6 KJV).

"Arise, O Lord; save me, O my God: for thou hast smitten all mine enemies upon the cheek bone; thou hast broken the teeth of the ungodly" (Ps. 3:7 KJV).

"He hath also prepared for him the instruments of death; he ordaineth his arrows against the persecutors" (Ps. 7:13 KJV).

"Thou hast rebuked the heathen, thou hast destroyed the wicked, thou hast put out their name for ever and ever" (Ps. 9:5 KJV).

"Let a cry be heard from their houses, when thou shalt bring a troop suddenly upon them: for they have digged a pit to take me, and hid snares for my feet" (Jer. 18:22 KJV).

"O thou enemy, destructions are come to a perpetual end: and thou hast destroyed cities; their memorial is perished with them" (Ps. 9:6 KJV).

"Let them be confounded that persecute me, but let not me be confounded: let them be dismayed, but let not me be dismayed: bring upon them the day of evil, and destroy them with double destruction" (Jer. 17:18 KJV).

"Break thou the arm of the wicked and the evil man: seek out his wickedness till thou find none" (Ps. 10:15 KJV).

"The Lord is King for ever and ever: the heathen are perished out of his land" (Ps. 10:16 KJV).

"Upon the wicked he shall rain snares, fire and brimstone, and an horrible tempest: this shall be the portion of their cup" (Ps. 11:6 KJV).

"The Lord examines both the righteous and the wicked. He hates those who love violence" (Ps. 11:5 NLT).

"Thine hand shall find out all thine enemies: thy right hand shall find out those that hate thee" (Ps. 21:8 KJV).

"He will rain down blazing coal and burning sulfur on the wicked, punishing them with scorching winds" (Ps. 11:6 NLT).

"You will throw them in a flaming furnace when you appear. The Lord will consume them in his anger; fire will devour them" (Ps. 21:9 NLT).

"Their fruit shalt thou destroy from the earth, and their seed from among the children of men" (Ps. 21:10 KJV).

"Because they regard not the works of the Lord, nor the operation of his hands, he shall destroy them, and not build them up" (Ps. 28:5 KJV).

"Praise the Lord! For he has heard my cry for mercy" (Ps. 28:6 NLT).

"You brought me up from the grave, O Lord. You kept me from falling into the pit of death" (Ps. 30:3 NLT).

"But my enemies say nothing but evil about me. "How soon will he die and be forgotten?" they ask" (Ps. 41:5 NLT).

"But thou, O Lord, be merciful unto me, and raise me up, that I may requite them" (Ps. 41:10 KJV).

"Let them be confounded and put to shame that seek after my soul: let them be turned back and brought to confusion that devise my hurt" (Ps. 35:4 KJV).

"Let the lying lips be put to silence; which speak grievous things proudly and contemptuously against the righteous" (Ps. 31:18 KJV).

"Let them be ashamed and brought to confusion together that rejoice at mine hurt: let them be clothed with shame and dishonour that magnify themselves against me" (Ps. 35:26 KJV).

"Let them be as chaff before the wind: and let the angel of the Lord chase them" (Ps. 35:5 KJV).

"Let their way be dark and slippery: and let the angel of the Lord persecute them" (Ps. 35:6 KJV).

"Let not the foot of pride come against me, and let not the hand of the wicked remove me" (Ps. 36:11 KJV).

"Draw me not away with the wicked, and with the workers of iniquity, which speak peace to their neighbors, but mischief in their hearts" (Ps. 28:3 KJV).

"Do not be afraid of them, for I am with you to deliver you, declares the Lord" (Jer. 1:8 ESV).

"Evil shall slay the wicked: and they that hate the righteous shall be desolate" (Ps. 34:21 KJV).

"There are the workers of iniquity fallen: they are cast down, and shall not be able to rise" (Ps. 36:12 KJV).

"The face of the Lord is against them that do evil, to cut off the remembrance of them from the earth" (Ps. 34:16 KJV).

"The Lord bringeth the counsel of the heathen to nought: he maketh the devices of the people of none effect" (Ps. 33:10 KJV).

"Many sorrows shall be to the wicked; but he that trusteth in the LORD, mercy shall compass him about" (Ps. 32:10 KJV).

"He shall receive the blessing from the LORD, and righteousness from the God of his salvation" (Ps. 24:5 KJV).

"And the word of the LORD of hosts came unto me, saying" (Zech. 8:18 KJV).

"Be glad in the LORD, and rejoice, ye righteous: and shout for joy, all ye that are upright in heart" (Ps. 32:11 KJV).

"Cry out and shout, thou inhabitant of Zion: for great is the Holy One of Israel in the midst of thee" (Isa. 12:6 KJV).

"Keep me as the apple of the eye, hide me under the shadow of thy wings" (Ps. 17:8 KJV).

"As for me, I will behold thy face in righteousness: I shall be satisfied, when I awake, with thy likeness" (Ps. 17:15 KJV).

"The LORD redeemeth the soul of his servants: and none of them that trust in him shall be desolate" (Ps. 34:22 KJV).

*In Jesus name, amen.*

## Notes

_____
_____
_____

# The Righteous Vindicated

## (Prayer)

"Rejoice not against me, O mine enemy: when I fall, I shall arise; when I sit in darkness, the LORD shall be a light unto me" (Mic. 7:8 KJV).

"When my soul fainted within me I remembered the LORD: and my prayer came in unto thee, into thine holy temple" (Jon. 2:7 KJV).

"Therefore I will look unto the LORD; I will wait for the God of my salvation: my God will hear me" (Mic. 7:7 KJV).

"For mine enemies speak against me; and they that lay wait for my soul take counsel together" (Ps. 71:10 KJV).

"Saying, God hath forsaken him: persecute and take him; for there is none to deliver him" (Ps. 71:11 KJV).

"Thus saith the LORD GOD, it shall not stand, neither shall it come to pass" (Isa. 7:7 KJV).

"I have blotted out, as a thick cloud, thy transgressions, and, as a cloud, thy sins: return unto me; for I have redeemed thee" (Isa. 44:22 KJV).

"Fret not thyself because of evildoers, neither be thou envious against the workers of iniquity" (Ps. 37:1 KJV).

"For they shall soon be cut down like the grass, and wither as the green herb" (Ps. 37:2 KJV).

"Because I am righteous, I will see you. When I awake, I will see you face to face and be satisfied" (Ps. 17:15 NLT).

"O God, when thou wentest forth before thy people, when thou didst march through the wilderness" (Ps. 68:7 KJV). *Selah.*

"Through thee will we push down our enemies: through thy name will we tread them under that rise up against us" (Ps. 44:5 KJV).

"Arise, O Lord, disappoint him, cast him down: deliver my soul from the wicked, which is thy sword" (Ps. 17:13 KJV).

"Thus saith the Lord God; Because the enemy hath said against you, Aha, even the ancient high places are ours in possession" (Ezek. 36:2 KJV).

"Therefore, as the tongue of fire devours the stubble, and as dry grass sinks down in the flame, so their root will be as rottenness, and their blossom go up like dust; for they have rejected the law of the Lord of hosts, and have despised the word of the Holy One Israel" (Isa. 5:24 ESV).

"Woe to those who call evil good and good evil, who put darkness for light and light for darkness, who put bitter for sweet and sweet for bitter!" (Isa. 5:20 ESV).

"Woe to those who are wise in their own eyes, and shrewd in their own sight!" (Isa. 5:21 ESV).

"Their sorrows shall be multiplied that hasten after another god: their drink offerings of blood will I not offer, nor take up their names into my lips" (Ps. 16:4 KJV).

"Moreover the word of the Lord came unto me, saying" (Ezek. 36:16 KJV).

"And he shall spread forth his hands in the midst of them, as he that swimmeth spreadeth forth his hands to swim: and he shall bring down their pride together with the spoils of their hands" (Isa. 25:11 KJV).

"Then my enemies will see that the Lord is on my side. They will be ashamed that they taunted me, saying, "So where is the Lord - that God of yours?" With my own eyes I will see their downfall; they will be trampled like mud in the streets" (Mic. 7:10 NLT).

"The scoffer will be gone, the arrogant will disappear, and those who plot evil will be killed" (Isa. 29:20 NLT).

"Those who convict the innocent by their false testimony will disappear. A similar fate awaits those who use trickery to pervert justice and who tell lies to destroy the innocent" (Isa. 29:21 NLT).

"You have preserved my life because I am innocent; you have brought me into your presence forever" (Ps. 41:12 NLT).

"And the word of the Lord came unto me, saying" (Ezek. 38:1 KJV).

"See, I care about you, and I will pay attention to you. Your ground will be plowed and your crops planted" (Ezek. 36:9 NLT).

"The Lord of Heaven's Armies is here among us; the God of Israel is our fortress" (Ps. 46:11 KJV).

## (Interlude)

"The eyes of the Lord are on the righteous, and his ears are attentive to their cry" (Ps. 34:15 NIV).

"He is before all things, and in him all things hold together" (Col. 1:17 NIV).

"He causes wars to end throughout the earth. He breaks the bow and snaps the spear; he burns the shields with fire" (Ps. 46:9 NLT).

"Therefore thus saith the Lord God; I have lifted up mine hand, Surely the heathen that are about you, they shall bear their shame" (Ezek. 36:7 KJV).

"Gather my saints together unto me; those that have made a covenant with me by sacrifice" (Psalm 50:5 KJV).

"They won't need to cut wood from the fields or forests, for these weapons will give them all the fuel they need. They will plunder those who planned to plunder them, and they will rob those who planned to rob them, says the Sovereign Lord" (Ezek. 39:10 NLT).

"And I will multiply upon you man and beast; and they shall increase and bring fruit: and I will settle you after your old estates, and will do better unto you than at your beginnings: and ye shall know that I am the Lord" (Ezek. 36:11 KJV).

"And this shall be a sign unto thee, Ye shall eat this year such things as grow of themselves, and in the second year that which springeth of the same; and in the third year sow ye, and reap, and plant vineyards, and eat the fruits thereof" (2 Kings 19:29 KJV).

"And in that day shall ye say, Praise the Lord, call upon his name, declare his doings among the people, make mention that his name is exalted" (Isa. 12:4 KJV).

"I will praise thee for ever, because thou hast done it: and will wait on thy name; for it is good before thy saints" (Ps. 52:9 KJV).

"For you are my hiding place; you protect me from trouble. You surround me with songs of victory" (Ps. 32:7 NLT).

## (Interlude)

*In Jesus name, amen.*

## Notes

_____
_____
_____

# God's Provision and Protection

## (Prayer)

"O Lord, God of my salvation, I cry out to you by day. I come to you at night" (Ps. 88:1 NLT).

"Now hear my prayer; listen to my cry" (Ps. 88:2 NLT).

"Turn your ear to listen to me; rescue me quickly. Be my rock of protection, a fortress where I will be safe" (Ps. 31:2 NLT).

"O Lord, I have come to you for protection; don't let me be disgraced. Save me, for you do what is right" (Ps. 31:1 NLT).

"You are my rock and my fortress. For the honor of your name, lead me out of this danger" (Ps. 31:3 NLT).

"Quicken me, O Lord, for thy name's sake: for thy righteousness' sake bring my soul out of trouble" (Ps. 143:11 KJV).

"Pull me from the trap my enemies set for me, for I find protection in you alone" (Ps. 31:4 NLT).

"In your unfailing love, silence all my enemies and destroy all my foes, for I am your servant" (Ps. 143:12 NLT).

"Don't let me be disgraced, O Lord, for I call out to you for help" (Ps. 31:17 NLT).

"Silence their lying lips—those proud and arrogant lips that accuse the godly" (Ps. 31:18 NLT).

"Bring disgrace and destruction on my accusers. Humiliate and shame those who want to harm me" (Ps. 71:12 NLT).

"But I will keep on hoping for your help; I will praise you more and more" (Ps. 71:14 NLT).

"I will remember the deeds of the LORD; yes, I will remember your wonders of old" (Ps. 77:11 NLT).

"I will ponder all your work, and meditate on your mighty deeds" (Ps. 77:12 NLT).

"Then I said, 'I will appeal to this, to the years of the right hand of the Most High'" (Ps. 77:10 ESV).

"O LORD, you know; remember me and visit me, and take vengeance for me on my persecutors. In your forbearance take me not away; know that for your sake I bear reproach" (Jer. 15:15 ESV).

"The word of the LORD came to me. He said" (Ezek. 38:1 ERV).

"The LORD is righteous in all his ways and holy in all his works" (Ps. 1454:17 KJV).

"The LORD is gracious, and full of compassion; slow to anger, and of great mercy" (Ps. 145:8 KJV).

"O God, your ways are holy. Is there any god as mighty as you?" (Ps. 77:13 NLT).

"You are the God of great wonders! You demonstrate your awesome power among the nations" (Ps. 77:14 NLT).

"Then this further message came to me from the LORD" (Ezek. 36:16 NLT).

"O my people, listen to my instructions. Open your ears to what I am saying" (Ps. 78:1 NLT).

"For the mountains shall depart, and the hills be removed; but my kindness shall not depart from thee, neither shall the covenant of my peace be removed, saith the LORD that hath mercy on thee" (Isa. 54:10 KJV).

"For this is as the waters of Noah unto me: for as I have sworn that the waters of Noah should no more go over the earth; so have I sworn that I would not be wroth with thee, nor rebuke thee" (Isa. 54:9 KJV).

"In righteousness shalt thou be established: thou shalt be far from oppression; for thou shalt not fear: and from terror; for it shall not come near thee" (Isa. 54:14 KJV).

"And the work of righteousness shall be peace; and the effect of righteousness quietness and assurance for ever" (Isa. 32:17 KJV).

"And my people shall dwell in a peaceable habitation, and in sure dwellings, and in quiet resting places" (Isa. 32:18 KJV).

"Every valley shall be exalted, and every mountain and hill be made low: and the crooked shall be made straight, and the rough places plain" (Isa. 40:4 KJV).

"When the poor and needy seek water, and there is none, and their tongue faileth of thirst, I the Lord will hear them, I the God of Israel will not forsake them" (Isa. 41:17 KJV).

"For I the Lord thy God will hold thy right hand, saying unto thee, Fear not; I will help thee" (Isa. 41:13 KJV).

"The Lord is on my side; I will not fear: what can man do unto me?" (Ps. 118:6 KJV).

"And now, O Lord God, thou art that God, and thy words be true, and thou hast promised this goodness unto thy servant" (2 Sam. 7:28 KJV).

"Cause me to hear thy lovingkindness in the morning; for in thee do I trust: cause me to know the way wherein I should walk; for I lift up my soul unto thee" (Ps. 143:8 KJV).

"And enter not into judgment with thy servant: for in thy sight shall no man living be justified" (Ps. 143:2 KJV).

*In Jesus name, amen.*

## Notes

_____
_____
_____

# A Solitude Cry for Help

## (Prayer)

"O God, do not be far from me; O my God, come quickly to help me!" (Ps. 71:12 AMP).

"For my enemies have spoken against me; Those who watch for my life have consulted together" (Ps. 71:10 AMP).

"You know my reproach and my shame and my dishonor [how I am insulted]; My adversaries are all before you [each one fully known]" (Ps. 69:19 AMP).

"Unto thee lift I up mine eyes, O thou that dwells in the heavens" (Ps. 123:1 KJV).

"Answer me when I call, O God of my righteousness! You have given me relief when I was in distress. Be gracious to me and hear my prayer!" (Ps. 4:1 ESV).

"Save me, O God! For the waters have come up to my neck" (Ps. 69:1 ESV).

"I am weary with my crying out; my throat is parched. My eyes grow dim with waiting for my God" (Ps. 69:3 ESV).

"O God, you know my folly; the wrongs I have done are not hidden from you" (Ps. 69:5 ESV).

"I am the favorite topic of town gossip, and all the drunks sing about me" (Ps. 69:12 NLT).

"But I keep praying to you, LORD hoping this time you will show me favor" (Ps. 69:13 NLT).

"Don't let floods overwhelm me, or the deep waters swallow me, or the pit of death devour me" (Ps. 69:15 NLT).

"Rescue me from the mud; don't let me sink any deeper! Save me from those who hate me, and pull me from these deep waters" (Ps. 69:14 NLT).

"The ropes of death entangled me; floods of destruction swept over me" (Ps. 18:4 NLT).

"You know of my shame, scorn, and disgrace. You see all that my enemies are doing" (Ps. 69:19 NLT).

"Their insults have broken my heart, and I am in despair. If only one person would show some pity; if only one would turn and comfort me" (Ps. 69:20 NLT).

"Listen to my prayer, O God. Do not ignore my cry for help!" (Ps. 55:1 NLT).

"Please listen and answer me, for I am overwhelmed by my troubles" (Ps. 55:2 NLT).

"Day and night I have only tears for food, while my enemies continually taunt me, saying, "where is this God of yours?" (Ps. 42:3 NLT).

"Why am I discourage? Why is my heart so sad? I will put my hope in God! I will praise him again—my Savior and my God!" (Ps. 42:5 NLT).

"The word of the Lord came to me. He said" (Ezek. 35:1 ERV).

"Praise him for his mighty acts: praise him according to his excellent greatness" (Ps. 150:2 KJV).

"Praise him with the sound of the trumpet: praise him with the psaltery and harp" (Ps. 150:3 KJV).

"Praise him with the timbrel and dance: praise him with stringed instruments and organs" (Ps. 150:4 KJV).

"Praise him upon the loud cymbals: praise him upon the high sounding cymbals" (Ps. 150:5 KJV).

"Let every thing that hath breath praise the Lord. Praise ye the Lord" (Ps. 150:6 KJV).

"For the Lord delights in his people; he crowns the humble with victory" (Ps. 149:4 NLT).

"Give thanks to the Lord and proclaim his greatness. Let the whole world know what he has done" (1 Chron. 16:8 NLT).

## PRAY IN GOD'S WORD FOR ENCOURAGEMENT AND CHANGE

"Let the faithful rejoice that he honors them. Let them sing for joy as they lie on their beds" (Ps. 149:5 NLT).

"God, I praise you forever for what you have done. I will speak your name before your followers because it is so good!" (Ps. 52:9 ERV).

"How great is our Lord! His power is absolute! His understanding is beyond comprehension!" (Ps. 147:5 NLT).

"He takes no pleasure in the strength of a horse or in human might" (Ps. 147:10 NLT).

"No, the Lord's delight is in those who fear him, those who put their hope in his unfailing love" (Ps. 147:11 NLT).

"How precious also are thy thoughts unto me, O God! how great is the sum of them!" (Ps. 139:17 KJV).

"It is like the precious ointment upon the head, that ran down upon the beard, even Aaron's beard: that went down to the skirts of his garments" (Ps. 133:2 KJV).

"As the dew of Hermon, and as the dew that descended upon the mountains of Zion: for there the Lord commanded the blessing, even life for evermore" (Ps. 133:3 KJV).

"My soul shall be satisfied as with marrow and fatness; and my mouth shall praise thee with joyful lips" (Ps. 63:5 KJV).

"O death, where is thy sting? O grave, where is thy victory?" (1 Cor. 15:55 KJV).

"For our light affliction, which is but for a moment, worketh for us a far more exceeding and eternal weight of glory" (2 Cor. 4:17 KJV).

"But thanks be to God, which giveth us the victory through our Lord Jesus Christ" (1 Cor. 15:57 KJV).

"Thus will I bless thee while I live: I will lift up my hands in thy name" (Ps. 63:4 KJV).

"In Your righteousness deliver me and rescue me; Incline Your ear to me and save me" (Ps. 71:2 AMP).

"Answer my prayers, O Lord, for your unfailing love is wonderful. Take care of me, for your mercy is so plentiful" (Ps. 69:16 NLT).

*In Jesus name, amen.*

# CRAIG WILLIAMS

# Notes

# The Lord Is Our Intercessor

## (Prayer)

"Who is he that condemneth? It is Christ that died, yea rather, that is risen again, who is even at the right hand of God, who also maketh intercession for us" (Rom. 8:34 KJV).

"The Lord is my light and my salvation—so why should I be afraid? The Lord is my fortress, protecting me from danger, so why should I tremble?" (Ps. 27:1 NLT).

"Rescue me from my enemies, O God. Protect me from those who have come to destroy me" (Ps. 59:1 NLT).

"They have set an ambush for me. Fierce enemies are out there waiting, Lord, though I have not sinned or offend them" (Ps. 59:3 NLT).

"I have done nothing wrong, yet they prepare to attack me. Wake up! See what is happening and help me!" (Ps. 59:4 NLT).

"Listen to the filth that comes from their mouths; their words cut like swords. "After all, who can hear us?" they sneer" (Ps. 59:7 NLT).

"I am only a foreigner in the land. Don't hide your commands from me!" (Ps. 119:19 NLT).

"But this is what the Lord says: I would no more reject my people than I would change my laws that govern night and day, earth and sky" (Jer. 33:25 NLT).

"For the mountains shall depart, and the hills be removed; but my kindness shall not depart from thee, neither shall the covenant of my peace be removed, saith the Lord that hath mercy on thee" (Isa. 54:10 KJV).

"For this is what the Sovereign Lord says: I myself will search and find my sheep" (Ezek. 34:11 NLT).

"If the Spirit of him who raised Jesus from the dead dwells in you, he who raised Christ Jesus from the dead will also give life to your mortal bodies through his Spirit who dwells in you" (Rom. 8:11 ESV).

"I have set the Lord always before me; because he is at my right hand, I shall not be shaken" (Ps. 16:8 ESV).

"God has spoken in his Temple: 'I will win the war and rejoice in victory! I will divide this land among my people. I will give them Shecham. I will give them Succoth Valley'" (Ps. 60:6 ERV).

"Likewise the Spirit helps us in our weakness. For we do not know what to pray for as we ought, but the Spirit himself intercedes for us with groanings too deep for words" (Rom. 8:26 ESV).

"Do not be afraid of them, for I am with you to deliver you, declares the Lord." (Jer. 1:8 ESV).

"No weapon that is fashioned against you shall succeed, and you shall refute every tongue that rises against you in judgment. This is the heritage of the servants of the Lord and their vindication from me, declares the Lord" (Isa. 54:17 ESV).

"You will live in joy and peace. The mountains and hills will burst into song, and the trees of the field will clap their hands!" (Isa. 55:12 NLT).

"And ye shall eat in plenty, and be satisfied, and praise the name of the Lord your God, that hath dealt wondrously with you: and my people shall never be ashamed" (Joel 2:26 KJV).

"Where once there were thorns, cypress trees will grow. Where nettles grew, myrtles will sprout up. These events will bring great honor to the Lord's name; they will be an everlasting sign of his power and love" (Isa. 55:13 NLT).

"So shall my word be that goeth forth out of my mouth: it shall not return unto me void, but it shall accomplish that which I please, and it shall prosper in the thing whereto I sent it" (Isa. 55:11 KJV).

"Ye are blessed of the LORD which made heaven and earth" (Ps. 115:15 KJV).

"Make me to know your ways, O LORD; teach me your paths" (Ps. 25:4 ESV).

"Then the word of the LORD came to me, saying" (Jer. 18:5 KJV).

"He that hath clean hands, and a pure heart; who hath not lifted up his soul unto vanity, nor sworn deceitfully" (Ps. 24:4 KJV).

"I prayed to the LORD my God and made confession, saying, "O Lord, the great and awesome God, who keeps covenant and steadfast love with those who love him and keep his commandments" (Dan. 9:4 ESV).

"O Lord, hear; O Lord, forgive. O Lord, pay attention and act. Delay not, for your own sake, O my God, because your city and your people are called by your name." (Dan. 9:19 ESV).

"You are a hiding place for me; you preserve me from trouble; you surround me with shouts of deliverance" (Ps. 32:7 ESV). *Selah.*

"Arise, O LORD; O God, lift up your hand; forget not the afflicted" (Ps. 10:12 ESV).

"In pride and arrogance the wicked hotly pursue and persecute the afflicted; Let them be caught in the plots which they have devised" (Ps. 10:2 AMP).

"Be gracious to me, O God, be gracious and merciful to me, For my soul finds shelter and safety in You, And in the shadow of your wings I will take refuge and be confidently secure Until destruction passes by" (Ps. 57:1 AMP).

"For there is one God, and one mediator between God and men, the man Christ Jesus" (1 Tim. 2:5 KJV).

"And now, O LORD, for what do I wait? My hope is in you" (Ps. 39:7 ESV).

"Deliver me from all my transgressions. Do not make me the scorn of the fool!" (Ps. 39:8 ESV).

"You are my strength; I wait for you to rescue me, for you, O God, are my fortress" (Ps. 59:9 NLT).

"Yes, joyful are those who live like this! Joyful indeed are those whose God is the LORD" (Ps. 144:15 NLT).

"In his unfailing love, my God will stand with me. He will let me look down in triumph on all my enemies" (Ps. 59:10 NLT).

*In Jesus name, amen.*

## Notes

_____
_____
_____

# God's Protection for His Servants

## (Prayer)

"Hear my cry, O God; attend unto my prayer" (Ps. 61:1 KJV).

"Hear my voice, O God, in my prayer: preserve my life from fear of the enemy" (Ps. 64:1 KJV).

"Hide me from the secret counsel of the wicked; from the insurrection of the workers of iniquity" (Ps. 64:2 KJV).

"For thou hast been a shelter for me, and a strong tower from the enemy" (Ps. 61:3 KJV).

"Behold, God is my salvation; I will trust, and not be afraid: for the Lord Jehovah is my strength and my song; he also is become my salvation" (Isa. 12:2 KJV).

"He gives power to the weak and strength to the powerless" (Isa. 40:29 NLT).

"Have respect therefore to the prayer of thy servant, and to his supplication, O Lord my God, to hearken unto the cry and the prayer which thy servant prayeth before thee" (2 Chron. 6:19 KJV).

"Thus says the Lord God: 'It shall not stand, and it shall not come to pass'" (Isa. 7:7 ESV).

"Who has done such mighty deeds, summoning each new generation from the beginning of time? It is I, the Lord, the First and the Last. I alone am he" (Isa. 41:4 NLT).

"Yes, I will certainly keep you safe from these wicked men. I will rescue you from their cruel hands" (Jer. 15:21 NLT).

"For by me thy days shall be multiplied, and the years of thy life shall be increased" (Prov. 9:11 KJV).

"Be not afraid of sudden fear, neither of the desolation of the wicked, when it cometh" (Prov. 3:25 KJV).

"The Lord will not suffer the soul of the righteous to famish: but he casteth away the substance of the wicked" (Prov. 10:3 KJV).

"For the Lord shall be thy confidence, and shall keep thy foot from being taken" (Prov. 3:26 KJV).

"I will give to the Lord the thanks due to his righteousness, and I will sing praise to the name of the Lord, the Most High" (Ps. 7:17 ESV).

"He only is my rock and my salvation: he is my defense; I shall not be moved" (Ps. 62:6 KJV).

"Lord, you alone are my inheritance, my cup of blessing. You guard all that is mine" (Ps. 16:5 NLT).

"A single day in your courts is better than a thousand anywhere else! I would rather be a gatekeeper in the house of my God than live the good life in the homes of the wicked" (Ps. 84:10 NLT).

"For the Lord God is a sun and shield: the Lord will give grace and glory: no good thing will he withhold from them that walk uprightly" (Ps. 84:11 KJV).

"Because thou hast been my help, therefore in the shadow of thy wings will I rejoice" (Ps. 63:10 KJV).

"My soul followeth hard after thee: thy right hand upholdeth me" (Ps. 63:8 KJV).

"But those that seek my soul, to destroy it, shall go into the lower parts of the earth" (Ps. 63:9 KJV).

"O my God, make them like a wheel; as the stubble before the wind" (Ps. 83:13 KJV).

"Let their eyes go blind so they cannot see, and let their backs be bent forever" (Rom. 11:10 NLT).

"Rise up, O God, and scatter your enemies. Let those who hate God run for their lives" (Ps. 68:1 NLT).

"But let the godly rejoice. Let them be glad in God's presence. Let them be filled with joy" (Ps. 68:3 NLT).

"Do not stay so far from me, for trouble is near, and no one else can help me" (Ps. 22:11 NLT).

"My enemies surround me like a pack of dogs; an evil gang closes in on me. They have pierced my hands and feet" (Ps. 22:16 NLT).

"Like lions they open their jaws against me, roaring and tearing into their prey" (Ps. 22:13 NLT).

"Lord, how long wilt thou look on? rescue my soul from their destructions, my darling from the lions" (Ps. 35:17 KJV).

"Save me from the sword; spare my precious life from these dogs" (Ps. 22:20 NLT).

"Turn away my reproach which I dread, For Your ordinances are good" (Ps. 119:39 AMP).

"Thus saith the Lord Jehovah, It shall not stand, neither shall it come to pass" (Isa. 7:7 ASV).

"There shall no evil happen to the just: but the wicked shall be filled with mischief" (Prov. 12:21 KJV).

"All the horns of the wicked also will I cut off; but the horns of the righteous shall be exalted" (Ps. 75:10 KJV).

"That thy foot may be dipped in the blood of thine enemies, and the tongue of thy dogs in the same" (Ps. 68:23 KJV).

"Yes, the Lord is for me; he will help me. I will look in triumph at those who hate me" (Ps. 118:7 NLT).

He will send help from heaven to rescue me, disgracing those who hound me.

## (Interlude)

"My God will send forth his unfailing love and faithfulness" (Ps. 57:3 NLT).

"Do not let those gloat over me who are my enemies without cause; do not let those who hate me without reason maliciously wink the eye" (Ps. 35:19 NIV).

"Do not let them think, 'Aha, just what we wanted!' or say, 'We have swallowed him up'" (Ps. 35:25 NIV).

"Let their table become a snare before them: and that which should have been for their welfare, let it become a trap" (Ps. 69:22 KJV).

"Let their eyes be dimmed so that they cannot see, And make their loins shake continually [in terror and weakness]" (Ps. 69:23 AMP).

"Pour out Your indignation on them, And let [the fierceness of] Your burning anger overtake them" (Ps. 69:24 AMP).

"Let their habitation be desolate; and let none dwell in their tents" (Ps. 69:25 KJV).

"For they persecute him whom thou hast smitten; and they talk to the grief of those whom thou hast wounded" (Ps. 69:26 KJV).

"Add [unforgiven] iniquity to their iniquity [in Your book], And may they not come into Your righteousness" (Ps. 69:27 AMP).

"May all who gloat over my distress be put to shame and confusion; may all who exalt themselves over me be clothed with shame and disgrace" (Ps. 35:26 NIV).

"I wait quietly before God, for my victory comes from him" (Ps. 62:1 NLT).

"He alone is my rock and my salvation, my fortress where I will never be shaken" (Ps. 62:2 NLT).

*In Jesus name, amen.*

## Notes

_____
_____
_____

# Reflections

# Desperation

## (Prayer)

"Listen to my prayer, O God. Do not ignore my cry for help!" (Ps. 55:1 NLT).

"Please listen and answer me, for I am overwhelmed by my troubles" (Ps. 55:2 NLT).

"Let the day of my birth be erased, and the night I was conceived" (Job 3:3 NLT).

"As for that night, let darkness seize it; Let it not rejoice among the days of the year; Let it not be counted in the number of the months" (Job 3:6 AMP).

"Because it did not shut the doors of my mother's womb, Nor hide trouble from my eyes" (Job 3:10 AMP).

"Why is the light of day given to a man whose way is hidden, And whom God has hedged in?" (Job 3:23 AMP).

"For the thing which I greatly fear comes upon me, And that of which I am afraid has come upon me" (Job 3:25 AMP).

"For all the day long have I been stricken, And punished every morning" (Ps. 73:14 AMP).

"Upon You have I relied and been sustained from my birth; You are He who took me from my mother's womb and You have been my benefactor from that day. My praise is continually of You" (Ps. 71:6 AMP).

"Your righteousness, O God, reaches to the [heights of the] heavens, You who have done great things; O God, who is like You, [who is your equal]?" (Ps. 71:19 AMP).

"But I am poor and needy: make haste unto me, O God: thou art my help and my deliverer; O Lord, make no tarrying" (Ps. 70:5 KJV).

"For you have heard my vows, O God. You have given me an inheritance reserved for those who fear your name" (Ps. 61:5 NLT).

"Give ear to my words, O Lord, consider my meditation" (Ps. 5:1 KJV).

"I know that You can do all things, And that no thought or purpose of Yours can be restrained" (Job 42:2 AMP).

"'Hear, please, and I will speak; I will ask You, and You instruct [and answer] me'" (Job 42:4 AMP).

"I have heard of thee by the hearing of the ear: but now mine eye seeth thee" (Job 42:5 KJV).

"Hearken unto the voice of my cry, my King, and my God: for unto thee will I pray" (Ps. 5:2 KJV).

"Have respect therefore to the prayer of thy servant, and to his supplication, O Lord my God, to hearken unto the cry and the prayer which thy servant prayeth before thee" (2 Chron. 6:19 KJV).

"Thine, O Lord, is the greatness, and the power, and the glory, and the victory, and the majesty: for all that is in the heaven and in the earth is thine; thine is the Kingdom, O Lord, and thou art exalted as head above all" (1 Chron. 29:11 KJV).

"Both riches and honour come of thee, and thou reignest over all; and in thine hand is power and might; and in thine hand it is to make great, and to give strength unto all" (1 Chron. 29:12 KJV).

"Withhold not good from them to whom it is due, when it is in the power of thine hand to do it" (Prov. 3:27 KJV).

"Then the word of the Lord came to me" (Jer. 13:8 ESV).

"I will deliver you out of the hand of the wicked, and redeem you from the grasp of the ruthless." (Jer. 15:21).

"'For I know the plans and thoughts that I have for you,' says the Lord, 'plans for peace and well-being and not for disaster to give you a future and a hope'" (Jer. 29:11 AMP).

"Then you will call on me and you will come and pray to Me, and I will hear [your voice] and I will listen to you" (Jer. 29:12 AMP).

"Therefore I say unto you, what things soever ye desire, when ye pray, believe that ye receive them, and ye shall have them" (Mark 11:24 KJV).

"Honour the LORD with your wealth And with the first fruits of all your crops (income)" (Prov. 3:9 AMP).

"Then your barns will be abundantly filled And your vats will overflow with new wine" (Prov. 3:10 KJV).

"Study this book of instruction continually. Meditate on it day and night so you will be sure to obey everything written in it. Only then will you prosper and succeed in all you do" (Josh. 1:8 NLT).

"Blessed [fortunate, prosperous, and favored by God] is the man who makes the LORD his trust, And does not regard the proud nor those who lapse into lies" (Ps. 40:4 AMP).

"And he shall be like a tree planted by the rivers of water, that bringeth forth his fruit in his season; his leaf also shall not wither; and whatsoever he doeth shall prosper" (Ps. 1:3 KJV).

"The LORD will guide you continually, giving you water when you are dry and restoring your strength. You will be like a well-watered garden, like an ever-flowing spring" (Isa. 58:11 NLT).

"Therefore with joy shall ye draw water out of the wells of salvation" (Isa. 12:3 KJV).

"Knowing that of the LORD ye shall receive the reward of the inheritance: for ye serve the LORD Christ" (Col. 3:24 KJV).

"Cast not away therefore your confidence which hath great recompense of reward" (Heb. 10:35 KJV).

"I delight to do Your will, O my God; Your law is within my heart" (Ps. 40:8 AMP).

"He has made everything beautiful in its time. He has also set eternity in the human heart; yet no one can fathom what God has done from beginning to end" (Eccles. 3:11 NIV).

"Let the people praise thee, O God; Let all the people praise thee" (Ps. 67:5 KJV).

"Then shall the earth yield her increase; And God, even our own God, shall bless us" (Ps. 67:6 KJV).

"That our garners may be full, affording all manner of store: that our sheep may bring forth thousands and ten thousands in our streets" (Ps. 144:13 KJV).

"And May our oxen be loaded down with produce. May there be no enemy breaking through our walls, no going into captivity, no cries of alarm in our town squares" (Ps. 144:14 NLT).

"Let my vindication come from you; may your eyes see what is right" (Ps. 17:2 NIV).

"When my heart was grieved and my spirit embittered" (Ps. 73:21 NIV).

"I was senseless and ignorant; I was a brute beast before you" (Ps. 73:22 NIV).

"Yet I am always with you; you hold me by my right hand" (Ps. 73:23 NIV).

"Being fully persuaded that God had power to do what he had promised" (Rom. 4:21 NIV).

"I will praise you as long as I live, and in your name I will lift up my hands" (Ps. 63:4 NIV).

"I cling to you; your right hand upholds me" (Ps. 63:8 NIV).

"My soul [my life, my very self] clings to You; Your right hand upholds me" (Ps. 63:8 AMP).

"For You have been my help. And in the shadow of Your wings [where I am always protected] I sing for joy" (Ps. 63:7 AMP).

"But those who seek my life to destroy it will [be destroyed and] go into the depths of the earth [into the underworld]" (Ps. 63:9 AMP).

"They will be given over to the power of the sword; They will be a prey for foxes" (Ps. 63:10 AMP).

"There are the workers of iniquity fallen: they are cast down, and shall not be able to rise" (Ps. 36:12 KJV).

"For you have rescued me from my troubles and helped me triumph over my enemies" (Ps. 54:7 NLT).

*In Jesus name, amen.*

CRAIG WILLIAMS

# Notes

# Supplication for God's Help against Attackers

## (Prayer)

"Bend down, O Lord, and hear my prayer; answer me, for I need your help" (Ps. 86:1 NLT).

"Bless be the Lord, who bears our burden day by day, The God who is our salvation!" (Ps. 68:19 AMP). *Selah.*

"Lord, hear my voice: let thine ears be attentive to the voice of my supplications" (Ps. 130:2 KJV).

"Be good to your servant, that I may live and obey your word" (Ps. 119:17 NLT).

"As I learn your righteous regulations, I will thank you by living as I should!" (Ps. 119:7 NLT).

"Then this message came to me from the Lord" (Ezek. 7:1 NLT).

"Unto the upright there ariseth light in the darkness: he is gracious, and full of compassion, and righteous" (Ps. 112:4 KJV).

"Joyful are people of integrity, who follow the instructions of the Lord" (Ps. 119:1 NLT).

"Joyful are those who obey his laws and search for him with all their hearts" (Ps. 119:2 NLT).

"Save us, O Lord our God, and gather us from among the heathen, to give thanks unto thy holy name, and to triumph in thy praise" (Ps. 106:47 KJV).

"Do not abhor us, for thy name's sake, do not disgrace the throne of thy glory: remember, break not thy covenant with us" (Jer. 14:21 KJV).

"Teach me your decrees, O Lord; I will keep them to the end" (Ps. 119:33 NLT).

"For the zeal of thine house hath eaten me up; and the reproaches of them that reproached thee are fallen upon me" (Ps. 69:9 KJV).

"Be thou my strong habitation, whereunto I may continually resort: thou hast given commandment to save me; for thou art my rock and my fortress" (Ps. 71:3 KJV).

"Listen to my prayer, O God. Do not ignore my cry for help!" (Ps. 55:1 NLT).

"Please listen and answer me, for I am overwhelmed by my troubles" (Ps. 55:2 NLT).

"My enemies shout at me, making loud and wicked threats. They bring trouble on me and angrily hunt me down" (Ps. 55:3 NLT).

"Take hold of shield and buckler, and stand up for mine help" (Ps. 35:2 KJV).

"Draw out also the spear, and stop the way against them that persecute me: say unto my soul, I am thy salvation" (Ps. 55:3 KJV).

"They are always twisting what I say; they spend their days plotting to harm me" (Ps. 56:5 NLT).

"Please, Lord, prove that your power is as great as you have claimed. For you said" (Num. 14:17 NLT).

"To the faithful you show yourself faithful; to those with integrity you show integrity" (Ps. 18:25 NLT).

"To the pure you show yourself pure, but to the crooked you show yourself shrewd" (Ps. 18:26 NLT).

"And the Lord said, I have pardoned according to thy word" (Num. 14:20 KJV).

"Then this message came to me from the Lord" (Ezek. 11:14 NLT).

"The Lord has taken away the judgments against you; he has cleared away your enemies. The King of Israel, the Lord, is in your midst; you shall never again fear evil" (Zeph. 3:15 ESV).

"I will give thanks to the Lord with my whole heart; I will recount all of your wonderful deeds" (Ps. 9:1 ESV).

"Thou hast also given me the shield of thy salvation: and thy gentleness hath made me great" (2 Sam. 22:36 KJV).

"For you have maintained my just cause; you have sat on the throne, giving righteous judgment" (Ps. 9:4 ESV).

"You went out to rescue your chosen people, to save your anointed ones. You crushed the heads of the wicked and stripped their bones from head to toe" (Hab. 3:13 NLT).

"He delivered me from mine enemies: yea, thou liftest me up above those that rise up against me: thou hast delivered me from the violent man" (Ps. 18:48 KJV).

"Endless ruin has overtaken my enemies, you have uprooted their cities; even the memory of them has perished" (Ps. 9:6 NIV).

"This shall be their lot in return for their pride, because they taunted and boasted against the people of the Lord of hosts" (Zeph. 2:10 ESV).

"As for God, his way is perfect; the word of the Lord is tried: he is a buckler to all them that trust in him" (2 Sam. 22:31 KJV).

"Blessed be God, which hath not turned away my prayer, nor his mercy from me" (Ps. 66:19 KJV).

*In Jesus name, amen.*

## Notes

_____
_____
_____

# Assurance from God

## (Prayer)

"I will proclaim the name of the Lord; how glorious is our God!" (Deut. 32:3 NLT).

"Let the heavens be glad, and let the earth rejoice, and let them say among the nations, "The Lord reigns!" (1 Chron. 16:31 ESV).

"Hear me, O Lord, and listen to the voice of my adversaries" (Jer. 18:19 ESV).

"For mine enemies speak against me; and they that lay wait for my soul take counsel together" (Ps. 71:10 KJV).

"Their mouths are full of cursing, lies, and threats. Trouble and evil are on the tips of their tongues" (Ps. 10:7 NLT).

"Heartless, unappeasable, slanderous, without self-control, brutal, not loving good" (2 Tim. 3:3 ESV).

"Treacherous, reckless, swollen with conceit, lovers of pleasure rather than lovers of God" (2 Tim. 3:4 ESV).

"Saying, God hath forsake him: persecute and take him; for there is none to deliver him" (Ps. 71:11 KJV).

"Professing themselves to be wise, they became fools" (Rom. 1:22 KJV).

"They repay me evil for good, and hatred for my friendship" (Ps. 109:5 NIV).

"Therefore deliver up their children to famine; give them over to the power of the sword; let their wives become childless and wid-

## PRAY IN GOD'S WORD FOR ENCOURAGEMENT AND CHANGE

owed. May their men meet death by pestilence, their youths be struck down by the sword in battle" (Jer. 18:21 ESV).

"May a cry be heard from their houses, when you bring the plunderer suddenly upon them! For they have dug a pit to take me and laid snares for my feet" (Jer. 18:22 ESV).

"Then this message came to me from the LORD" (Ezek. 11:14 NLT).

"They will fight against you, but they shall not prevail against you, for I am with you, declares the LORD, to deliver you" (Jer. 1:19 ESV).

"'No weapon that is formed against you will succeed; And every tongue that rises against you in judgment you will condemn. This [peace, righteousness, security, and triumph over opposition] is the heritage of the servants of the LORD, and this is their vindication from Me,' says the LORD" (Isa. 54:17 AMP).

"Take good heed therefore unto yourselves, that ye love the LORD your God" (Josh. 23:11 KJV).

"I love them that love me; and those that seek me early shall find me" (Prov. 8:17 KJV).

"That I may cause those that love me to inherit substance; and will fill their treasures" (Prov. 8:21 KJV).

"Riches and honour are with me; yea durable riches and righteousness" (Prov. 8:18 KJV).

"'"Behold, I am the LORD, the God of all flesh. Is anything too hard for me?" (Jer. 32:27 ESV).

"Ah Lord LORD! behold, thou hast made the heaven and the earth by thy great power and stretched out arm, and there is nothing too hard for thee" (Jer. 32:17 KJV).

"Blessed is the one whose sin the Lord will never count against them." (Rom. 4:8 NIV).

"Again a message came to me from the LORD" (Ezek. 12:1 NLT).

"Through him we have also obtained access by faith into this grace in which we stand, and we rejoice in hope of the glory of God" (Rom. 5:2 ESV).

"And hope does not put us to shame, because God's love has been poured into our hearts through the Holy Spirit who has been given to us" (Rom. 5:5 ESV).

"Therefore being justified by faith, we have peace with God through our Lord Jesus Christ" (Rom. 5:1 KJV).

"Like your name, O God, your praise reaches to the ends of the earth; your right hand is filled with righteousness" (Ps. 48:10 NIV).

"Blessed be the Lord God, the God of Israel, who only doeth wondrous things" (Ps. 72:18 KJV).

"For all the promises of God in him are yea, and in him Amen, unto the glory of God by us" (2 Cor. 1:20 KJV).

"You are the God who performs miracles; you display your power among the peoples" (Ps. 77:14 NIV).

"For he satisfies the thirsty and fills the hungry with good things" (Ps. 107:9 NIV).

"For every child of God defeats this evil world, and we achieve this victory through our faith" (1 John 5:4 NLT).

"Remember your word to your servant, for you have given me hope" (Ps. 119:49 NIV).

*In Jesus name, amen.*

## Notes

_____
_____
_____

# Lord, Rescue Me

## (Prayer)

"My God, my God, why have you abandoned me? why are you so far away when I groan for help?" (Ps. 22:1 NLT).

"Why standest thou afar off, O Lord? why hidest thou thyself in times of trouble" (Ps. 10:1 KJV).

"Every day I called to you, my God, but you do not answer. Every night you hear my voice, but I find no relief" (Ps. 22:2 NLT).

"How long wilt thou forget me, O Lord? for ever? How long wilt thou hide thy face from me?" (Ps. 13:1 KJV).

"How long shall I take counsel in my soul, having sorrow in my heart daily? how long shall mine enemy be exalted over me?" (Ps. 13:2 KJV).

"Be not far from me; for trouble is near; for there is none to help" (Ps. 22:11 KJV).

"I am scorned by all my enemies and despised by my neighbors-even my friends are afraid to come near me. When they see me on the street, they run the other way" (Ps. 31:11 NLT).

"Like lions they open their jaws against me, roaring and tearing into their prey" (Ps. 22:13 KJV).

"My life is poured out like water, and all my bones are out of joint. My heart is like wax, melting within me" (Ps. 22:14 KJV).

"My strength has dried up like sunbaked clay. My tongue sticks to the roof of my mouth. You have laid me in the dust and left me for dead" (Ps. 22:15 KJV).

"My future is in your hands. Rescue me from those who hunt me down relentlessly" (Ps. 31:15 NLT).

"Have mercy on me, Lord, for I am in distress. Tears blur my eyes. My body and soul are withering away" (Ps. 31:9 NLT).

"Because of the voice of the enemy, because of the oppression of the wicked: for they cast iniquity upon me, and in wrath they hate me" (Ps. 55:3 KJV).

"So many are saying, "God will never rescue him!" (Ps. 3:2 NLT).

## (Interlude)

"Fearfulness and trembling are come upon me, and horror hath overwhelmed me" (Ps. 55:5 KJV).

"But I will keep on hoping for your help; I will praise you more and more" (Ps. 71:14 NLT).

"For thou art the God of my strength: why dost thou cast me off? Why go I mourning because of the oppression of the enemy?" (Ps. 43:2 KJV).

"I will say unto God my rock, why hast thou forgotten me? Why go I mourning because of the oppression of the enemy?" (Ps. 42:9 KJV).

"I am sick at heart. How long, O Lord, until you restore me?" (Ps. 6:3 NLT).

"Remove thy stroke away from me: I am consumed by the blow of thine hand" (Ps. 39:10 KJV).

"You have allowed me to suffer much hardship, but you will restore me to life again and lift me up from the depths of the earth" (Ps. 71:20 NLT).

"I come to you for protection, O Lord my God. Save me from my persecutors-rescue me!" (Ps. 7:1 NLT).

"Save me and rescue me, for you do what is right. Turn your ear to listen to me, and set me free" (Ps. 71:2 NLT).

"Please, Lord, rescue me! Come quickly, Lord, and help me" (Ps. 40:13 NLT).

## PRAY IN GOD'S WORD FOR ENCOURAGEMENT AND CHANGE

"Protect me! Rescue my life from them! Do not let me be disgraced, for in you I take refuge" (Ps. 25:20 NLT).

"Return, O Lord, and rescue me. Save me because of your unfailing love" (Ps. 6:4 NLT).

"My God, rescue me from the power of the wicked, from the clutches of cruel oppressors" (Ps. 71:4 NLT).

"O God, don't stay away. My God, please hurry to help me" (Ps. 71:12 NLT).

"Consider and hear me, O Lord my God: lighten mine eyes, lest I sleep the sleep of death" (Ps. 13:3 KJV).

"O Lord, all my longing is before you; my sighing is not hidden from you" (Ps. 38:9 ESV).

"Arise, O Lord! Rescue me, my God! Slap all my enemies in the face! Shatter the teeth of the wicked!" (Ps. 3:7 NLT).

"Don't let the proud trample me or the wicked push me around" (Ps. 36:11 NLT).

"Unto thee, O Lord, do I lift up my soul" (Ps. 25:1 KJV).

"O Lord, I will honor and praise your name, for you are my God. You do such wonderful things! You planned them long ago, and now you have accomplished them" (Isa. 25:1 NLT).

"You will restore me to even greater honor and comfort me once again" (Ps. 71:21 NLT).

"I will bless the Lord, who hath given me counsel: my reins also instruct me in the night seasons" (Ps. 16:7 KJV).

"I know the Lord is always with me. I will not be shaken, for he is right beside me" (Ps. 16:8 NLT).

"Therefore my heart is glad, and my glory rejoiceth: my flesh also shall rest in hope" (Ps. 16:9 KJV).

"For you have rescued me from my troubles and helped me triumph over my enemies" (Ps. 54:7 NLT).

"I will tell about your righteous deeds all day long, for everyone who tried to hurt me has been shamed and humiliated" (Ps. 71:24 NLT).

*In Jesus name, amen.*

## Notes

# God's Sheltered Protection and Promises

## (Prayer)

"The Lord is my light and my salvation; whom shall I fear? The Lord is the strength of my life; of whom shall I be afraid?" (Ps. 27:1 KJV).

"The godly are showered with blessings; the words of the wicked conceal violent intentions" (Prov. 10:6 NLT).

"The wicked arrogantly hunt down the poor. Let them be caught in the evil they plan for others" (Ps. 10:2 NLT).

"For they brag about their evil desires; they praise the greedy and curse the Lord" (Ps. 10:3 NLT).

"They think, "Nothing bad will ever happen to us! We will be free of trouble forever!" (Ps. 10:6 NLT).

"Lord, you have heard the vile names they call me. You know all about the plans they have made" (Lam. 3:61 NLT).

"You have seen the wrong they have done to me, Lord. Be my judge, and prove me right" (Lam. 3:59 NLT).

"Arise, O Lord! Punish the wicked, O God! Do not ignore the helpless!" (Ps. 10:12 NLT).

"Your unfailing love is better than life itself; how I praise you!" (Ps. 63:3 NLT).

"What joy for those you choose to bring near, those who live in your holy courts. What festivities await us inside your holy Temple (Ps. 65:4 NLT).

"Therefore say unto them, Thus saith the Lord God; there shall none of my words be prolonged any more, but the word which I have spoken shall be done, saith the Lord God" (Ezek. 12:28 KJV).

"It is better to take refuge in the LORD than to trust in people" (Ps. 118:8 NLT).

"The Lord gives the word, and a great army brings the good news" (Ps. 68:11 NLT).

"Come and see what our God has done, what awesome miracles he performs for people!" (Ps. 66:5 NLT).

"And he has identified us as his own by placing the Holy Spirit in our hearts as the first installment that guarantees everything he has promised us" (2 Cor. 1:22 NLT).

"The word of the LORD also came to me, saying" (Ezek. 12:1 KJV).

"For he will rescue you from every trap and protect you from deadly disease" (Ps. 91:3 NLT).

"He will cover you with his feathers. He will shelter you with his wings. His faithful promises are your armor and protection" (Ps. 91:4 NLT).

"You will not fear the terror of night, nor the arrow that flies by day" (Ps. 91:5 NIV).

"Nor the pestilence that stalks in the darkness, nor the plague that destroys at midday" (Ps. 91:6 NIV).

"A thousand shall fall at thy side, and ten thousand at thy right hand; but it shall not come nigh thee" (Ps. 91:7 KJV).

"Only with thine eyes shalt thou behold and see the reward of the wicked" (Ps. 91:8 KJV).

"I will take revenge; I will pay them back. In due time their feet will slip. Their day of disaster will arrive, and their destiny will overtake them" (Deut. 32:35 NLT).

"For this I will praise you, O LORD, among the nations, and sing to your name" (Ps. 18:49 ESV).

## PRAY IN GOD'S WORD FOR ENCOURAGEMENT AND CHANGE

"Your promises revive me; it comforts me in all my troubles" (Ps. 119:50 NLT).

"As soon as I pray, you answer me; you encourage me by giving me strength" (Ps. 138:3 NLT).

"You faithfully answer our prayers with awesome deeds, O God our savior. You are the hope of everyone on earth, even those who sail on distant seas" (Ps. 65:5 NLT).

"Though we are overwhelmed by our sins, you forgive them all" (Ps. 65:3 NLT).

"Oh, that my actions would consistently reflect your decrees!" (Ps. 119:5 NLT).

"Then I will not be ashamed when I compare my life with your commands" (Ps. 119:6 NLT).

"I will keep on obeying your instructions forever and ever" (Ps. 119:44 NLT).

"And the word of the LORD came unto me, saying" (Ezek. 12:21 KJV).

"There is joy for those who deal justly with others and always do what is right" (Ps. 106:3 NLT).

"Thus saith the LORD, As the new wine is found in the cluster, and one saith, Destroy it not; for a blessing is in it: so will I do for my servants' sakes, that I may not destroy them all" (Isa. 65:8 KJV).

"Because he hath set his love upon me, therefore will I deliver him: I will set him on high, because he hath known my name" (Ps. 91:14 KJV).

"He shall call upon me, and I will answer him: I will be with him in trouble; I will deliver him, and honor him" (Ps. 91:15 KJV).

"With long life will I satisfy him, and shew him my salvation" (Ps. 91:16 KJV).

"Thy testimonies that thou hast commanded are righteous and very faithful" (Ps. 119:138 KJV).

"Therefore my heart is glad, and my glory rejoiceth: my flesh also shall rest in hope" (Ps. 16:9 KJV).

"Thy vows are upon me, O God: I will render praises unto thee" (Ps. 56:12 KJV).

"O Lord my God, I cried unto thee, and thou hast healed me" (Ps. 30:2 KJV).

"I will extol thee, O Lord; for thou hast lifted me up, and hast not made my foes to rejoice over me" (Ps. 30:1 KJV).

"O Lord, thou hast brought up my soul from the grave: thou hast kept me alive, that I should not go down to the pit" (Ps. 30:3 KJV).

"Let my soul live and praise you, and let your rules help me" (Ps. 119:175 ESV).

"For the scriptures saith, Whosoever believeth on him shall not be ashamed" (Rom. 10:11 KJV).

"Thou wilt shew me the path of life: in thy presence is fulness of joy; at thy right hand there are pleasures for evermore" (Ps. 16:11 KJV).

"Moreover the word of the Lord came to me, saying" (Ezek. 12:17 KJV).

"And I give unto them eternal life; and they shall never perish, neither shall any man pluck them out of my hand" (John 10:28 KJV).

"For all of God's promises have been fulfilled in Christ with a resounding "Yes! And through Christ, our 'Amen' (which means 'Yes') ascends to God for his glory" (2 Cor. 1:20 NLT).

"He fills my life with good things. My youth is renewed like the eagle's!" (Ps. 103:5 NLT).

*In Jesus name, amen.*

## Notes

_____
_____
_____

# Help for the Righteous and Wrath to the Wicked

## (Prayer)

"This is what the Sovereign Lord says: The enemy said of you, 'Aha! The ancient heights have become our possession'" (Ezek. 36:2 NIV).

"They sharpen their tongues like swords and aim their bitter words like arrows" (Ps. 64:3 NLT).

"Their own tongues will ruin them, and all who see them will shake their heads in scorn" (Ps. 64:8 NLT).

"But let the righteous be glad; let them rejoice before God: Yea, let them exceedingly rejoice" (Ps. 68:3 KJV).

"You have tested us, O God; you have purified us like silver" (Ps. 66:10 NLT).

"Hasten, O God, to save me; come quickly, Lord, to help me" (Ps. 70:1 NIV).

"Hear me, Lord, my plea is just; listen to my cry. Hear my prayer - it does not rise from deceitful lips" (Ps. 17:1 NIV).

"Show me the wonders of your great love, you who save by your right hand those who take refuge in you from their foes" (Ps. 17:7 NIV).

"Then this message came to me from the Lord" (Ezek. 12:26 NLT).

"Who hath ears to hear, let him hear" (Matt. 13:9 KJV).

"Verily, verily, I say unto you, He that heareth my word, and believeth on him that sent me, hath everlasting life, and shall not come into condemnation; but is passed from death unto life" (John 5:24 KJV).

"O Lord, I have longed for your rescue, and your instructions are my delight" (Ps. 119:174 NLT).

"Thy word have I hid in mine heart, that I might not sin against thee" (Ps. 119:11 KJV).

"My heart aches with longing; I want to know your judgments at all times" (Ps. 119:20 GNT).

"Free me from their insults and scorn, because I have kept your laws" (Ps. 119:22 GNT).

"For, lo, they lie in wait for my soul: the mighty are gathered against me; not for my transgression, nor for my sin, O Lord" (Ps. 59:3 KJV).

"They come out at night, snarling like vicious dogs as they prowl the streets" (Ps. 59:6 NLT).

"Listen to their insults and threats. Their tongues are like swords in their mouths, yet they think that no one hears them" (Ps. 59:7 GNT).

"Thou therefore, O Lord God of hosts, the God of Israel, awake to visit all the heathen: be not merciful to any wicked transgressors" (Ps. 59:5 KJV). *Selah.*

"Shall not God search this out? For he knoweth the secrets of the heart" (Ps. 44:21 KJV).

"I cried unto thee; save me, and I shall keep thy testimonies" (Ps. 119:146 KJV).

"Stir up thyself, and awake to my judgment, even unto my cause, my God and my Lord" (Ps. 35:23 KJV).

"Lord, how long wilt thou look on? Rescue my soul from their destructions, my darling from the lions" (Ps. 35:17 KJV).

"Break their teeth, O God, in their mouth: break out the great teeth of the young lions, O Lord" (Ps. 58:6 KJV).

"Let them melt away as waters which run continually: when he bendeth his bow to shoot his arrows, let them be as cut in pieces" (Ps. 58:7 KJV).

"As snails which melteth, let every one of them pass away: like the untimely birth of a woman, that they may not see the sun" (Ps. 58:8 KJV).

"In the day when I cried thou answeredst me, and strengthenedst me with strength in my soul" (Ps. 138:3 KJV).

"God will sweep them away, both young and old, faster than a pot heats over burning thorns" (Ps. 58:9 NLT).

"The righteous shall rejoice when he seeth the vengeance: he shall wash his feet in the blood of the wicked" (Ps. 58:10 KJV).

"For the Lord taketh pleasure in his people: he will beautify the meek with salvation" (Ps. 149:4 KJV).

"So that a man shall say, Verily there is a reward for the righteous: verily he is a God that judgeth in the earth" (Ps. 58:11 KJV).

*In Jesus name, amen.*

## Notes

_____
_____
_____

# Betrayal

## (Prayer)

"I cry out to God Most High, to God who will fulfill his purpose for me" (Ps. 57:2 NLT).

"All my longings lie open before you, Lord; my sighing is not hidden from you" (Ps. 38:9 NIV).

"I am surrounded by fierce lions who greedily devour human prey—whose teeth pierce like spears and arrows, and whose tongues cut like swords" (Ps. 57:4 NLT).

"My heart is in anguish within me; the terrors of death have fallen on me" (Ps. 55:4 NIV).

"Fear and trembling overwhelmed me, and I can't stop shaking" (Ps. 55:5 NLT).

"My heart pounds, my strength fails me; even the light has gone from my eyes" (Ps. 38:10 NIV).

"Oh, that I had wings like a dove; then I would fly away and rest!" (Ps. 55:6 NLT).

"I would fly far away to the quiet of the wilderness" (Ps. 55:7 NLT).

(Interlude)

"How quickly I would escape- far from this wild storm of hatred" (Ps. 55:8 NLT).

"It is not an enemy who taunts me—I could bear that. It is not my foes who so arrogantly insults me—I could have hidden from them" (Ps. 55:12 NLT).

"Instead, it is you—my equal, my companion and close friend" (Ps. 55:13 NLT).

"They visit me as if they were my friends, but all the while they gather gossip, and when they leave, they spread it everywhere" (Ps. 41:6 NLT).

"Declare me innocent, O God! Defend me against these ungodly people. Rescue me from these unjust liars" (Ps. 43:1 NLT).

"Even my best friend, the one I trusted completely, the one who shared my food, has turned against me. (Ps. 41:9 NLT).

"I prayed, 'Don't let my enemies gloat over me or rejoice at my downfall'" (Ps. 38:16 NLT).

"[My companion] has put forth his hands against those who were at peace with him; he has broken and profaned his agreement [of friendship and loyalty]" (Ps. 55:20 AMPC).

"His words are as smooth as butter, but in his heart is war. His words are as soothing as lotion, but underneath are daggers!" (Ps. 55:21 NLT).

"Why should I fear when trouble comes, when enemies surround me?" (Ps. 49:5 NLT).

"For God hath not given us the spirit of fear; but of power, and of love, and of a sound mind" (2 Tim. 1:7 KJV).

"Why am I discouraged? Why is my heart so sad? I will put my hope in God! I will praise him again- my savior and my God!" (Ps. 42:11 NLT).

"My God, rescue me from the power of the wicked, from the clutches of cruel oppressors" (Ps. 71:4 NLT).

"For you are my safe refuge, a fortress where my enemies cannot reach me" (Ps. 61:3 NLT).

"Let me live forever in your sanctuary, safe beneath the shelter of your wings!" (Ps. 61:4 NLT).

CRAIG WILLIAMS

# (Interlude)

*In Jesus name, amen.*

# Notes

_____
_____
_____

# Longing for God's Help

## (Prayer)

"Save me, O God; For the waters are come in unto my soul" (Ps. 69:1 KJV).

"I am weary of my crying: my throat is dried: Mine eyes fail while I wait for my God" (Ps. 69:3 KJV).

"O God, thou knowest my foolishness; And my sins are not hid from thee" (Ps. 69:5 KJV).

"Let not them that wait on thee, O Lord God of hosts, be ashamed for my sake: Let not those that seek thee be confounded for my sake, O God of Israel" (Ps. 69:6 KJV).

"Because for thy sake I have borne reproach; Shame hath covered my face" (Ps. 69:7 KJV).

"As it is written, For thy sake we are killed all the day long; We are accounted as sheep for the slaughter" (Rom. 8:36 KJV).

"For the zeal of thine house hath eaten me up; And the reproaches of them that reproached thee are fallen upon me" (Ps. 69:9 KJV).

"Truly my soul waiteth upon God: From him cometh my salvation" (Ps. 62:1 KJV).

"How long wilt thou forget me, O LORD? For ever? How long wilt thou hide thy face from me?" (Ps. 13:1 KJV).

"How long shall I take counsel in my soul, Having sorrow in my heart daily?" (Ps. 13:2 KJV).

"Consider and hear me, O LORD my God: Lighten mine eyes, lest I sleep the sleep of death" (Ps. 13:3 KJV).

"Lest mine enemy say, I have prevailed against him; And those that trouble me rejoice when I am moved" (Ps. 13:4 KJV).

"The wicked walk on every side, When the vilest men are exalted" (Ps. 12:8 KJV).

"They speak vanity every one with double heart do they speak" (Ps. 12:2 KJV).

"But as for me, my prayer Is unto thee, O LORD, in an acceptable time: O God, in the multitude of thy mercy Hear me, in the truth of thy salvation" (Ps. 69:13 KJV).

"Deliver me out of the mire, and let me not sink: Let me be delivered from them that hate me, and out of the deep waters" (Ps. 69:14 KJV).

"Let not the waterflood overflow me, neither let the deep swallow me up, And let not the pit shut her mouth upon me" (Ps. 69:15 KJV).

"Hear me, O LORD; for thy lovingkindness is good: Turn unto me according to the multitude of thy tender mercies" (Ps. 69:16 KJV).

"And hide not thy face from thy servant; For I am in trouble: Hear me speedily" (Ps. 69:17 KJV).

"Draw nigh unto my soul, and redeem it: Deliver me because of mine enemies" (Ps. 69:18 KJV).

"Thou hast known my reproach, and my shame, and my dishonour: Mine adversaries are all before thee" (Ps. 69:19 KJV).

"Reproach hath broken my heart; and I am full of heaviness: And I looked for some to take pity, but there was none; And for comforters, but I found none" (Ps. 69:20 KJV).

"For the wicked boasteth of his heart's desire, And blesseth the covetous, whom the LORD abhorreth" (Ps. 10:3 KJV).

"The wicked in his pride doth persecute the poor: Let them be taken in the devices that they have imagined" (Ps. 10:2 KJV).

"Let their table become snare before them: And that which should have been for their welfare, let it become a trap" (Ps. 69:22 KJV).

"Let their eyes be darkened, that they see not; And make their loins continually to shake" (Ps. 69:23 KJV).

"Pour out thine indignation upon them, And let thy wrathful anger take hold of them" (Ps. 69:24 KJV).

"Let their habitation be desolate; And let none dwell in their tents" (Ps. 69:25 KJV).

"For they persecute him whom thou hast smitten; And they talk to the grief of those whom thou hast wounded" (Ps. 69:26 KJV).

"Add iniquity unto their iniquity: And let them not come into thy righteousness" (Ps. 69:27 KJV).

"Let them be blotted out of the book of the living, And not be written with the righteous" (Ps. 69:28 KJV).

"The LORD trieth the righteous: But the wicked and him that loveth violence his soul hateth" (Ps. 11:6 KJV).

"But I have trusted in thy mercy; My heart shall rejoice in thy salvation" (Ps. 13:5 KJV).

"For the righteous LORD loveth righteousness; His countenance doth behold the upright" (Ps. 11:7 KJV).

"O God, I will offer you what I have promised; I will give you my offering of thanksgiving" (Ps. 56:12 GNT).

"My God loves me and will come to me; he will let me see my enemies defeated" (Ps. 59:10 GNT).

*In Jesus name, amen.*

## Notes

_____

_____

_____

# The Lord Is Our Covering in Battle

## (Prayer)

"In the LORD put I my trust: how say ye to my soul, Flee as a bird to your mountain?" (Ps. 11:1 KJV).

"My enemies make trouble for me all day long; they are always thinking up some way to hurt me!" (Ps. 56:5 GNT).

"But you laugh at them, LORD; you mock all the heathen" (Ps. 59:8 GNT).

"Then this message came to me from the LORD" (Ezek. 17:1 NLT).

"I am the LORD, the God of all the peoples of the world, Is anything too hard for me?" (Jer. 32:27 NLT).

"Proud people are coming against me, O God; a cruel gang is trying to kill me- people who pay no attention to you" (Ps. 86:14 GNT).

"For, lo, the wicked bend their bow, they make ready their arrow upon the string, that they may privily shoot at the upright in heart" (Ps. 11:2 KJV).

"Help, LORD; for the godly man ceaseth; for the faithful fail from among the children of men" (Ps. 12:1 KJV).

"The LORD gave me another message. He said" (Jer. 2:1 NLT).

"I am the LORD your God; I strengthen you and tell you, 'Do not be afraid; I will help you." (Isa. 41:13 GNT).

"How could one person chase a thousand of them, and two people put ten thousand to flight, unless their Rock had sold them, unless the Lord had given them up?" (Deut. 32:30 NLT).

"Moreover the word of the Lord came unto me, saying" (Ezek. 17:11 KJV).

"Two people are better off than one, for they can help each other succeed" (Eccles. 4:9 NLT).

"For where two or three are gathered together in my name, there am I in the midst of them" (Matt. 18:20 KJV).

"Again I say unto you, That if two of you shall agree on earth as touching any thing that they shall ask, it shall be done for them of my Father which is in heaven" (Matt. 18:19 KJV).

"Then another message came to me from the Lord" (Ezek. 18:1 NLT).

"The Lord is good, a strong refuge when trouble comes. He is close to those who trust in him" (Nah. 1:7 NLT).

"Be strong and of a good courage, fear not, nor be afraid of them: for the Lord thy God, he it is that doth go with thee: he will not fail thee, nor forsake thee" (Deut. 31:6 KJV).

"For we wrestle not against flesh and blood, but against principalities, against powers, against the rulers of the darkness of this world, against spiritual wickedness in high places" (Eph. 6:12 KJV).

"Therefore, put on the complete armor of God, so that you will be able to [successfully] resist and stand your ground in the evil day [of danger], and having done everything [that the crisis demands], to stand firm [in your place, fully prepared, immovable, victorious]" (Eph. 6:13 AMP).

"Stand therefore, having your loins girt about with truth, and having on the breastplate of righteousness" (Eph. 6:14 KJV).

"And your feet shod with the preparation of the gospel of peace" (Eph. 6:15 KJV).

"Above all, taking the shield of faith, wherewith ye shall be able to quench all the fiery darts of the wicked" (Eph. 6:16 KJV).

"And take the helmet of salvation, and the sword of the Spirit, which is the word of God" (Eph. 6:17 KJV).

"Then this message came to me from the LORD" (Ezek. 17:1 NLT).

"The LORD thy God in the midst of thee is mighty; he will save, he will rejoice over thee with joy; he will rest in his love, he will joy over thee with singing" (Zeph. 3:17 KJV).

"The LORD shall preserve thee from all evil: he shall preserve thy soul" (Ps. 121:7 KJV).

"The LORD shall preserve thy going out and thy coming in from this time forth, and even for evermore" (Ps. 121:8 KJV).

"I will exalt you, my God and King, and praise your name forever and ever" (Ps. 145:1 NLT).

"Behold, God is my helper and ally; The LORD is the sustainer of my soul [my upholder]" (Ps. 54:4 AMP).

"Do not let the oppressed retreat in disgrace; may the poor and needy praise your name" (Ps. 74:21 NIV).

"Remember your covenant promises, for the land is full of darkness and violence" (Ps. 74:20 NLT).

"Arise, O God, and defend your cause. Remember how these fools insult you all day long" (Ps. 74:22 NLT).

"Don't overlook what your enemies have said or their growing uproar" (Ps. 74:23 NLT).

"It is God alone who judges; he decides who will rise and who will fall" (Ps. 75:7 NLT).

"For God alone my soul waits in silence; from him comes my salvation" (Ps. 62:1 ESV).

*In Jesus name, amen.*

## Notes

_____
_____
_____

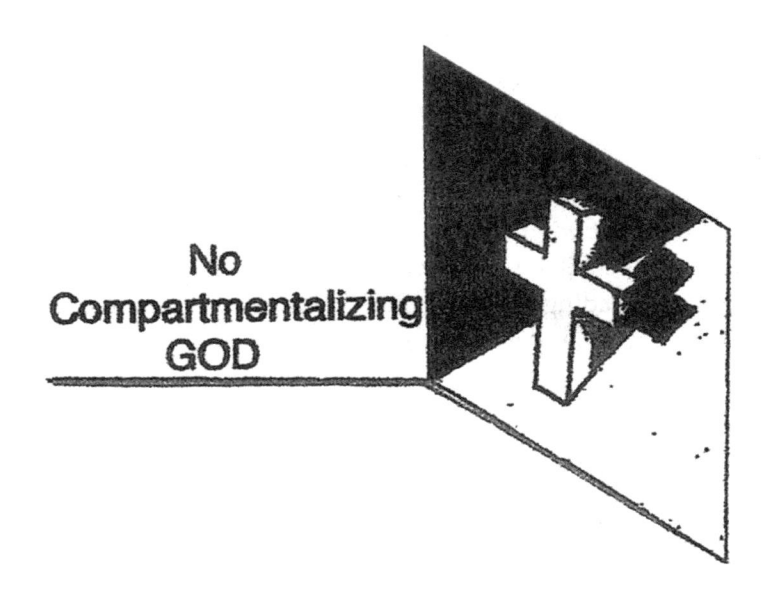

# Introduction to the Author

The true unadulterated author of this book is God the Father; Jesus Christ the Son, our Lord and Savior; and the precious Holy Spirit, who is our Comforter. God is the author of us all and everything we come to know about creation.

> Then God said, "Let Us (Father, Son, Holy Spirit) make man in Our image, according to Our likeness [not physical, but a spiritual personality and moral likeness]; and let them have complete authority over the fish of the sea, the birds of the air, the cattle, and over the entire earth, and over everything that creeps and crawls on the earth." (Gen. 1:26 AMP)

Jesus said in John 16:7 KJV: "Nevertheless I tell you the truth; It is expedient for you that I go away; for if I go not away, the Comforter will not come unto you; but if I depart, I will send him unto you." It is he, the Comforter, the third person of God, the Tri-unity, if you will, that inspired, encouraged, and led me in writing this book, *Pray in God's Word for Encouragement and Change.*

Reading the Bible will renew you and change your life for the better. For me, reading the Word of God has enlightened my desire to seek Him more, live and walk out my life as Jesus did. To be Christlike.

> To put off your old self, which belongs to your former manner of life and is corrupt through deceitful desires and to be renewed in the Spirit of your minds and to put on the new self, created after the likeness of God in true righteousness and holiness. (Eph. 4:22–24 ESV)

To show more love, encouragement, and operating in self-control no matter what mood I am in. To experience the joy of being in a relationship with Jesus.

To be patient with others and easily forgive an offense.

To show kindness to all and help the disenfranchised, the poor, the elderly, the orphan, the prisoner, and the widow.

"And the King shall answer and say unto them, Verily I say unto you, Inasmuch as ye have done it unto one of the least of these my brethren, ye have done it unto me" (Matt. 25:40 KJV).

Living in this world, no matter your gender, race, or what family you belong to, you will perpetually encounter three life changing events. You will experience, heading into a storm, being in a storm or coming out of a storm. The only solace in all three situation is that God will be with us in the storm, and He is trying to bring something good to us. "But the boat by this time was long way from the land, beaten by the waves, for the wind was against them. And in the fourth watch of the night he came to them, walking on the sea" (Matt. 14:24–25 ESV). Our experience will be different. The storm is personalized.

## PRAY IN GOD'S WORD FOR ENCOURAGEMENT AND CHANGE

The goodness of God has taught me to be thankful no matter what comes my way. "In every thing give thanks: for this is the will of God in Christ Jesus concerning you" (1 Thess. 5:18 KJV).

To rely on the peace of God, which eclipse all understanding.

"And the peace of God, which passeth all understanding, shall keep your hearts and minds through Christ Jesus" (Phil. 4:7 KJV).

To be faithful to God because He is always faithful to me.

"If we are faithless, He remains faithful (true to His word and His righteous character), for He cannot deny Himself" (2 Tim. 2:13 AMP).

That means so much to me because when I stumble on my journey through this world, this present life, God is always guaranteed to be there. Which in turn helps me to long-suffer with others. Long-suffering is essential in how we interact to each other with all our different personalities.

"With all lowliness and meekness, with long-suffering, forbearing one another in love" (Eph. 4:2 KJV).

It all starts and ends with God's love for us.

"In this was manifested the love of God towards us, because that God sent his only begotten Son into the world, that we might live through him" (1 John 4:9 KJV).

"This is real love—not that we loved God, but that He loved us and sent His Son as a sacrifice to take away our sins" (1 John 4:10 NLT).

I surrender all to Christ, whom I thank for being the Author and finisher of my faith.

"Looking unto Jesus, the Author and finisher of our faith, who for the joy that was set before Him endured the cross, despising the shame, and has sat down at the right hand of the throne of God" (Heb. 12:2 KJV).

In this world, a person can find any number of resources, but there is only one source, God. All our resources start with God.

> For by Him all things were created in heaven and on earth, [things] visible and invisible, whether thrones or dominions or rulers

or authorities; all things were created and exist through Him [that is, by His activity] and for Him. And He Himself existed and is before all things, and in Him all things hold together. [His is the controlling, cohesive force of the universe.] (Col. 1:16–17 AMP)

He is also the head [the life-source and leader] of the body, the church; and He is the beginning, the firstborn from the dead, so that He Himself will occupy the first place [He will stand supreme and be preeminent] in everything. (Col. 1:18 AMP)

God is the source of our strength, our power, our capacity to withstand all manner of evil and perplexed adversity. God has given us, believers of Christ Jesus, his marvelous light, shining in our hearts, even though we are fragile, we have a great treasure. The enemy attacks us daily, pressing in on us with troubles and confusion, but thank you, LORD, we are not crushed or driven to despair.

"We are hunted down, but never abandoned by God. We get knocked down, but we are not destroyed" (2 Cor. 4:9 NLT).

For the believer in Christ Jesus, every encounter, every trial, we are being reinforced in our faith, our hope, our thoughts and actions, our existence, that God only works things for our good. Our soul, is being transformed into the image of God. I press on with all vigilance because God's power sustains me.

"For therein is the righteousness of God revealed from faith to faith: as it is written, The just shall live by faith" (Rom. 1:17 KJV).

"Therefore we do not lose heart. Though outwardly we are wasting away, yet inwardly we are being renewed day by day" (2 Cor. 4:16 NIV). Through the transcending power of God's love for me, I am saved, and so will you, once you receive him.

*Be blessed!*

# Reflections

# Source Notes

*Special praise, honor, glory, and thanksgiving to our LORD Jesus Christ.*

"The heavens proclaim the glory of God. The skies display his craftsmanship" (Ps. 19:1 NLT).

"The unfolding of your words gives light; it gives understanding to the simple" (Ps. 19:130 NIV).

Amplified (AMP)
American Standard Version (ASV)
Amplified Classic (AMPC)
Eastern Standard Version (ESV)
Easy-to Read Version (ERV)
Good News Translation (GNT)
God Word Translation (GWT)
King James Version (KJV)
New King James Version (NKJV)
New English Translation (NET)
New International Translation (NLT)
Message Bible (MSG)
and
Wikipedia (History of the first English Bible)

"To the only wise God, through Jesus Christ, be glory forever more! Amen" (Rom. 16:27 AMP).

# The Reason for Our Faith

*"The message of the cross is foolish to those who are headed for destruction! But we who are being saved know it is the very power of God"* (1 Cor. 1:18 NTL).

*"For it is written, I will destroy the wisdom of the wise, and will bring to nothing the understanding of the prudent"* (1 Cor. 1:19 KJV)

# Bless My Day, Lord

A prayer of faith in the LORD, to walk daily in the fruits of the Spirit.

Pray:

"This I recall to my mind, therefore have I hope" (Lam. 3:21 KJV).

*I have the Joy of the LORD today*:

"Listen to my voice in the morning, LORD. Each morning I bring my requests to you and wait expectantly" (Ps. 5:3 NLT).

"O God, you take no pleasure in wickedness; you cannot tolerate the sins of the wicked" (Ps. 5:4 NLT).

"But let all who take refuge in you rejoice; let them sing joyful praises forever. Spread your protection over them, that all who love your name may be filled with joy" (Ps. 5:11 NLT).

*In Jesus name,*

*I am loved by God, so I will show love today*:

"Herein was the love of God manifested in us, that God hath sent his only begotten Son into the world that we might live through him" (1 John 4:9 ASV).

"Hereby we know that we abide in him and he in us, because he hath given us of his Spirit" (1 John 4:13 ASV).

*In Jesus name,*

*I have the peace of Christ Jesus today, for God has defeated all my enemies*:

"May the evil plans of my enemies be turned against them. Do as you promised and put an end to them" (Ps. 54:5 NLT).

"The Lord shall fight for you, and ye shall hold your peace" (Exod. 14:14 KJV).

"Peace I leave with you: my peace I give to you. Not as the world gives do I give to you. Let not your hearts be troubled, neither let them be afraid" (John 14:27 ESV).

"Give all your worries and cares to God, for he cares about you" (1 Pet. 5:7 NLT).

*In Jesus name,*

*God is patient, help me O' Lord, to be patient today, for:*
"Whoever is patient has great understanding, but one who is quick- tempered displays folly" (Prov. 14:29 NIV).

*In Jesus name,*

*Today I will be kind to my neighbor:*
"My shield is with God, Who saveth the upright in heart" (Ps. 7:10 ASV).

"He hath shewed thee, O man, what is good; and what doth the Lord require of thee, but to do justly, and love mercy, and to walk humbly with thy God?" (Mic. 6:8 KJV).

"And be renewed in the spirit of your mind" (Eph. 4:23 KJV).

"Wherefore putting away lying, speak the truth, each one to his neighbor: for we are members one of another" (Eph. 4:25 KJV).

"And be ye kind one to another, tenderhearted, forgiving one another, even as God for Christ's sake hath forgiven you" (Eph. 4:32 KJV).

*In Jesus name,*

*Today, I have Goodness and favor with God and man:*
"I had fainted, Unless I had believed to see the goodness of the Lord in the land of the living" (Ps. 27:13 KJV).

"The meek will he guide in judgment: And the meek will he teach his way" (Ps. 25:9 KJV).

"Jesus grew in wisdom and in stature and in favor with God and all people" (Luke 2:52 NLT).

"So shalt thou find favour and good understanding In the sight of God and man" (Prov. 3:4 KJV).

"For he raised us from the dead along with Christ and seated us with him in the heavenly realms because we are united with Christ Jesus" (Eph. 2:6 NLT).

"And don't forget to do good and share with those in need. These are the sacrifices that please God" (Heb. 13:16 NLT).

*In Jesus name, amen.*

*Today I have faith that God will take care of all my troubles*:
"I will call to you whenever I'm in trouble, and you will answer me" (Ps. 86:7 NLT).

"The LORD hears thee in the day of trouble; the name of the God of Jacob defend thee" (Ps. 20:1 KJV).

"The works of his hands are faithful and just; all his precepts are trustworthy" (Ps. 111:7 ESV).

"Faithful is he that calleth you, who also will do it" (1 Thess. 5:24 KJV).

"Wait on the LORD: Be of good courage, and he shall strengthen thine heart: wait, I say, on the LORD" (Ps. 27:14 KJV).

In Jesus name,

*Today, I am Gentle, for my LORD is gentle*:
"For we also once were foolish, disobedient, deceived, serving divers lusts and pleasures, living in malice and envy, hating one another" (Titus 3:3 ASV).

"Now therefore, thus says the LORD of hosts, "Consider your ways and thoughtfully reflect on your conduct!" (Hag. 1:5 AMP).

"To speak evil of no man, to be no brawlers, but gentle, shewing all meekness unto all men" (Titus 3:2 KJV).

In Jesus name,

*Today, the LORD long-suffered for me*:

"But he was pierced for our transgressions; he was crushed for our iniquities; upon him was the chastisement that brought us peace, and with his wounds we are healed" (Isa. 53:5 ESV).

"My flesh and my heart faileth: But God is the strength of my heart, and my portion for ever" (Ps. 73:26 KJV).

"O Lord, I will honor and praise your name, for you are my God. You do such wonderful Things! You planned them long ago, and now you have accomplished them" (Isa. 25:1 NLT).

"Trust in the Lord forever, for the Lord himself is the Rock eternal" (Isa. 26:4 NIV).

*In Jesus name, amen Lord!*

# Covered Prayer

Lord, I pray that:

"You guide me with your instruction and at the end you will receive me with honor" (Ps. 73:24 GNT).

"What else do I have in heaven but you? Since I have you, what else could I want on earth?" (Ps. 73:25 GNT).

"Listen to my prayer; rescue me as you promised" (Ps. 119:170 NLT).

"You are my defender and protector; I put my hope in your promise" (Ps. 119:114 GNT).

"Give me strength, as you promised, and I shall live; don't let me be disappointed in my hope!" (Ps. 119:116 GNT).

"Make your face shine on your servant and teach me your decrees" (Ps. 119:135 NIV).

"Hold me, and I will be safe, and I will always pay attention to your commands" (Ps. 119:117 GNT).

"Rescue me, O Lord, from liars and from all deceitful people" (Ps. 120:2 NLT).

"Promise that you will help your servant; don't let the arrogant oppress me!" (Ps. 119:122 GNT).

"As you have promised, keep me from falling; don't let me be overcome by evil" (Ps. 119:133 GNT).

"Your justice is eternal, and your instructions are perfectly true" (Ps. 119:142 GNT).

"Be good to me, your servant, so that I may live to obey your word" (Ps. 119:17 ERV).

"Happy are those who obey the LORD, who live by his commands" (Ps. 128:1 GNT).

"A man who obeys the LORD will surely be blessed like this" (Ps. 128:4 GNT).

"Your work will provide for your needs; you will be happy and prosperous" (Ps. 128:2 GNT).

"Your wife will be like a fruitful vine in your home, and your children will be like young olive trees around your table" (Ps. 128:3 GNT).

"How great are your actions, LORD! How deep are your thoughts!" (Ps. 92:5 GNT).

"Even though I am a free man with no master, I have become a slave to all people to bring many to Christ" (1 Cor. 9:19 NLT).

"I do all this for the sake of the gospel, that I may share in its blessings" (1 Cor. 9:23 NIV).

*In Jesus name, amen.*

# Closing Prayer

It is my desire that everyone reading *Pray in God's Words for Encouragement and Change* will be motivated to read the Bible. To be empowered, renewed, and valiant in the fear (reverence) of God to share the gospel with everyone they come in contact with.

*In Jesus name, amen.*

The encouraging word of God says:

> That's the whole story. Here now is my final conclusion: Fear God and obey his commands, for this is everyone's duty. God will judge us for everything we do, including every secret thing, whether good or bad. (Eccles. 12:13–14 NLT)

"For if you live according to the flesh, you will die; but if by the Spirit you put to death the misdeeds of the body, you will live" (Rom. 8:13 NIV).

For every one of us reading *Pray in God's Word for Encouragement and Change*, I pray, Lord:

"Let us then with confidence draw near to the throne of grace, that we may receive mercy and find grace to help in time of need" (Heb. 4:16 ESV).

"The God of peace will soon crush Satan under your feet. The grace of our Lord Jesus be with you" (Rom. 16:20 NIV).

"To the only wise God be glory forever through Jesus Christ! Amen" (Rom. 16:27 NIV).

*Shalom!*

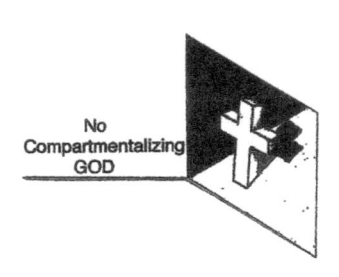

"For everything comes from him and exists by his power and is intended for his glory. All glory to him forever! Amen" (Rom. 11:36 NLT).

# About the Author

Born and raised in St. Catherine Jamaica Craig was carefree, blissful until his dad had trouble finding work as an electrician and his mother's job couldn't not sustain the family, so Craig's mother went to the United States, in search of a better life for her family. Craig's mom was and still is an emphasis of strength, determination, and resilience for Craig, because her courage, strength, and the ability to make tough decisions shaped Craig's life. With any obstacle, Craig now knows through Christ Jesus, he has the victory and the confidence that no matter what the circumstances are, GOD has only good for him. A few years after leaving Jamaica, Craig's mom Esmie, filed the necessary paperwork to have Craig and her husband join her in America in the winter of 1985, they settled in Rockville MD and became citizens shortly thereafter.

Craig excelled in school academics and athletics, graduating from high school with a 3.9 GPA and a D1 offer for football. Due to his father being injured in a car accident, Craig quit college and attended and completed with honors along with being class valedictorian at a four-year trade school and finished with a 4.0 GPA. Positioning himself to help his family.

Today Craig is a retired 602 steamfitter for HVAC, divorced single parent of 8, raising four young boys, under 15. Craig considers his children his greatest achievement. Throughout his life, Craig has endured many setbacks, heartbreaks, and trials, but because of his faith in Christ Jesus he has overcome them all. On August 30, 2008, at 12pm Craig died after lung surgery to correct the histoplasmosis infection he got from pigeon droppings on the job. Craig was a government contractor for 10 years. His family was notified by hospital staff/surgeon of his death, only for his family to receive word a short time after that he came back to life. Craig gave his testimony of witnessing doctors trying to save him then when that failed, they put a blue sheet over him (head to toe). While witnessing all this from an elevated position above his body, he spoke of being at peace and with a presence next to him talking to him, he asked that figure why is my body lying there, then he woke up on life support. GOD performed a miracle. Craig then was involved in a car accident, not his fault. In fact, Craig has been involved in several car accidents none of which was his fault, but that is not the oddest thing, the oddest thing is that the accidents happened every four years like clockwork. 2005, 2009, 2013. Craig thought the cycle was over until it happened in 2019 while parked at a Chick-fil-A. He had 3 cervical spine surgeries done. He needs back surgery, but God has been sustaining him. During this period the family home was foreclosed on, and they were homeless for a year.

Throughout all these bad circumstances, Craig will be the first to tell you, we live on purpose, so for him to go through this, it's God will that I go through this because as Christian's, followers of Christ Jesus and our relationship with God, takes us from faith to faith. This has inspired Craig to write Pray in God's word for encouragement and change. I don't know what challenges you are facing today, or how long you've been battling your difficult situation, but remember not to quit, always pray, read your Bible daily and stay reassured by reading "Pray in GOD's word for encouragement and change ". It will definitely help in any conflict we encounter. God brought Craig back from death and used Craig's tragedy to inspire him to bring the message in this book to help anyone who is lost and struggling without any sign or hope of change. God is the answer, and his message is clear "Come unto me, all ye that labor and are heavy laden, and I will give you rest. Take my yoke upon you and learn of me; for I am meek and lowly in heart: and ye shall find rest unto your souls". (Matt. 11:28-29 KJV)
Be blessed.